RAMAYANA
THE
GAME
OF LIFE

Rise of the Sun Prince

BOOK 1

RAMAYANA
—THE—
GAME
OF LIFE

Rise of the Sun Prince

BOOK 1

SHUBHA VILAS

JAICO PUBLISHING HOUSE

Ahmedabad Bangalore Bhopal Bhubaneswar Chennai
Delhi Hyderabad Kolkata Lucknow Mumbai

Published by Jaico Publishing House
A-2 Jash Chambers, 7-A Sir Phirozshah Mehta Road
Fort, Mumbai - 400 001
jaicopub@jaicobooks.com
www.jaicobooks.com

RAMAYANA: THE GAME OF LIFE
Rise of the Sun Prince – Book 1
ISBN 978-81-8495-530-9

First Jaico Impression: 2014
Third Jaico Impression: 2014

Printed by
Rashmi Graphics
#3, Amrutwel CHS Ltd., C.S. #50/74
Ganesh Galli, Lalbaug, Mumbai-400 012
E-mail: tiwarijp@vsnl.net

DEDICATION

To a dear friend, Gaurakrsna, who left me forever, but not before emboldening me sufficiently to rewrite the *Ramayana*.

To my mother, Chitra, and my father, Badri Narayanan, to whom I owe the deepest foundations of my life.

To my *paramguru*, Srila Prabhupada, whose teachings and books have influenced my life immensely.

To my guru, Radhanath Swami, whose words of wisdom have inspired my heart, whose love and kindness has touched my soul.

To my guide, who has been a beacon light of direction, a treasure house of wisdom and an unflagging source of encouragement.

To my brother, well-wishers and friends, who have been the supporting pillars in all my endeavors. From them I have learnt to love and serve selflessly.

CONTENTS

	Acknowledgments	ix
	Author's Note	xi
Chapter 1	The Angry Curse Turns into Glorious Verse	1
Chapter 2	A Sad Monarch in a Happy Kingdom	17
Chapter 3	A Flood of Sweetness	39
Chapter 4	Happiness — Not Always Satisfaction	69
Chapter 5	Laws of Progressive Living	89
Chapter 6	A River of Tales	119
Chapter 7	You Rise When Your Pride Falls	135
Chapter 8	Virtues and the Virtuous	167
Chapter 9	Might is Not Always Right	201
	Appendix	213

ACKNOWLEDGMENTS

Walking through life, I have always seen myself as a student, surrounded by teachers who have touched and enhanced my life immensely. I would like to express my heartfelt gratitude for all that I have been fortunate enough to learn from them.

To name all of them here would be impossible; however, some of the most prominent teachers in my life have been: H.D.G. A.C. Bhaktivedanta Swami Srila Prabhupada, the founder of the Hare Krsna Movement, and H.H. Radhanath Swami, the author of the international bestseller *The Journey Home - Autobiography of an American Swami.*

I am indebted to Valmiki *muni,* the author of the *Ramayana.* And Kamba *muni,* who further enriched the flavor of the original with his amazing poetry. I have learnt a lot about the intricacies of the *Ramayana* from Sri Velukkudi Krishnan Swami and K.S. Narayanacharya, C. Sita Ramamurti and Sri S. Appalacharyulu. I would also like to appreciate all those who have worked on the website - www.valmikiramayan.net - to make the epic accessible to the world.

My special gratitude to Dr. Shrilekha Hada, for her tireless zeal and invaluable inputs in developing every aspect of the book. My thanks also to Mrs. Natasha Vasudev for her kind help in further editing the book.

I personally owe a million thanks to Meera Menon, whose meticulousness shows through in every sentence of this book, whose thought-provoking enquiries have helped me go deeper into the *Ramayana.*

And of course, my warm thanks to the entire team of Jaico, especially Mr. Akash Shah, Sandhya Iyer, Lakshmi Krishnan, Nita Satikuwar and Vijay Thakur - their intense efforts and sincere dedication are visible on every page of the book. This journey with them has been about not only working on a book but also bonding deeply with the Jaico family.

Author's Note

When was the last time you came across a novel that you felt like reading all over again? Have you ever met characters in a story who appear different to you every time you read about them? Most stories can be enjoyed once, at the most twice; they have nothing new to offer after the second read. But unlike regular stories, the *Ramayana* grows more interesting with every reading. An all-encompassing story, it adds value to every kind of reader and addresses every human need. Here, we find adventure and romance, mysticism and sinister plots, struggles and immortal values, poetry and intellectual analogies, and so much more.

Some books teach ideals and some books entertain. *Ramayana: The Game of Life* is an attempt to present this timeless story in a way that is entertaining to the heart and enlightening to the intellect.

A good game is full of twists and turns at every stage and promises to thrill with its absolute unpredictability of results. But no one wants the same to happen in real life. Life should be extremely predictable and smooth – this is what most of us are comfortable with. Stories like the *Ramayana* present the realities of life in the most exciting manner. This magical epic arms us with valuable tools to deal with the various twists and turns of our own lives. The simple wisdom to be found in dharmic tales like the *Ramayana* is always fresh and gives us the clarity we often need, while being rooted in time-tested traditional values.

Those who are looking only for the story of the *Ramayana* will find it here, packed with plenty of exciting drama and action. This book keeps Valmiki's *Ramayana* front and center, yet explores other versions, gently weaving in aspects of *Kambar Ramayana*'s beautiful poetic analogies and folk tales that are in philosophical alignment with Valmiki's *Ramayana*. Those who seek to relate the story to their own lives will find in the footnotes, practical learnings gleaned from various facets of the story. These *sutras* will help them navigate and steer the ship of life through stormy seas and clear skies alike.

Essentially, every one of us falls into one of three categories in the game of life: positive contributor, negative destroyer or protective mediator. So here we find all the sages headed by the iconic Vishwamitra striving to contribute positively to society through the Vedic sacrifice even as the demons, headed by Maricha and Subahu, try to destroy the positive forces by casting spells of intense negativity. And Rama and Lakshmana work to protect the positive from the corrupting influence of the negative by wielding a protective shield of arrows. This, for instance, is a classic scene taken from the game of life. Which role do you want to play?

Book One of the six-volume *Ramayana: The Game of Life*, which draws extensively from *Valmiki Ramayana*'s *Bala Kanda*, is entitled *Rise of the Sun Prince*. The coming together of myriad forces that it takes to give rise to a perfect hero are brought out through the early life of Rama. As Rama carefully weighs the pros and cons of so many of His decisions and words, we catch a glimpse of the loftiness of a real hero. What is more, we also begin to value the simplicity of being a good student.

In *Rise of the Sun Prince*, we are exposed to the struggles of an imperfect teacher, one who relentlessly fights his internal battles to rise above his shortcomings. And this, in a way, is the central hero of this book - Vishwamitra, the ever-angry sage. As the teacher mentors his pupils, Rama and Lakshmana, they, too, mentor him on another sphere. As the story advances, we witness the angry sage and imperfect teacher blossoming into a focused spiritualist and perfect student, learning the laws of progressive living.

We palpably feel the angst of Dasaratha, his struggle as a father on the one hand and a king on the other. How does a loving father resolve his conflicting role as a dutiful king, especially when his duty obstructs his love?

This book also unravels the story of Sita, whose life revolves around a bow. For a girl, handling the delicate balance between love and tradition is like walking a tightrope between life and death. Are traditions made to die or are they made to live on? This is a question only the heart-moving saga of the marriage of Sita and Rama can answer.

Rise of the Sun Prince reveals to us the range of principles that underlie the healthy relationships in our lives – between parents and children, between husband and wife, between brothers, between a leader and his followers, between a teacher and his students.

The *Ramayana* is not a book; it is a way of life. I invite you to delve into *Ramayana: The Game of Life...* to master your own game of life.

CHAPTER 1

THE ANGRY CURSE TURNS INTO
GLORIOUS VERSE

The illustrious Valmiki *muni*, in all humility and without any preconceived notions, asked his teacher Narada *muni*, "Who is a hero?" His question invoked compassion in Narada *muni* and stirred his teaching instincts.[1]

To remove any ambiguity from his question, Valmiki further asked, "Is there a person in this world who is full of good virtues and is at the same time powerful, grateful, truthful, determined and also compassionate? Is there a person who displays exemplary conduct, ardently wishes and works for the good of all, is wise, competent beyond doubt and good-looking? Is there a person who is self-satisfied,

---

[1] The Vedic books of knowledge are in the form of questions and answers. Knowledge is transferred when an eager and inquisitive person humbly seeks answers from a resourceful and qualified teacher. The scriptures are compared to a cow that provides milk. Here, milk symbolizes the essence of the scriptures and the wisdom of life. A qualified teacher is like the milkman who deftly milks the cow and pours the milk into a vessel keeping its capacity in mind; he imparts knowledge according to a student's abilities. The student is compared to the vessel; his humility is the empty space in the vessel and his eagerness is its depth. A student with preconceived notions is like a full vessel. Such a student cannot assimilate or retain fresh information anymore than a full vessel can hold more milk.

who has control over his anger, whose beauty casts a spell over everyone, who is free from envy and whose courage never fails him?"

The depth of his question revealed Valmiki's yearning and long search for a true hero. He was unwilling to worship one with even a single blemish and wanted to know if there existed a man who possessed all the 24 virtues.[2]

As soon as he heard the question, Narada *muni* knew exactly who possessed all these qualities, and the mere thought of Him stirred up a volcanic eruption of infinite gratitude and devotion in his heart. To his student, Narada *muni* replied, "The qualities you have enquired about are rare and not easily found in a single person." He then sought time away from Valmiki to be better equipped to answer his question. Narada *muni* wanted to delve deeper into his heart to arrive at an accurate answer.

Why did Narada *muni* need time? Did he need time to analyze the millions of people in this world to find who best fit the description of a perfect man? No! He already knew the answer. He needed time

---

[2] Everyone needs a hero to look up to and adore. Most people identify with just one or two of their hero's qualities. Some identify with external beauty although he may be ugly from within; some with wealth although he may be poor at heart; some with intelligence although he may be cruel in dealings; some with courage although he may be exploitative; and some may identify with determination although he may readily succumb to anger. We all desire for a perfect hero, but we settle for one with many imperfections and possibly just one aspect of excellence that attracts us the most. Valmiki listed all the virtues that a person ought to possess. It was this all-perfect man – should such a man exist – that Valmiki wished to worship.

because the answer to Valmiki's question had caused turbulence within his heart.[3]

Embedded deep within Narada *muni's* heart were multiple thoughts of this person who embodied a vast ocean of qualities and attributes. Amid all this turbulence, Narada *muni* needed time to calm his nerves. The surge of emotions from his heart broke into his mind, and in this ecstasy, caused his body to melt, his knees to tremble, his heart to palpitate and his eyes to rotate. The myriad effects on his body needed to be controlled and allayed before he could speak.

Narada *muni* slowly opened tear-laden eyes and revealed to Valmiki that the hero he sought – the one who possessed all these qualities – was none other than Lord Rama.[4]

And on the pretext of explaining the qualities of Lord Rama, he narrated the entire *Ramayana* – the saga of Lord Rama.[5]

---

[3] Valmiki's question was like a churning rod dipped into the core of these emotions. The moment Valmiki hurled the question at Narada *muni*, the answer swiveled its way to the top of his consciousness, just as vigorous churning whips the cream to the top. If this was the result of merely remembering his hero, what would be the impact of following in His footsteps?

[4] A drizzle is not enough to make a barren land fertile; continuous showers are needed to moisten the earth for the sweetest of sugarcanes to grow. Similarly, a heart as hard as rock and devoid of *bhakti* needs a million showers of devotional rain to blossom with gratitude. Remembering Lord Rama can be the much-needed shower to melt a cold, unemotional heart and help it bloom in *bhakti*.

[5] It is believed that chanting the core 92 verses (Verses 1.8 to 1.100), as Narada *muni* had, is equivalent to reciting the entire *Ramayana* comprising 24,000 verses.

the riverside encounter

After narrating the *Ramayana* to Valmiki, Narada *muni* left once more on his ceaseless travels and his selfless occupation of serving the world with his wisdom. Valmiki gazed in awe after his teacher. Every reunion with Narada *muni* had left him inspired. The great sage's purity, absorption of higher truths, wisdom, self-control and selflessness were qualities Valmiki wished to emulate.[6]

Valmiki was no ordinary disciple of Narada *muni*. He too had a host of disciples who flocked to his hermitage for training and guidance. Valmiki was convinced that he was just an instrument in his teacher's hands and felt that he was only serving as their guru on the great *muni's* behalf. And so he remained humble despite the glory that came his way.

On the departure of his teacher, Valmiki decided to take a bath. Forsaking his usual ritual of bathing in the Ganga, he went instead to the river Tamasa, accompanied by his disciple, Bharadwaja.[7] As he stepped into the river, it seemed to him that the water pooling there

---

[6] A student learns by listening to a good teacher and observing a great one. A good teacher teaches through words and a great one teaches through actions. A good teacher is appreciated and a great one emulated.

[7] Was it really by chance that he went to the Tamasa instead? It does not seem so. Whether the choice of river was coincidental or the result of intervention by a higher power needs exploration. Sages are predictable, doing the same thing every day, at the same time, at the same place and in the same way. They like consistency and are easily satisfied with little. In fact, consistency is the sign of stability and inner strength; therefore, we understand that Valmiki's change of path was influenced by a higher power for a higher cause.

was dirty. Immediately, he stepped out and went to a cleaner part of the river. Pleased with the quality of water here, he said to Bharadwaja, "The river is like the mind of a noble man: free from the filth of craving. It is clean, pure and shines with goodness. It is calm and radiates happiness all around."

Valmiki gazed appreciatively at the beauty surrounding the riverbank. He saw two *krouncha* birds (a bird which looks like a crane), a mated pair, calling out to each other. He watched their courting ritual and soon was engrossed in the scene.[8] Suddenly, an arrow zoomed across the sky. Like unkind words from the mouth of a cruel man, the arrow pierced through the heart of the male *krouncha*, killing it instantly. In agony, the female shrieked, bereaved so cruelly from her partner. Her immense pain wrung Valmiki's heart.[9]

Sickened by the sight and overwhelmed with grief, he could not contain his curse. "Oh, unfortunate hunter! [10] Because you have killed this male bird and separated it from its companion when they were

---

[8] Loyalty ignites undying love. The *krouncha* birds choose their partners for life and never separate until death. If they do get separated, the lonesome bird never couples with any other. Such is their loyalty.

[9] The forest is a blend of beauty and cruelty, which together bring fresh insight. Monotony kills learning.

[10] The circle of indifference has the self at the center, the natural outcome of which is apathy; the circle of compassion, on the other hand, has others at the center, the natural outcome of which is empathy. How is sweetness possible in a state of fury? His fury was expressed not to seek self-glorification but to show compassion toward the suffering of a living being.

approaching the peak of their passion, you will be condemned for all ages to come. Let all inauspiciousness befall you."[11]

No sooner than he uttered the words, Valmiki realized the extremity of his reaction.[12] He regretted having cursed the hunter on an impulse and allowing sudden rage to get the better of him. "Violence quintessentially defines a hunter. Why did I have to curse him?" he admonished himself.[13]

Lamenting his harsh response, Valmiki tried to remember the exact phrasing of his curse. As he recalled the words, his lips curled into a smile, belying the worry lining his forehead. He realized that something mystical had occurred. The Sanskrit curse was in fact a rhyme in perfect meter and tune! Perfect in every way, the curse could be set to music. Notwithstanding the meaning, the composition was unique and perfect. Bharadwaja, until now the silent bystander, had noticed how his spiritual master's emotions had swung from intense rage to deep remorse to beguiling delight. Bharadwaja was wise enough not to judge a great soul for his occasional peculiar behavior.[14]

---

[11] In Sanskrit, *soka* is the word for lamentation and *sloka* for verse. Valmiki's *soka* came out in the form of a *sloka*. This verse had such sweet cadence, although it was a curse. As Valmiki cursed the hunter, he recited some of his best poetry!

[12] Negative words that are hurled at others boomerang and hurt oneself the most. Even though Valmiki lost his temper for a good reason, he was the one most disturbed by it.

[13] The one who allows anger to affect him reacts, and the one who shields himself from anger responds. The one who reacts suffers alone, and the one who responds can alleviate others' suffering.

[14] Do not judge the behavior of great people; there is meaning even in their eccentricity. In case of ordinary people, there is eccentricity even in normal behavior.

Just then, Valmiki asked him if he had noticed that his curse was perfect poetry, and Bharadwaja couldn't but agree whole-heartedly. How mystical – a sweet-sounding curse!

Captivated by this unexpected brilliance, Valmiki continued with his bath, pondering over his verse. Bharadwaja gazed at him. Although Valmiki spent his entire day teaching his disciples, the curse kept playing at the back of his mind. He could not fathom what the curse-verse meant or why it sounded this sweet. Worse still, he was befuddled by the incessant repetitions inside his head and his helplessness in shutting them out.

the solution to valmiki's dilemma

Amid this helplessness, the answer came in the form of an unexpected visitor. Lord Brahma (the creator of the universe) was standing, imposing in all his glory, at the gate to Valmiki's *ashram*. An awestruck Valmiki rushed to welcome Brahma and watched as the four-headed god, resplendent like molten gold, alighted from his swan carrier. Four pairs of unblinking lotus petal–shaped eyes gazed at Valmiki and his four mouths smiled graciously.

Valmiki wondered to what he owed this divine presence. Unlike for others, Brahma had appeared of his own accord at Valmiki's doorstep. And Valmiki knew that great universal controllers such as Brahma do not appear on planet Earth without a reason; they appear only when they are pleased by extreme austerities and penances. Valmiki could think of no reason for Brahma to grace him with this visit. He wondered what then made Brahma choose to do so...

Whatever the reasons, Valmiki was overjoyed to see Brahma. He ushered him into the *ashram* with great respect and obeisance.

Formalities completed, Brahma asked Valmiki to take a seat. Valmiki was seated in front of the most powerful entity in the universe, but yet again his mind was helplessly drawn toward the *krouncha* bird incident. Involuntarily, as if goaded by some inner power, Valmiki began to recite the *sloka*-curse he had compiled.

It was then that Brahma revealed the real purpose of his visit, "The curse you uttered this morning is actually a verse because I wanted these words to spill out of your mouth in the manner they did. I want you to render the entire saga of Lord Rama's life in the same meter and composition as this verse. Those details about Lord Rama's life that you don't yet know shall be revealed to you. Whatever words you compose will be perfect and will truly glorify the stories of Lord Rama."

Brahma continued, "For as long as mountains and rivers flourish on Earth, the legend of Rama will flourish in this world. And for as long as the *Ramayana* flourishes, the world will know and celebrate you along with the *Ramayana*."

With this, Lord Brahma disappeared just as mysteriously and suddenly as he had appeared, leaving Valmiki *muni* and his disciples dumbfounded. Soon Valmiki's disciples began reciting the curse-verse. As the chanting reached a crescendo, Valmiki resolved, "Yes! I must begin writing the *Ramayana* immediately, in the same meter."[15]

As soon as Brahma left, Valmiki began preparing to write the

---

[15] Great people have the ability to convert a curse into a blessing. Valmiki could not comprehend how negativity could actually be a blessing. Whenever one goes through a negative experience in life, one cannot possibly see a shred of positivity in it. Brahma represents the guide who can help us see positivity in a highly negative situation. In fact, Brahma was able to bring out the hidden talent in Valmiki.

Ramayana. Before he began, he wondered, "Why me? Why was I chosen to perform this most fortunate task? What is so special about me that Brahma chose to assign this task to me of all the great souls in the universe?"

Just then, he turned toward the radiant beauty of one who had been a resident of his *ashram* for a while now. Her beauty and aristocracy radiating through Her simple attire. She was Sita, the mother of the universe. Yes, the very Sita who was Lord Rama's consort and the queen of Ayodhya; She was the same Sita who was the essence of Lord Rama's story. Valmiki reasoned that Brahma had chosen him to write the *Ramayana* possibly because Lord Rama had chosen **his** *ashram* to host Sita.

Valmiki then played back all the events of his life that had led to his becoming the sage that he was known to be. He took a deep breath and shut his eyes. His mind instantly transported him to a day in the distant past when he was merely a bow-and-arrow-wielding, scowl-faced and ferocious-looking wild hunter clad in deer skin. He was Ratnakar, the cruel and infamous sadist.

a sage is born

One day, while on a wild hunt, Ratnakar stopped in his tracks when he spotted a saffron-clad sage radiating an aura of tranquility. Ratnakar momentarily forgot his purpose and began gawking at Narada *muni*. A second later, he was back on track, chasing the fleeing animal. Narada *muni* spoke in a melodious, soft, lilting voice: "Why are you accumulating so many sins by inflicting suffering upon the innocent? Don't you understand that what goes around comes around? Every sin that is committed is definitely going to fructify in the form of a future suffering you have to undergo." The voice froze Ratnakar to a halt. Gathering his composure, he promptly attempted to justify his actions: "I do this with the sole aim of feeding my family."

Narada *muni* told him that if that was his aim, his family should be willing to share the burden of his sins. Ratnakar beamed, confident that his family members loved him enough to take the fall with him. Smiling knowingly, Narada *muni* asked Ratnakar to validate his belief. Ratnakar rushed to his family and asked them if they would share the consequence of the sins he accumulated while trying to provide for them. Their brutal response shocked Ratnakar. Crestfallen, he went back to Narada *muni*. Ratnakar could now be "helped." Prostrate at Narada *muni*'s feet, Ratnakar asked him to solve his dilemma. The fear that his sins would engulf him aggravated Ratnakar's anxiety, and he implored the *muni* for guidance.

Narada *muni* offered a simple yet effective solution. He asked Ratnakar to chant the various holy names of Lord Rama constantly, but Ratnakar failed in his attempt. Narada *muni* realized that he was full of sin; however, he was not among those who gave up. He thought up a unique way to help Ratnakar chant. He asked Ratnakar to chant constantly the word *mara* instead. This was easy for Ratnakar to repeat because his life was so closely connected to the word *mara*, which means death. Ratnakar sat down instantly and began chanting, *mara, mara, mara...* with complete sincerity. The chant created a word loop that magically transformed into Rama, Rama, Rama![16]

---

[16] Narada *muni*'s prescription suited Ratnakar's diseased condition. An advisor is like an able doctor who does not prescribe before diagnosing the disease.

Days became weeks, and weeks turned into years, but Ratnakar continued chanting *mara*, never once getting up, eating or even sleeping. Ants began to crawl all over his still body and gradually made a huge anthill upon it. Besieged by ants, Ratnakar was almost invisible. Many years later, when traveling through the forest once again, Narada *muni* stopped for he thought he distinctly heard the Rama chant emanating from somewhere close. He traced the humming sound to an anthill.

The bewildered *muni* sprinkled some holy water and the anthill dissolved, uncovering a devout figure seated in the lotus posture, eyes shut tight and lips constantly chanting *Rama*. "Ratnakar!" Narada *muni* gasped. Ratnakar opened his eyes to the soothing voice of his spiritual master. Valmiki *muni* stirred out of his past and into the present. His eyes swelled with tears of gratitude on seeing his savior, Narada *muni*. Soon he was at his master's feet, seeking blessings. Narada *muni* was so moved by his disciple's determination and virtuous appearance that he embraced Ratnakar and blessed him with a new name – Valmiki *muni*, the sage who emerged from an anthill.

Valmiki *muni* could not thank his teacher enough for teaching him to praise Lord Rama by unceasingly chanting the supremely pure holy name. He now knew why *he* was chosen to write the *Ramayana*. Narada *muni*'s forgiveness and mercy had armed him with unwavering strength for meditation and relentless chanting of the holy name. Chanting the holy name had purified him and spiritually elevated him enough to attract the mercy of Lord Rama. Lord Rama's mercy in turn presented him with the opportunity to serve Mother Sita. And, it was Mother Sita's mercy that empowered him to write the *Ramayana*. Valmiki acknowledged, "I am a product of mercy, and let that same higher power use me as an instrument to compose the *Ramayana*."

the poet finds his calling

As he sat down to write this epic, the entire *Ramayana* unfolded itself to Valmiki *muni* as if it were a live saga. Not only was he able to visualize the entire story, he was also able to experience every emotion of every character in the epic.[17,18]

After composing the *Ramayana*, which is a mammoth of an epic with 24,000 verses across 640 chapters and 6 books, Valmiki set about thinking about how to overcome the challenge of making it accessible to the world.

After much deliberation, Valmiki decided to use music to popularize this epic. The entire *Ramayana* was a single-meter composition. All Valmiki had to do was to find someone gifted enough to sing the entire saga in the perfect melody, pitch and intonation that reflected the emotions of all the characters. His thoughts raced in search of that perfect voice for this epic song.

As Valmiki sat pondering, he spotted Lava and Kusha, the two

---

[17] Spiritual knowledge is revealed not researched. Knowledge of physical sciences involves competence; however, knowledge of scriptural sciences involves character. Valmiki was chosen to author the *Ramayana* not so much because he was the most competent person to write it but because his character was flawless. Good character always attracts blessings.

[18] No knowledge can be gained without sufficient austerity. Austerities experienced in gaining knowledge of physical sciences include going to school, studying and giving up social life, whereas those experienced in learning scriptural sciences include following a disciplined lifestyle, such as waking up early, having a cold water bath, controlling stimuli that enter through the senses and chanting God's holy names for self-purification. The difference between the two types of austerities lies in the fact that one leads to unlimited information, the other to tangible internal transformation.

virtuous sons of Mother Sita. The two boys were humility, devotion, character and competence personified. They walked up to Valmiki and bowed in obeisance. Their velvet voices convinced Valmiki that he had found not one but two answers to his question.

Valmiki chose Lava and Kusha – his disciples and the sons of Sita and Rama – to be the first ones to be trained to sing the epic ballad. He meticulously explained the various nuances in the *Ramayana* to them and rehearsed every episode to help them perfect their delivery.[19]

After learning the *Ramayana*, Lava and Kusha began traversing the land, presenting its contents to various assemblies of sages and citizens. Everywhere they sang the ballad, appreciation, gifts and praises followed. The narration filled the heart of every listener with inexplicable ecstasy. One of the sages who heard them granted a unique blessing – that the boys would one day sing to the very person they were singing about. The essence of this benediction was lost on them.

The brothers soon became very popular across Ayodhya. Lord Rama eventually heard about their popularity and invited them to His assembly to hear the *Ramayana*. He invited His own brothers and ministers to hear these glorious brothers sing the *Ramayana*.

---

[19] Valmiki wrote the *Ramayana* when Rama was 40 years old. The chronology of Lord Rama's life is thus: Rama was married to Sita at the age of 12. They lived happily together for 12 years in their palace. At the age of 25, Rama's coronation ceremony had to be cancelled. Rama and Sita were exiled and went on to live in the forest for 14 years. Till the age of 39, Rama remained in the forest. At the age of 39 or 40, Rama was king of Ayodhya. It was at that time that Valmiki started writing the *Ramayana*. Valmiki then taught the *Ramayana* to Rama's sons, Lava and Kusha.

At this point, Lord Rama had no idea that these twin brothers were His own sons, born of His wife Sita, whom He had left long ago, during Her pregnancy, at the *ashram* of Valmiki *muni*.

Lord Rama praised the brothers and encouraged them before they began singing.[20] He told His brothers that the narration was about great personalities and should be listened to carefully.[21] Unbeknownst to Lord Rama, His own sons were to narrate their father's story to Him!

Lord Rama sat all alone on a huge golden throne with no Mother Sita by His side. She had made Valmiki's *ashram* Her home. The throne was placed on a raised platform, 18 steps above ground level. All of Lord Rama's subjects were seated below in their respective seats.

Everyone eagerly waited for the performance to begin. When the narration began, everyone was engrossed. Lava and Kusha were singing the *Ramayana* to the tune of the *veena*. Lord Rama could hear His own story unfurl. He seemed unaware of the many intricate details about His life that these boys seemed to know so well.

---

[20] It is interesting how Rama deals with people and with Himself. When a person is about to perform something challenging, he or she needs encouragement. An appreciative audience goads the performer. Rama is shown as being sensitive to the needs of performers.

[21] Self-praise is destructive; therefore, Rama does not reveal that this is a narration about Himself. Instead, He calls it a narration of great personalities. Scholars say that Rama was referring to mother Sita here as a great person. In fact, Rama was of the opinion that His story is glorious only because it revolves around mother Sita. Scholars say that the word *Ramayana* (*Rama* + *ayana*) actually should have been *Ramaayan* (*Ramaa* + *ayana*). The word *ayana* means – the story of a particular character. So, *Ramayana* means the story of Lord Rama. And the word *Ramaayan* refers to the story of *Ramaa*, which is another name of mother Sita.

Lord Rama suddenly felt lonely on His throne. Who wants to enjoy something pleasant all alone? He looked down at the audience and seeing them relish the narration in the loving company of their friends, He realized how lonely He was at the top.

Lord Rama wanted to descend from His throne, sit with His followers and hear the narration. But it was impossible because the awe and reverence they had for Him would not let that happen. So Lord Rama sneaked down the steps, unnoticed by others. As He climbed down, gradually moving toward the audience, He held on to His jewelry and clothes to avoid making any noise, creating any disturbance or drawing any attention toward Himself. Everyone in the assembly was too absorbed in the *Ramayana* to notice Lord Rama.[22]

Soon Lord Rama was part of the general audience. Everybody was immersed in the narration, patting one another, laughing and thoroughly enjoying the story. So engrossed were they that when Lord Rama patted a person, that person patted Rama back! When the narration ended, the audience looked for Lord Rama on the throne. To their horror, He wasn't there! They started searching for Lord Rama and were shocked to see Him sitting right next to them.

---

[22] Valmiki very beautifully mentioned that attraction to the *Ramayana* was greater than the attraction to Rama. The *Ramayana* attracted even Lord Rama! It's no wonder then that the *Ramayana* appeals to everyone even today.

CHAPTER 2

A SAD MONARCH IN A HAPPY KINGDOM

a miracle called ayodhya

Lava and Kusha's story began with a description of the kingdom of Kosala, which was by the Sarayu river. At the center of this kingdom was its capital city, Ayodhya, the abode of the great king, Dasaratha. King Dasaratha was the crowning glory of the luminous Solar dynasty. Manu, the first king of the Ikshvaku dynasty, had laid the foundation of this massive city.[1]

Ayodhya means unconquerable, and it was impenetrable to both external and internal enemies. While other kings and kingdoms were the external enemies, vices such as lust, anger, pride, illusion, greed and envy formed the internal enemies. Most cities are equipped to fend off only external enemies, but Ayodhya could counter internal enemies too. In the perfect city of Ayodhya, whose citizens had flawless character and strong values, internal attacks were unheard of.

A deep, wide moat ran alongside the walls surrounding the city, making the security system of Ayodhya impossible to breach. The moat was so deep and wide that clouds would mistake it for the ocean

---

[1] The city was 12 *yojanas* long and 3 *yojanas* broad. 1 *yojana* = approx. 10 miles.

and absorb water from it; but then when they tried to float up, these water-heavy clouds would fail to cross over the high boundary walls of the city. Drained and weary, they would drop the rain back into the moat.

Powerful weapons like daggers, swords, bows, battle-axes, rods, *chakras*, *tomaras*, *musalas* and *vajras* were embedded in the walls. These could kill mosquitoes (the smallest of creatures) and *garudas* (the largest of creatures) with equal ease. Some of the embedded weapons were unique to Ayodhya in that these had as much power to stave off wild catastrophic winds as to strike at the vile minds of those who dared harbor evil thoughts against the people of the city.

The highly secure city of Ayodhya was also picturesque. Under King Dasaratha's rule, the city became as beautiful and opulent as Amaravati, the heavenly abode of Indra. Beautiful gateways and arches speckled the city and most homes had well-laid-out front yards. The outskirts were teeming with orchards and gardens.

Ayodhya's layout resembled the board game *Astapadi*, which meant that the city was designed like a dice table, with wide streets running in eight directions from centrally located palaces. The densely populated city was filled with houses; no place was left unutilized. Buildings were constructed on leveled lands.

The city was so vast that nobody could claim to have seen its boundaries! Even the Sarayu river could not define the boundaries of Ayodhya despite several rivulets flowing into it. The palaces in Ayodhya were whiter than the moon. Some had floors studded with *chandrakanta* stones (a special precious stone, lesser known today), some had pillars made of sandalwood, rafters made of red gold and walls of emerald. There were twenty million such palaces! Ayodhya's skyscrapers were studded with precious jewels.

Ayodhya was also a trade center, and people from across the world flocked to the city for business.

ayodhya's body

Music was an intrinsic part of Ayodhya, so much so that the king sponsored musicians to play continuous soul-stirring music across different districts of the capital.[2]

King Dasaratha's brilliance and foresight could be gauged from the way he made systematic arrangements to make the kingdom self-sufficient. Rice grain was always in surplus and drinking water was as sweet as sugarcane juice. That Dasaratha had immense foresight could be seen in Ayodhya's ground-breaking irrigation system. Ayodhya had two types of water-storage systems – the first *devamatraka* (entirely dependent on rains sent by demigods or *devas*) and the other *nadimatraka* (dependent on effective water storage systems).[3] Ayodhya depended on the *nadimatraka* system of irrigation, which facilitated rainwater harvesting to ensure abundant water supply through years and years of drought.

In fact, Ayodhya once faced an eleven-year drought and no one even noticed that it hadn't rained through all those years! There was abundant water for everything. It was only in the twelfth year that everyone began taking notice and worrying. Word reached the king,

---

[2] Music is a balm that supplies positive emotions, which calms agitation and inspires innovation.

[3] Today's society adopts the *devamatraka* system of irrigation, which is heavily dependent on the rains.

and Dasaratha then consulted astrologers to find out the exact reason for the drought. When told that the Shani *graha's* (planet) fiery gaze had left his kingdom parched, Dasaratha decided to set things right immediately.[4]

An enraged Dasaratha mounted his chariot and headed toward Shani.[5] As the king came close to the planet, Shani glared at him. His stern gaze alone was enough to topple Dasaratha's chariot. From then on it was a hopeless free fall. Dasaratha had totally lost control.

A giant vulture named Jatayu who was flying by saw Dasaratha's plight and flew downward to grab him. He spread out his wings like a safety net and Dasaratha, along with his chariot, fell on it. So colossal was Jatayu that only one of his wings was enough to catch Dasaratha, his chariot and all his horses!

Jatayu decided to help Dasaratha counter Shani. With Jatayu by his side, Dasaratha set off to take on Shani, yet again. Dasaratha's dogged determination pleased Shani, and he agreed to shift his gaze away from Ayodhya. Joy at last! The rains had returned to Ayodhya.

Dasaratha could not thank Jatayu enough for having saved his life and helped him. So he asked Jatayu to take the liberty of seeking any

---

[4] Foresight is the hallmark of a leader; it enables a leader to build effective systems. The leader's quality lies not just in building such systems but also in ensuring effective functioning of those systems. An interesting type of leadership is "servant leadership", where the leader feels that being anointed leader is a gift to serve more people. Such a leader finds every opportunity to serve as god sent. Dasaratha had created a flawless system, but when it was not as effective as anticipated, he considered it his responsibility to rectify it at any cost, even at the cost of his life.

[5] The name Dasaratha means one whose chariot can move in ten directions.

benediction of his choice.[6] Dasaratha was least expecting what was to come. Jatayu requested that when Dasaratha begot a son, he should become the son of Jatayu. Although he was yearning for a son, at this point, Dasaratha had none. So he had no hesitation in agreeing to what, at the time, seemed a non-possibility.[7]

ayodhya's soul

Ayodhya was glorified as a place with no lock shops and people who did not donate for charity. This seems like a skewed glorification of the city; in fact, these appear more likes flaws. But what it actually does is glorify the city, in that a highly secure Ayodhya was bereft of lock shops because nothing needed locking! No one had a wrong motive or felt the need to rob because everyone was prosperous and self-sufficient. As for no one being charitable, whom would people donate to if there were no needy souls?

Dasaratha's ocean of charities engulfed Ayodhya's poverty, so no beggars walked the streets. Dasaratha crossed the ocean of knowledge by plunging deep into the scriptures, he crossed the ocean of enemies

---

[6] Promises should be made in accordance with one's capacity to keep them and not with overconfidence. Not knowing what Jatayu would ask, Dasaratha told him to ask for anything. Only God can grant all boons. A human with unlimited flaws can no doubt imitate God by making such a statement, but cannot substantiate it without experiencing great pain and personal loss. This results in a change of mood from gratitude to annoyance for the one who promises.

[7] At a later point in the *Ramayana*, however, this promise would hold a different meaning for both the giver and the taker. What was to prove very costly for Dasaratha would become a saving grace for Jatayu.

by cutting across them through deft use of his sword and he crossed the ocean of vices by immersing himself in spiritual practices.[8]

The physical strength of Ayodhya came not just from brute force, but from years of discipline. Ayodhya's soldiers were skilled in all kinds of weapons and military tactics. Ayodhya was compared to a cave teeming with countless lions. On principle, the skilled archers of Ayodhya neither killed a lone, helpless person nor a fleeing one. They were experts in sonic archery, yet they did not practice it.

The soldiers were deeply loyal to their king and were ever ready to make any sacrifice for him because they loved him and did not fear him. The strong-willed soldiers of Ayodhya were so courageous that they would rather face death than run away from a battle.

ripple effect

There is a story behind why Ayodhya's army did not practice sonic archery. In his youth, Dasaratha used to venture out on hunting expeditions, where he loved using the powerful method of sonic archery as often as possible. He was in fact looking for one such opportunity when he heard a sound, much like the rumbling of a tiger or like an elephant drinking water from a river. He shot an eager

---

[8] For a leader, four things are essential – physical strength, intellectual strength, emotional strength and spiritual strength. Physical strength is acquired by having a powerful army; intellectual strength by studying the scriptures and being guided by a wise counsel; emotional strength by being kind, generous and sensitive toward those weaker; and spiritual strength by taking some time off from worldly pursuits to pursue one's goal in life and taking refuge in higher powers.

arrow in that direction.[9] Little did he realize that the sound was that of a pot being dunked into the river; an eager-to-serve son was filling water for his thirsty parents. The arrow hit its mark. A blood-curdling, agonizing scream followed. It was the dying boy's cry of despair and misery.

Almost simultaneously, reverberating through the forest was Dasaratha's scream of guilt.[10] He realized that his skill had inexorably destroyed him. Dasaratha ran to meet his dying destiny, to offer whatever little help he could, to prove his sincerity and to secure some pardon for his arrogance. Before him was a young boy writhing in pain, an arrow pierced right through his chest. The boy implored Dasaratha, begging to know what could possibly have been his fault to have been fatally attacked this way.

Dasaratha tried to offer an explanation only to know of the boy's predicament.[11] The boy was the only child of his old, blind and invalid parents. His life was dedicated to serving them, and they lived a life of gratitude, dependent on their only son. Even as he was dying this very moment, further down the banks, the old couple was waiting with parched throats for their son to bring them some water. As the boy began to inch closer to death, his pain became more excruciating at the thought of who would look after his parents after he was no more. No sooner than he told Dasaratha about his concern, he passed away.

---

[9] Acting without seeing the reality is a sign of overconfidence.

[10] Dasaratha's pain was probably more excruciating than the pain the arrow caused the boy. The pain of guilt is the toughest to deal with.

[11] To justify one's actions is the easiest part of life. Acting responsibly and being accountable to others who may have to pay for your actions (foreseen or unforeseen) is very difficult. Being able to respect the predicament of each individual, not judge and shoot arrows of harsh words or unkind deeds is a sign of maturity.

A heavy-hearted Dasaratha carried water in that pot to the eagerly waiting ill-fated parents. When the old couple heard the rustle of the footsteps of a stranger and not their son's approach them, inexplicable fear gripped them.[12] When Dasaratha told the couple of his dreadful mistake, their wounded hearts let out a curse: Dasaratha, too, would die of the pain of separation from his son. Dasaratha fell at their feet, begging for forgiveness.[13] Alas, those were the old parents' last words before they joined their son in his pyre.

A despondent Dasaratha returned to Ayodhya. He had learnt a very important lesson: Never to let passion prevail over reason. He vowed that day never to practice sonic archery, lest it bring upon another painful curse and even more painful memories.[14]

Ayodhya's intellectual prowess consisted of brahmanas or Vedic scholars who had immense control over their senses. They lived a life governed by strict spiritual discipline. Everything they asked of others, they demonstrated in person. They were strict with themselves and accommodated others' shortcomings, even as they encouraged them

---

[12] Fearing the worst is incomparable to the trauma that one goes through when the truth is revealed.

[13] One begs forgiveness for a mistake one commits. It is extremely important to think before making that mistake. Passion makes reasoning difficult. Dasaratha's passion for hunting made him overconfident; before shooting the arrow, he did not use reason. Now that the consequences of his action were waiting for him, he resorted to reasoning. If we allow our passion to prevail over reasoning, we are in for a curse instead of a blessing.

[14] To lament for one's mistake is important, but far more important is to learn from that mistake. To make mistakes does not imply lack of intelligence but a lack of foresight. Not repeating mistakes is a sign of intelligence.

to perfection. They did not beg for survival, instead they survived on donations they received as tokens of gratitude from their students for imparting knowledge to them. In fact, before accepting any donation, they verified that the money was earned through righteous means. Because of their wisdom and knowledge, their behavior and their purity, they commanded absolute respect.[15]

Dasaratha's in-depth knowledge of the Vedas, expertise in military sciences, far-sightedness in administration, purity of mindset and kindness and empathy were qualities that made his kingdom flawless.

Consequently, the citizens were content, happy, pure, always truth-abiding and affluent. Jealous, unscholarly, ugly men, thieves, liars, atheists and the sick had no place in the kingdom.[16]

dasaratha's leadership model

Of all the assets Dasaratha possessed, the one he valued most and depended on always was the Big M – the brains behind his

---

[15] A person worthy of respect is a person worthy of being followed. Respect is one of life's greatest jewels. Just as diamonds are given only to people who can understand and afford their value, the jewel of respect is handed over only to those worthy of it. Respect cannot be demanded, but only commanded. To command respect, an individual's words and actions have to be in alignment with the highest truths. Only then does a person become truly respectable.

[16] We often wonder if it is at all possible to have a competition-free society. Here is a role model in Ayodhya. When everyone, from the king to the common person, is striving to live a life of purity and service, it is definitely possible.

success.[17] Dasaratha's strength was in fact this Big M – a council of ministers (*mantris* or mentors) carefully chosen by him. He had eight ministers – Dristi, Jayantha, Vijaya, Suraashtra, Raashtravardhana, Akopa, Dharmapaala and Sumantra.

These eight ministers were men of pure mind and great integrity. Their love for the country and its people, along with their loyalty to the king, encouraged them to use their foresight in devising policies and plans to help their country progress. They were learned, affluent, modest and unpretentious men with exemplary skills. Their words complemented their actions. Their self-control was such that when provoked, angered, or even tempted with wealth or sex, they did not yield. Not only did they embrace truth, they also inspired others to value it at all times. They appreciated virtues in the elders and showed them respect, overlooking their lapses. They were resourceful and assessed people and situations very quickly, and at the first whiff of trouble, they took immediate action.[18] Their intelligence was so keen that they never failed to live up to the expectations of doing the right thing at the right time. They were equipoised in war and in peace.

---

[17] Success is sure to follow a leader if he can create tangible as well as intangible assets. Tangible assets are essentially his abundant treasury and an unconquerable army. Intangible assets include the confidence of people in the leader's power and ability. It is this intangible asset that is the soul of leadership, which leads to loyalty and unquestioned cooperation. To capitalize on tangible and intangible assets effectively, the leader has to depend heavily on a third type of asset, known as the Big M. The Big M represented those people known as Ministers, Mentors or *Mantris* of the king. A strong temptation of a leader is to become autocratic or to act solely based on desires, aspirations and perceptions.

[18] Indecision is a deadly disease in leadership; however, the ministers kept themselves immune from this disease by timely action.

In addition to these common qualities, each of Dasaratha's ministers had a specialty. Surprisingly, their names were metaphors for the special qualities they possessed.

Dristi means vision; he was farsighted. Since he had the wisdom to see ahead of time, he was the architect of Ayodhya's fortune.

Vijaya means victory; he always led Ayodhya's army to victory.

Jayantha literally means the one who ensures that victory remains. He ensured proper jurisdiction and control over the vast dominions that Vijaya expanded.[19]

Suraashtra's (also known as Arthasadaka) responsibility was to keep the royal treasury full by collecting taxes from the citizens on time, thus ensuring financial stability in the state.[20]

Siddhartha (also known as Raashtravardhana) was responsible for fulfilling all the needs of the citizens and the king. He knew the art of resources management. He kept everyone happy and at the same time ensured that the state's resources were not depleted.[21]

Akopa (also known as Asoka) means one who does not allow grief or lamentation. His role was to ensure that no citizen was remorseful or disgruntled. He made himself available to the people at all times,

---

[19] Expansion is important but not at the cost of continuity. Equally if not more important than the team that expands is the team that ensures continuity.

[20] The state should collect taxes like a honeybee collects nectar in small portions from many, many flowers to make honey and not extracting so much from one flower that it dies.

[21] Classifying needs and wants is the first step toward stability. The second is fulfilling those needs compulsively and wants selectively.

allowing them to speak their hearts out without the fear of being misjudged or mistreated.[22]

Dharmapaala (also known as Mantrapala) means one who guides according to *dharma* or truth. He was the policy maker in Ayodhya, adept in statecraft. In fact, he recommended policies for all departments and personally supervised their implementation. He promoted a strong and stable government at home and a policy of friendship and goodwill with other states.

Sumantra was the oldest and wisest; he headed the cabinet. He was Dasaratha's confidant. A natural leader and the simplest of all the ministers, he commanded great respect and his words were considered the absolute truth.

In addition to the eight ministers, the Big M consisted of two venerable saints named Vasistha and Vamadeva who were experts in everything religious.

The combination of tangible and intangible assets and the support of the Big M made Dasaratha the perfect, invincible leader.[23]

---

[22] The need to be heard runs very deep in all human beings. This need becomes most pressing when one is discontent. When one feels unheard or ignored, one emotionally links this discontent to feeling neglected and not wanted. Most people do not look for solutions, they only want empathy. The prime duty of a good leader is to make every subject feel heard. This creates stability and a sense of belongingness.

[23] However great an individual may be, it is impossible to achieve any kind of success alone. The power of a team cannot be discounted. Those who do not believe in a team are afflicted by the disease of insecurity. Deep insecurity about working with those stronger than themselves stems from the fear of being overshadowed. Such people prefer to surround themselves with weaker people and sycophants. When one dreams of a big goal, the team one chooses must be bigger than the dreams envisioned. Else, it will only remain a dream.

dasaratha's void

Dasaratha seemed to be a complete man. He had everything a man could aspire for and probably more. Physical strength, beautiful wives, opulence beyond imagination, magnificent palaces, followers who would do anything for him, and a kingdom that extended across the globe.[24]

Yes, Dasaratha had everything indeed; yet, he was dissatisfied. The presence of everything in his life was overshadowed by the absence of a son. Just as a small coin that can cover the eye to block out the brightness of the majestic sun, the absence of a son eclipsed the grandeur of Dasaratha's limitless fortune and blessings. Dasaratha had 353 wives, but no son!

Kausalya, Sumitra and Keikeyi were the principal wives of Dasaratha. The king married the remaining 350 princesses under harsh circumstances. A powerful incarnation of Lord Vishnu named Parashuram once went on a rampage, destroying all *Kshatriyas* with vengeance, because of mistakes committed by some of them.

Parashuram traveled across the world eliminating *Kshatriyas* who crossed his path; however, he did not touch a *kshatriya* surrounded by women or one in the midst of a wedding. A king was called *Nari*

---

[24] Could a person who possessed so much, have any lacuna? The nature of this world is defined by limitations. There is always a pin pricking in some part of our life. The dimension of the prick is insignificant compared to the entire body. However, that small prick is capable of creating immense turmoil in the mind. Physical pain is much easier to tolerate than the mental pain of not having what you yearn the most. When the mind zooms in on a problem, it magnifies a small problem into gigantic proportions.

Kavaca because he saved himself by surrounding himself with naked women that nauseated Parashuram enough to spare the king.

Dasaratha, on the other hand, took refuge in weddings. Whenever he was informed about Parashuram's imminent arrival, he would initiate a wedding ceremony with the princess of the land he was in. Parashuram could not fight or kill Dasaratha because he was in the midst of a wedding. Parashuram passed by Ayodhya 350 times during his rampage, and Dasaratha evaded death as many times and ended up with 350 wives in addition to his three queens!

The pangs of agony at not having a son far surpassed the tremors of anguish that Dasaratha felt every time Parashuram came by to attack him.

material problems, spiritual solutions

Dasaratha called his Big M for a conference to find a way to overcome his grief. He thought an *ashwamedha yajna* (a horse sacrifice) would please the Lord enough to award him a son; however, before making a decision, he wanted the advice and blessings of all the great sages and wise men in his council.[25]

The great sages led by Vasistha seconded Dasaratha's idea and agreed to assist him in fulfilling his desire. The sages also warned him of the

---

[25] The mind is a connoisseur in converting trivial puddles into bottomless oceans. The boat of good advice is the hope that can help cross the ocean of grief. Undermining good advice is tantamount to disaster. Dasaratha was not just concerned with good advice, but also with the accompanying blessings.

dire consequences of any errors made when conducting this sacrifice. They agreed to protect the sacrifice against such lapses by keeping strict vigil on the performance and the purity of every individual and ritual involved.[26]

After all the advisors left, Sumantra approached Dasaratha and told him a hitherto unknown story. He narrated that long ago he had heard the great sage Sanat Kumar predicting that Dasaratha would perform this very *yajna*. Sanat Kumar had spoken about a unique and powerful sage named Rishi Shringa as being the chief director of the sacrifice. The wise Sanat Kumar had predicted that under the guidance of Rishi Shringa, the sacrifice would be a success and that Dasaratha would father illustrious sons.[27]

---

[26] Dasaratha wanted to solve his material problem with a spiritual solution, by taking shelter in and worshipping the Lord. However, solutions to problems are not always as easy as they seem. Seeing the unseen is an art that requires maturity and wisdom. Everyone knows the laws, but few know the lapses. Treading on a path of spirituality requires systematic guidance or else a lone mistake can undo even the best intentions. Dasaratha, therefore, capitalized on the strength of his big M to see him through such tricky moments.

[27] Why did Sumantra not speak about this sage and the *yajna* before? The reason was that Sumantra was a confidant; his job was to improve upon the ideas the king proposed, not take any initiatives regarding his personal affairs. A relationship is effective when both parties involved understand their limits and expectations. Though Sumantra knew what would be good for the king, it was inappropriate for him to make suggestions to him. Every king had a confidant like Sumantra; they were like treasure troves of information. On occasion, they would dig up required information for the king, or, they would keep their lips sealed and continue observing the affairs of the kingdom actively.

rishi shringa — a sage with a horn

Sumantra went on to narrate the history behind Rishi Shringa's greatness.

Rompada, the great king of Anga, was a very a dear friend of King Dasaratha so much so that Dasaratha had given up his own daughter Santa for adoption to King Rompada, assuming that he would father sons in the future. Once, Rompada's kingdom was crippled by drought. Great sages advised that if Rishi Shringa stepped into his kingdom, there would be bountiful rains immediately.

Rishi Shringa was so named because of this peculiar birth feature. *Shringa* means a horn. Rishi Shringa means a sage with a horn. Indeed, Rishi Shringa was born with a horn on his forehead! But to get Rishi Shringa to step into the kingdom was not an easy task because his father Vibandaka kept him cocooned from the material world. He forbade Rishi Shringa from entering any city or leaving behind the austere forest life of an ascetic. To make Rishi Shringa a great sage, Vibandaka kept him off all luxuries, comforts, women and even rich food.

So Rompada asked his ministers to devise a clever plan to trick Rishi Shringa into entering his kingdom. The ministers waited until Rishi Shringa's father was away. They then sent a group of female courtesans dressed as male sages to lure the hermit. The female courtesans began surrounding the hermitage with sweet melodious music. The innocent Rishi Shringa had no idea these sages were women and treated them as compatriots who had come to the forest. In return for respect and hospitality, the sages offered Rishi Shringa exquisite sweets and words of affection. The naïve Rishi Shringa thought the sweets were some kind of fruit. When it was time for his father to return, each courtesan embraced him and left the hermitage.[28]

After their departure, Rishi Shringa was like a lost man. He was emotionally disturbed and overcome with sadness and was always absorbed in the thoughts of these women. He had never ever experienced such turbulence before.[29]

The next day, the women returned and told him to accompany them to their hermitage. They promised to introduce Rishi Shringa to many other exalted sages. Rishi Shringa willingly accompanied them. Their hermitage was actually a moving boat, which quickly brought the unsuspecting Rishi Shringa into the kingdom of Rompada.

The moment Rishi Shringa stepped on the soil of Anga, the clouds burst and began pouring incessant rain. The downpour swelled Anga's parched hearts with the kind of joy a *chataka* bird feels when after waiting for long, the first drops of rain quenches its thirst.

A much-relieved and grateful Rompada fell at the feet of the great

---

[28] Rishi Shringa is compared to the mind of a living entity and the women disguised as ascetics are considered to be desirable objects. The nature of the mind is to interpret worldly temptation as good. His father represents intelligence. In the face of intelligence, desirable objects seem foolish, but when one is alone, the same desirable objects control and direct. If one's own intelligence is not strong enough to resist temptations, one should seek the company of one with stronger intelligence.

[29] From another perspective, Rishi Shringa teaches us that even if one is strong-willed, constant interaction with material objects can weaken the toughest of resolves. Without understanding the real nature of his son, Vibandaka forced him to follow an austere lifestyle. One has to be true to one's nature and not be hypocritical. If one is forced to do something one does not want to, it leads to hypocrisy. It is best to practice a lifestyle conducive to one's nature, keeping the higher principles in mind.

sage and offered his daughter Santa's hand in marriage to him. It was then that Rishi Shringa figured what had actually transpired: He would now be a married man and that he was instrumental in serving a greater purpose, although he was tricked into it. Rishi Shringa wisely decided not to take offense. King Rompada requested Rishi Shringa to stay in his kingdom.

Sumantra reminded Dasaratha that Santa was after all his own daughter and that made Rishi Shringa his son-in-law. So, if Dasaratha were to request Rishi Shringa, he would definitely not be able refuse because they were so closely related.[30]

Dasaratha wasted no time and set forth for Anga to request Rompada to allow Rishi Shringa to perform the sacrifice in Ayodhya.

The citizens of Ayodhya welcomed Rishi Shringa with much pomp and glory. Here was a sage who could usher into Ayodhya the rain of good fortune by facilitating Dasaratha's desire for sons.

the sacrifice

Rishi Shringa suggested that Dasaratha perform the *putrakamesti yajna* (a sacrifice to the Lord to fulfill one's desire for sons). Successful performance of the *putrakamesti yajna* required the king to be sinless. To ensure purity, Rishi Shringa suggested that the *ashwamedha yajna* be performed.[31]

---

[30] From Dasaratha's action, we learn how one act of kindness reaps fruit, eventually. Dasaratha giving away his daughter to a distressed Rompada was eventually the cause of Dasaratha's joy.

[31] *Asva* means *kala* or time and *medha* means purified. The performer of this *yajna* gets purified of all sins ever committed in any past life.

Arrangements for the *ashwamedha yajna* had in fact begun from the time Rishi Shringa arrived in Ayodhya. A powerful horse was selected and sent out to traverse the globe. The *ashwamedha yajna* was such that the king of every kingdom through which this horse passed had to either accept the sender of the horse as his master or fight to prove his supremacy. When the horse sent from Ayodhya passed through every kingdom of the world, no king dared challenge it, and everyone rightfully accepted Dasaratha as the unopposed monarch of the world.

The ritual horse took a whole year to return to Ayodhya. Meanwhile, preparations for the sacrificial ceremony were on full swing. Every king of the world was invited to this sacrifice. Vasistha insisted that Sumantra personally go and invite Dasaratha's close friends – Janaka the king of Mithila, Rompada the king of Anga, Kekeya the king of Kekeya (Keikeyi's father, the third wife of Dasaratha) and many others. Elaborate lodging arrangements were made to host the royal guests and their entourage comfortably.

Vasistha painstakingly monitored every aspect of the arrangement for the sacrifice.[32] He ensured that there were no lapses and that all those involved in the preparations did their best. His key instructions to all concerned were that nothing should be taken lightly; no invitee

---

[32] Inattention and neglect creates demons. When we carry out our duties with a carefree attitude, we give the various demons an opportunity to enter our life and harass us. Being focused is a sign of love, and love means paying attention to detail. When we do something out of love, there is no question of neglect and inattention. Vasistha loved Dasaratha, not because he gave him extensive facilities, but because he saw in him a leader striving to uphold the principles of true leadership. He did not do his duty as a matter of ritual but performed them with such intensity out of love.

should feel neglected; none who came to participate in the sacrifice should go hungry or thirsty. Women, children, old and ailing were given special consideration and their needs were attended to immediately. The food served was so wholesome and pure that even those with poor appetites overate and still longed for more. All the visitors were thoroughly satisfied and showered their blessings wholeheartedly.

The *ashwamedha yajna* was a double-edged sword, in that it could deliver great results and ensure an elevated life for the performer, but it could also prove disastrous if there were to be a single lapse. It was believed that *brahma rakshasas* attacked and destroyed the performer as soon as that single error was committed.[33] To avoid such mistakes, Vasistha appointed supervisors to keep strict vigil, to ensure that everyone executed their tasks sincerely, without neglecting their responsibilities.

dasaratha's benevolence

The *ashwamedha yajna* was thus successfully completed under Rishi Shringa's able guidance and Vasistha's alert management. After the *yajna*, the joyous Dasaratha showered all his wealth on the priests as charity. In his ecstasy, he exhausted all his wealth. Dasaratha gave

---

[33] *Brahma rakshasas* were *brahmanas* in their previous birth reborn as demons for sins they had committed in their past lives. Whenever such sacrifices took place, *brahma rakshasas* would start hovering over the sacrificial arena waiting for that single mistake. One of the greatest sins is fault-finding.

away everything he had because he was completely filled with joy.[34] When the priests received all his wealth, they addressed him as Raghunandana.

Why did the priests call Dasaratha so? Dasaratha's charitable disposition reminded them of his ancestor, a famous king named Raghu, also known for his extreme benevolence.

A story from King Raghu's life highlights this wonderful quality. Once King Raghu performed the Viswajit yajna,[35] in which he gave away all his possessions. The only possessions that remained were his clothes and some earthen pots and vessels. Hearing of his magnificence, a young scholar named Kautsa went to seek his help to discharge his obligation toward his spiritual master. Kautsa needed a princely amount of 140 million gold coins. Because Kautsa was a brahmana, King Raghu received him respectfully. When Kautsa learned that Raghu had given away everything and was reduced to poverty, he did not ask for anything. Raghu, however, insisted on serving Kautsa, not wanting the dishonor of dissatisfying a needy guest. After relentless persuasion, the young scholar told him what he wanted. Immediately, Raghu started praying to Kubera (the treasurer of demigods) for the wealth he needed. He also instructed his soldiers that if Kubera did not respond to his prayer, they should attack Kubera's kingdom. That very night, a heavy shower of gold coins filled the king's empty coffers. The scholar wanted only 140 million coins. Neither the scholar nor the king was willing to accept anything

---

[34] The result of being happy is that one wants to share it with others. A brahmana is not respected due to his birth but because he has the wealth of realized knowledge. When this wealth of knowledge is combined with humility, it becomes like a magnetic force that commands respect.

[35] A yagna that ensures victory over the world.

more because neither owned this wealth. Such was the magnanimity of the donor and the recipient.

Pleased with Dasaratha's attitude, the priests returned his riches to him saying that they were not competent enough to handle such opulence. They took only as much as they required for educational purposes and for sacrifices. Dasaratha took back the wealth and property and instead gave them millions of cows, gold coins and four times as many silver coins. The *brahmanas* in turn passed all this wealth on to Rishi Shringa and Vasistha. The two detached souls promptly divided the wealth equally among all the *brahmanas*.[36,37]

At the end of the *ashwamedha yajna*, Dasaratha became qualified to perform the *putrakamesti yajna*. Rishi Shringa spearheaded the *putrakamesti yajna* rituals. The altar of the *yajna* was eagle-shaped because Garuda, an eagle, was instrumental in getting nectar for the demigods whenever they were in trouble. Now that Dasaratha was in despair, the eagle-shaped altar was his hope for the celestial nectar – the ultimate magic potion that could usher in the sweet joy of male children into his life.

---

[36] Dasaratha exhibited the quality of detachment and the priests, that of self-control. Both are qualities that purify. Those who have a lot wealth are too attached to part with it. Those who do not have wealth are willing to go to any extent, even compromising on their principles, to get it. In abundance, sharing gives satisfaction, and in scarcity, being content gives satisfaction. Those with plenty that do not share become hard-hearted and those with little that are not content become envious.

[37] The *brahmanas* knew their capabilities and were honest about it. Many people wish to have unlimited power without realizing that with power comes responsibility.

CHAPTER 3

A FLOOD OF SWEETNESS

The *putrakamesti yajna* began at last! The sacrificial fire blazed powerfully, sending billowing fumes right up to the sky. As the sky became overcast with holy smoke, the demigods descended from the heavens to receive their share of the offering. The sacrifice was so pure that they felt drawn toward it. Although their heart was pounding with excitement, their minds were racing toward a demon named Ravana. His presence in this universe disturbed them so much that they took their concerns about the demon and his cruel ways to Brahma, the god of gods.

history of ravana

Ravana was eldest of the three sons and a daughter born to Kaikashi and Vishravas. Kaikashi was the daughter of Sumali, a *rakshasa*. Sumali wanted his daughter to marry a powerful *brahmana* so that their offspring have the best of both races – they would be *rakshasas* but with the powers of great *brahmanas*. This would ensure permanent rule of the *rakshasas* over the demigods. The pious Kaikashi did not share her father's opinion; however, being an obedient daughter, she married Vishravas, Sumali's choice of the ideal groom for her.

After the wedding, when Vishravas realized his wife's real intentions, he cursed that she would give birth to bloodthirsty *rakshasas*. Kaikashi had married Vishravas to appease her father, so she fell at his feet, imploring him to retract his curse. To pacify her, Vishravas bestowed her with another son who would be a great devotee of the Lord.

Kaikashi gave birth to a ten-headed and twenty-handed monster named Dasagriva or Dasanana. From his very birth, this decahedral monster was anger personified, and one who eventually turned into a cruel maniac. Ravana lived up to his name.[1] He derived great pleasure from making others cry. Next she gave birth to another son, who rapidly grew to become a giant. He devoured everything and everyone who crossed his path. He was named Kumbakarna.[2]

Next, a saintly boy was born; he was named Vibhishan.[3] Finally, an unattractive and deformed daughter with a vicious temper was born. She was named Surpanakha.[4]

Vishravas had another wife who gave birth to a son named Kubera,

---

[1] The word *ravana* means one who makes others cry.

[2] Kumba means pot and karna means ears, or the one whose ears were as gigantic as pots. If the ears are so huge how big would the body be. Ears represent the organ through which we acquire knowledge to destroy ignorance. Although Kumbakarna had such huge ears, the knowledge to help discriminate the right from the wrong never entered his ears. When right knowledge escapes the ears, garbage makes way into it. Kumbakarna was filled with rubbish, which is represented by his gigantic body.

[3] The word *bhishan* means fearful; hence Vibhishan meant one who is very fearful to behold. Vibhishan was very fearful of committing any act not sanctioned by the scriptures.

[4] *Nakha* means nails and surpa means *sharp*; it could also mean "like a winnowing fan." Surpanakha literally means the one who had sharp nails or one who had nails as big as winnowing fans. The sharp features of Surpanakha indicate the sharp nature (almost adamant) of her mindset. She was a person who wanted everything she desired.

who became the treasurer of the demigods. Kubera got possession of Lanka. Lanka was a very beautiful island, personally designed by Vishwakarma, the architect among demigods. He specifically chose this island as a recreational retreat for the demigods because of its scenic beauty and natural abundance.

a paradise named lanka

Lanka was built atop a mountain called Tri-kuta. Tri-kuta (means three peaks) was originally a piece of rock that broke off from Mount Meru. Once two *gandharvas*[5] were debating who was stronger – Vasuki (a gigantic celestial serpent) or Vayu (the wind god). The *gandharva* supporting Vasuki substantiated his claim by saying that Lord Vishnu personally always chose Vasuki to carry out herculean tasks such as churning the milk ocean[6] or rescuing the beings of the universe from the deluge when the Lord appeared as *matsya*, the fish incarnation.[7] The other *gandharva* wondered if Vayu could be stronger.

Vayu, who is omnipresent, happened to overhear this conversation

---

[5] *Gandharvas* were celestial beings with melodious voices.

[6] Vasuki was used as a rope for churning the milk ocean and the Mandhara mountain, which was placed on Lord Vishnu in his *kurma* or turtle incarnation, was used as the churning rod. Because Vasuki was a gigantic snake, he could coil around the mountain, and one end of his body was held by the demigods and the other by demons. And when Vasuki was pulled to and fro, the ocean ended up being churned.

[7] At the time of the great deluge or pralaya, Lord Vishnu in his Matsya incarnation pulled Manu's boat. Vasuki was used as the rope between the boat and Matsya's horn to prevent the boat from drifting away into oblivion.

and found it unbearable. It hurt his ego, and it became a matter of prestige for him to prove his superiority. Vayu decided to challenge Vasuki and prove his power over him. Thus began the clash of the titans.

When Vasuki was informed of the challenge, he readily agreed and proposed a test to prove their strength. He suggested that he would coil around Mountain Meru thrice and Vayu would have to blow as hard as possible to loosen his grip on the mountain and yank him off it. All was fine about this duel, except that they forgot to consult with Mount Meru and seek his permission to use his body as the testing ground.[8]

Vasuki coiled around Mount Meru thrice, and Vayu began blowing with all his might to get Vasuki to loosen his grip. The harder Vayu blew, the further Vasuki tightened his grip on Mount Meru. Mount Meru began writhing in agony because he was being both crushed by Vasuki's tight grip and rocked by Vayu's strong blows. Unable to bear the torture anymore, Mount Meru revolted and cried out piteously to Lord Brahma, the creator of the universe, to save him from this distress. Brahma heard Mount Meru's cries for help and appeared on the scene.

The profoundly wise Brahma explained to two gods how each one had unique strengths and weaknesses and how their strengths were to be utilized to serve and not compete.[9]

---

[8] The natural outcome of disagreement is insensitivity to one's surroundings.

[9] Rather than being engaged in one-upmanship, one should focus on how combined strength can enhance individual capabilities. When one engages in competition, it results in the destruction of the other and one becomes oblivious to the pain of the other.

Acknowledging their mistake, both Vayu and Vasuki put an end to the competition. As Vasuki eased his grip on Mount Meru, a huge piece of rock broke off and fell into the ocean. This enormous rock had three peaks, hence the name Tri-kuta. It was this rock – Lanka – that Vishwakarma chose as the paradise island for the recreation of demigods.

grabbing blessings

Rivalry between the two wives of Vishravas became the cause for a rift in the siblings' relationship. Kaikashi, Ravana's mother, began sowing seeds of dissent in her son's heart. She kindled the lowly feeling of envy in her son by taunting him about the opulence surrounding his half-brother Kubera. Even though she was not of pure mind, she asked all her sons to take refuge in prayers. She taught them the right tenets, but for the wrong purposes. Instigated by their mother and fuelled by the great aspirations within their hearts, Ravana, Kumbakarna, Surpanakha and Vibhishan left the comforts of their home to perform austerities.

Vishravas trained his son Ravana to become a scholar in the scriptures. Although Ravana was theoretically a scholar and had divine knowledge, he had no divine qualities.[10]

The three brothers and their sister performed tremendous austerities, neither eating nor sleeping, for many, many years to please Lord Brahma. When the deity they wanted to appease did not appear,

---

[10] It is not the divine knowledge you possess that makes you divine but what you do with it that does.

Ravana began chopping off his heads one after the other and began offering them into the sacrificial fire. When he was about to lop off his last head, Lord Brahma appeared before him to fulfill his desire. Immortality was what Ravana wanted. Brahma, however, was unable to give something that he himself did not possess. Ravana then tried to acquire the same boon by placing forth conditions that would indirectly ensure immortality.[11] He asked Brahma to grant him that none of the demigods, sages, *gandharvas*, *kinnaras*, *rakshasas* or *nagas* should be able to kill him. Brahma granted him this wish.[12]

boon or bane

Brahma's granting Ravana his wish threw the demigods in disarray, and they blamed him for their present unhappy predicament. Brahma assured them that he had acted in their best interests. He highlighted the big loophole in the boon, which a smug Ravana had missed because of a momentary lapse of intelligence.[13]

---

[11] Blessings are the outpouring of an appeased heart. The element of love is what makes a blessing special. When one is manipulative in his efforts to please another, he also is manipulated in return, without his knowledge.

[12] No one wants death. Deathlessness is a gift that comes after a lifetime of endeavor to please God, the giver of immortality. Everything valuable comes at a price. The price here is a life of devotion filled with genuine humility. A shortcut actually cuts your life short.

[13] Intelligence is a God-given faculty. Switching on and off this faculty is in the hands of God. No one can claim ownership for their ideas. Ravana, out of immense pride, had committed a blunder. His intelligence faculty was in switch-off mode at this point.

Ravana's extreme arrogance and pride made him forget to include humans and monkeys when choosing the entities for immunity from death. He believed that it would be an insult to his superior powers to ask protection from mortal humans and weak monkeys. Brahma told the demigods that this was the loophole that would result in Ravana's death.[14]

Brahma further explained that the moment he heard Ravana's demands, he instructed Saraswati to immediately sit on Kumbakarna's tongue and manipulate his desire. Kumbakarna wanted to ask for "*nitya-tvam*," or eternity, but as a result of Saraswati manipulating his tongue, he ended up asking for "*nidra-tvam*," or unlimited sleep. Instead of asking *Indraasana* (seat of Indra), he asked for *nidraasana* (bed for sleeping), and instead of asking for *nirdevatvam* (annihilation of the Devas), he asked for *nidratvam* (sleep). Brahma granted it immediately much to the dismay and frustration of Kumbakarna![15]

Kumbakarna begged Brahma to reverse the boon. Brahma relented and made a slight change – he could sleep for six months and be awake for the rest.

Since then, Kumbakarna led half a life of sleep. At the end of six months of sleep, waking Kumbakarna up was a humongous task. Even if his body was set on fire, elephants and camels were made to walk over his chest or bugles were sounded close to his ears, nothing could break his sleep. A huge army had to march all over his body. When the army marched past him shooting *astras* and creating a lot

---

[14] Ravana wanted to manipulate, but was manipulated instead.

[15] Most muscles in our body are involuntary, working automatically without our control or sanction. With such limited control, how can one feel in control of the world?

of noise, he would finally feel some sensation and stir slowly out of his slumber. On waking up, he would annihilate half the army.

To satiate the hunger of a colossal, mammoth body, he would ask for food immediately. He would satisfy his six-month hunger by eating incessantly through every waking moment before he went back to sleep again for the next six months. His education took place along with his eating. Pandits sat on either side and read books to him. He listened to the *shastras* as he ate. He also found time to become an expert archer.

Brahma then told the demigods about Surpanakha's boon. She desired that she be able to change her form at will. Brahma granted this wish.[16]

Brahma was stoked when narrating Vibhishan's boon. Vibhishan's request shocked not only the Supreme Creator but also the docile demon's own siblings. He asked for devotion to the Supreme Lord and that he should never deviate from the principles of truth at any point in his life. Ravana and Kumbakarna warned Vibhishan that he was not only ruining his own life but was also becoming a blot on the entire Rakshasa (Paulatsya) dynasty. They reminded him about the infinite powers of Brahma; however, Vibhishan was determined, and Brahma finally felt that his visit had been worthwhile.[17]

---

[16] Surpanaka, who was ugly both externally and internally, felt that by being able to change her external looks, she could hide her internal ugliness. However, internal ugliness has no relationship with external appearance as beauty resides inside a person.

[17] Not succumbing to peer pressure is an act of true courage. Further, more courage is required to fight the battle against temptation than to fight against opponents.

Once Brahma shared these details with the demigods, they were pacified. Yet, they thought it necessary to tell Brahma about the kind of atrocities Ravana was inflicting upon them. The most prominent demigods were made captives to cut vegetables in Ravana's kitchen. He bullied them into serving him all day. When he wanted a gentle breeze, he beckoned Vayu. When he wanted warmth, the sun god Surya had to appear even on a rainy day. The ocean god Varuna was made to guard Lanka. In the face of an enemy, Varuna had to create fierce waves to frighten them away. Rahu was made to hang upside down facing a wall so that he could never create any inauspiciousness in Ravana's life. Ravana had made the *navagrahas* (nine planets in charge for controlling astrological situations) prostrate on the steps leading up to his throne. He walked over before climbing up the steps to sit on his throne, indicating that not even the planets could control his life.

The demigods were flustered and agitated. Brahma told the harassed demigods that they should seek out Lord Vishnu and that He was the only one who could help them.

lord vishnu, the only hope

Even as Brahma's soothing words tried to calm the hapless demigods, Lord Vishnu, mounted on his carrier bird Garuda, personally appeared on the scene. In this instance, the Lord's eagerness and desire to protect His devotees took precedence over the devotees' praying and requesting the Lord to appear and protect them;

even before the demigods prayed to the Lord to help them, He manifested Himself.[18]

Lord Vishnu appeared resplendent in His yellow robes and the most exquisite dazzling jewelry. He was holding a conch (*panjajanya shankha*), a fiery, spinning, metal wheel (*sudarshana chakra*) and a mace (*kaumudaki*) in three of His four hands.[19] The Lord's arrival atop Garuda was like that of the arrival of the sun mounted on a black cloud to bestow the gift of rain as divine blessings of protection. Ravana had created a fire of anxiety, which was scalding Earth. The Lord was now expected to rain His cooling grace on Earth and quench the raging fire of anxiety by destroying Ravana.

Interestingly, when Lord Vishnu appeared in front of the demigods, He did not bring the lotus (*padma*) with Him. This was to convey that the time for creation had passed; the time of destruction of evil forces

---

[18]A distinct difference between Ravana's situation and that of the demigods is revealed here. To receive Brahma's favor, Ravana had to almost give up his life and even then ended up displeasing Brahma. But Lord Vishnu appeared to the demigods even before they prayed to him; they qualified for this favor because they served Vishnu through administration across the universe. Pleasing the Lord is a matter of not only prayer but also serving Him.

[19] The four symbols on Lord Vishnu's person depict His divine qualities. The lotus symbolizes creation, indicating that He is the creator of the universe. The wheel, known as *sudarshan chakra*, illuminates the world by dispelling the dark forces, indicating that He chases away ignorance and doubts with the light of knowledge. The mace, *kaumudaki*, indicates that He eradicates evil forces and protects His devotees. The conch, which is called *panchajanya*, symbolizes pure sound vibration, the blowing of which gives rise to hope in the heart of devotees and shatters the heart of the enemies. The sound of the conch precedes the appearance of the Lord, indicating that hope is in the vicinity.

had begun. The lotus was not required to destroy Ravana; the conch, wheel and the mace were enough. The hand, which held the lotus, was now held upwards, palm facing the demigods, showering blessings. The Lord thus assured the demigods, "Don't worry! I have come. Fear no more."[20]

Lord Vishnu announced to the demigods that He would soon descend to Earth and incarnate as sons of Dasaratha. He also instructed Brahma to ensure that all the demigods be sent to Earth as monkeys to assist Him in His activities. Lord Vishnu then disappeared.[21]

Brahma immediately got into action, delegating different roles to demigods to appear on Earth as monkeys. He instructed Surya to transform into Sugriva, Indra to transform into Vali, Kubera into Nila, Brihaspati into Taru, Varuna into Sushena, Vayu into Hanuman, and so on. Brahma himself decided to become a bear named Jambavan, who eventually was a source of inspiration and wisdom for all.[22]

---

[20] Another observation is that the Lord appeared riding an eagle carrier, Garuda. The sacrificial altar of Dasaratha's *putrakamesthi yajna* was also designed in the shape of an eagle. The Lord was thus indicating that He was going to descend from His carrier eagle to the *yajna* eagle. One eagle conveyed the offerings of Dasaratha to Lord Vishnu and another eagle carried Lord Vishnu's blessings to Dasaratha.

[21] When God decides to help us, He expects our cooperation according to His terms, not according to our terms. The most powerful universal controllers, the demigods were asked to become monkeys. They kept their egos aside to serve the Lord, which shows that their only intention was to serve, not how they serve.

[22] A good leader knows the art of delegation; in addition, he delegates to himself the most demanding role, that of being an inspiration.

nectar... at last!

Back on Earth, Dasaratha's sacrifice was in the last phase. Rishi Shringa offered the last oblation into the sacrificial fire of the *putrakamesthi yajna*. As soon as the purified butter was poured into the fire, an effulgent personality clad in black and red robes emerged. The tall-as-a-mountain red-faced personality with facial hair soft as the mane of a lion wore the most opulent of ornaments. His powerful arms held a golden vessel with a silver lid. The vessel dazzled and appeared to be illusionary. He held it close to his heart as he would hold his own wife.

In a booming voice like drum beats, he introduced himself as a representative of Prajapati, the demigod in charge of progeny. He declared the *putrakamesthi yajna* was a success and all the demigods were very pleased with Dasaratha. He handed over to Dasaratha the golden pot, receiving which was the peak of the sacrifice. After instructing Dasaratha to divide the nectarine sweet rice in the vessel among his principal queens, he disappeared into the sacrificial fire. Dasaratha, holding the golden vessel, suddenly felt like a beggar amid undeserving fortune.[23]

divine dessert divided

The aging Dasaratha felt like a young man again. The vessel of divine dessert seemed to be giving him a new lease of life and new hope. Resplendent with the effulgence of the vessel in his hands,

---

[23] Feeling undeserving and humility are enzymes that help us digest the heavy meal of success.

the exuberant Dasaratha ran to his queens. Of the 353 queens, Dasaratha chose the three queens qualified enough to receive the divine rice dessert.[24]

Dasaratha divided the nectarine rice dessert into two portions, giving half of it to Kaushalya, his first wife. Kaushalya also known as Hrilekha was the one who possessed and spread divine virtues. She had her share of the dessert as soon as she received it, wishing for a son who would eventually become the king of the world.

Dasaratha halved the remaining dessert yet again. This time he gave one half to Sumitra, his second wife. Sumitra was also known as Srilekha, one endowed with opulence and who shared this quality with those connected to her. Sumitra on receiving her share held it in her hands in a prayerful mood and did not consume the dessert.

Dasaratha further divided the remaining half into two portions, half of which he gave Keikeyi, his third wife. Keikeyi was Kirtilekha, one endowed with glory and fame and she, too, shared this quality with those around her. As soon as the dessert fell into her outstretched hands, she consumed it with the eagerness of the nestling feeding off its mother's beak, praying that her son becomes glorious.[25]

---

[24] In order to be the recipient of mercy, one requires qualification. Even if the best seed is sown in a barren field, it will yield no result. Since divine children were to be borne by the one who would consume the divine dessert, Dasaratha had been told to determine beforehand, which among his queens were most qualified.

[25] The order in which the queens had the divine dessert indicated their mood and the mood of their children. Kaushalya received and had the dessert first, clearly indicating that her son would be the Supreme Lord and the heir to the throne of Ayodhya. Keikeyi followed Kaushalya, eagerly having the dessert, which indicated that her child would be a follower of Kaushalya's son.

The last portion of the divine dessert was still left in the pot. After deep consideration, Dasaratha gave this last bit to Sumitra who still held her first portion in her hand.[26] Having received two portions of the divine rice dessert, Sumitra was filled with gratitude. She then consumed the divine dessert, praying for children who would be instruments of service to the Supreme Lord who was to be born. Her children epitomized service and cooperation. The twins set aside their personal desires and focused on serving their brothers.[27]

As soon as the three queens ate their share of the divine dessert, their hearts filled with the kind of joy they had never experienced before. Each could feel a divine presence in their wombs. They became radiant with the divine mercy of the Lord, and their beauty increased

---

[26] Interestingly, Dasaratha had the option of giving the last portion of the dessert to either of his wives; yet he chose to give it to Sumitra. Why? Kaushalya of course had the first major portion and was going to bear the Supreme Lord in her womb, so there was no question of one more child in the same womb. Although Keikeyi was Dasaratha's favorite and was the most beautiful, he felt that Sumitra's beauty was much greater because of her spirit of cooperation and service. Sumitra is called Srilekha not because of her opulence or wealth, but because of a good consciousness and desire to serve and assist others. Wherever there is the spirit of divine cooperation and non-enviousness, there is Sumitra's opulence. People like Sumitra help create a firm bonding within the family.

[27] Sumitra did not consume her share, rather she waited until Kaushalya and Keikeyi had theirs, thus indicating that she would have two sons who would be the followers of Kaushalya and Keikeyi's sons. Sumitra exhibited the quality of non-enviousness while consuming the divine dessert, a quality that was reflected in her sons.

infinitely.[28] The three queens bore the divine children in their wombs for 12 months.[29]

divine births in ayodhya

Each passing day of the 12 months of the gestation period, seemed like eons for Dasaratha. Toward the end of the 12 months, on the noon of *Navami* (ninth day in the bright fortnight or waxing moon) in the month of *Chaitra* (April–May), under the star *Punarvasu*,[30] when

---

[28] The proof of the presence of God in one's heart and the proof of advancement in spiritual life is that the person is filled with delight within. Such a person becomes beautiful with good qualities. Thus, the result of the presence of God is transformation of character.

[29] Ordinary children are born in ordinary ways and extraordinary children in extraordinary ways. Every aspect of these children was different. They were not conceived as regular babies are: they were born from their mothers consuming divine dessert; they were not born in 9 months, but appeared after 12. The Lord reserves His distinctness right from birth.

[30] Since the spring season is associated with blooming flowers and flowering trees, birth on *Navami* or the ninth day of the lunar calendar indicates being forever fresh. The number nine never loses its individuality and is eternal. If multiplied by any other number, the sum is nine again. For example, $9 \times 7 = 63$, $6 + 3 = 9$. Lord Rama's connection with nine indicates that the *Ramayana* and the character of Rama will never lose its freshness with the passing of time. Birth in the month of *Chaitra* (beginning of the spring season and the first month of the Vedic calendar) hinted that this child would be eternally fresh; the *Punarvasu* star is presided over by Aditi, the mother of demigods. *Diti* means the one who divides. *Aditi* means the opposite, one who views everyone and everything with equal vision. This child would go on to become supremely transparent in His actions, the most important quality for a leader.

all the auspicious planets were in constellation, Kaushalya gave birth to the first son.[31]

The infant's charm was beyond what words could express. His face was like the full moon, radiating effulgence that could put the moon to shame. He had smooth round cheeks and eyes like red-tinged lotus petals, His skin shone like green emeralds, soft black hair covered His head and His entire body was delicate, almost fragile, as if made up of the softest butter.

As soon as the child was born, the entire palace became a beehive of activity, with everyone scampering to inform others about the auspicious arrival. Sumitra and Keikeyi rushed to see the child. When they held the child in their hands, they could not stop marveling His beauty. Just then, both felt sudden movement in their own wombs. The two startled queens exchanged glances – they felt the children in their wombs trying to reach out to the child they were holding. They could understand from the outstretched skin on their stomachs that the delicate hands of their babies pressed against their womb were trying to reach out to grab the feet of the newborn. The two queens smiled, realizing that this newborn was going to unite the family.

Nothing compared to Dasaratha's delight on hearing the news of his first son's birth! For 12 months, this news had repeatedly played out in his head, and now it was finally buzzing in his ears. The distance from his palace to Kaushalya's seemed to be the longest he had ever covered. He felt extremely grateful toward Kaushalya.

---

[31] Valmiki referred to this son as Lord Vishnu Himself. The Supreme Lord has the entire universe within Himself. How surprising it is that Kaushalya held that same Supreme Lord in her womb for 12 months! According to Kamba, Kaushalya needed great skill to give birth to Lord Rama. What was her skill? The spirit of devotion is that skill needed to hold the Lord in her womb, the very Lord who is glorified in all great scriptures.

At long last he saw the child! What he saw left him spellbound. The beauty of the child mesmerized him, throwing him into a trance. He had wanted to thank Kaushalya, he had wanted to reward the one who had delivered the news to him, he had wanted to call for celebrations, but all of that was completely forgotten. All he could do was gaze at the child, hypnotized and transfixed, as the world around him melted away. When he held his son, he felt as if the entire universe was in his hands in its most charming form.[32]

As Dasaratha was immersed in the splendor of his first son, Keikeyi was taken to the maternity room. Early next morning, she gave birth to a beautiful son. This was the morning of *Dasami* (tenth day in the bright fortnight or waxing moon) in the month of *Chaitra* (April-May), under the *Pushyami* star. The same day at noon, Sumitra gave birth to twins under the star *Ashlesha*, whose presiding deity was the serpent. The children were born in the same order their mothers had consumed the dessert.

Ayodhya hadn't celebrated in a really long time. Every citizen of Ayodhya felt Dasaratha was their father because he cared for them more than their biological fathers would. He took care of their every need, and protected them. So his joys and sorrows were theirs, too. In all the years that Dasaratha remained childless, he was melancholic, so every citizen voluntarily decided to give up festivities or celebrations at home.[33]

---

[32] Through these years, Kaushalya had been the loyal and chaste wife, but Dasaratha had always neglected her, paying more attention to the beautiful Keikeyi. Now suddenly, he felt grateful to her. This is conditional gratitude. How easy it is to forget people who have done so much for you when your expectations are not met!

[33] Expectation of empathy from others comes from being empathetic.

Now, after so many years, the entire city burst into celebration. Celestial singers sang melodiously, dancers swayed joyously, musicians played their instruments tirelessly, flowers rained from the heavens incessantly and people streamed into the city from across the world to participate in the festivities. Onlookers tossed gems and valuables at the musicians in appreciation of their skills.

Dasaratha declared that there would be no tax collection for the following seven years. He declared his treasury open, and anyone could take as much as he or she wanted from it. He ordered a halt in the use of weaponry. He freed all prisoners. He distributed unlimited wealth among the *brahmanas* and requested them to continue performing auspicious rituals. Every temple in Ayodhya was well decorated, and the standard for deity worship was raised. He donated generously to the needy, the joy in his heart exploded through charity.[34]

decoding the names of the divine siblings

Eleven days after the birth of the children, the great sage Vasistha came to Dasaratha's palace to perform the naming ceremony for the

---

[34] Celebration means sharing your joy by making people around you happy. Making others happy invokes auspiciousness. When celebration is limited to pleasing only your own senses, it evokes envy in others, which in turn adds negativity to your joy. Distributing positivity is a positive way of ensuring continued positivity.

children. Observing the children carefully and praying, Vasistha bestowed upon the children their unique names.[35]

Born from Kaushalya, Vasistha spontaneously named the first born Rama, which means the one who gives pleasure. It appeared as if the child desired that name. Never before was Vasistha so overwhelmed when naming a child, it seemed as if he did not choose the name but the name chose itself.[36]

Vasistha named Keikeyi's child Bharata, which means the one with a big load on his head. It eventually came true as Bharata had to bear the burden of the kingdom when Rama left for the forest. The

---

[35] Vedic names are given according to the qualities of the personality. If studied carefully, these four sons exhibited qualities perfectly befitting their names. In fact, their qualities were similar to the mood of their mothers when consuming the celestial dessert. According to Vedic understanding, the consciousness of the mother at the time of conception accrues into the child; therefore, every event connected to the child is called a *samskara* or impression. Each event creates an impression in the mind of the child. Children are like wet cement; they carry these subtle impressions forever.

[36] The word Rama can give unlimited pleasure to the hearts of the listener and the speaker. This is remarkably contrary to the word Ravana that strikes terror in the minds of those who hear that name. While eating the dessert, Kaushalya had desired a perfect boy who would give pleasure to everyone and be an ideal leader; Rama was just the same! Rama gave much pleasure to His father, mother, step-mothers and all the citizens of Ayodhya. It was not merely pleasure related to His exquisite beauty but it was also that of His pleasing personality. Rama personally knew every citizen. He participated in their joys and sorrows. He was often found crying in the house of those going through a sad phase and was found celebrating in the house of those happy. His was a life of giving joy to others.

name Bharata meant that this boy had an infinite capacity to selflessly carry the heavy burden of responsibilities on his head.[37]

Sumitra's twins were named Lakshmana and Shatrughna. Lakshmana comes from the word Lakshmi, which means wealth.[38] Lakshmana had never aspired for material wealth, influence or power. Shatrughna means one who conquers his enemies.[39,40]

---

[37] Bharata was just like what Keikeyi had in mind at the time of eating the dessert. He was Rama's follower, adhering to his elder brother's instructions to the last letter. Bharata surrendered completely to his elder brother Rama, wanting to assist Rama in carrying His burdens. When Rama was exiled, Bharata had to rule the kingdom for 14 years. The servitude with which he ruled makes his name apt. For most people ruling a kingdom would be a pleasure, but for Bharata ruling the kingdom for 14 years was like a huge burden on his head. And he carried that burden of love to please his brother. His life was that of burden-bearing love.

[38] What wealth is this referring to? The real meaning of Lakshmana is one who is rich with the wealth of service to Rama. Lakshmana cultivated the attitude of service to his brother Rama. He became inseparable from Rama, and always looked for opportunities to serve Him. His very life is symbolic of his name. He was eager to collect this wealth of opportunities of service.

[39] Shatrughna barely fought any battles. There is record of him killing only a demon named Lavanasura. Given this fact, it seems very odd to call him a person who conquers his enemies. Shatrughna lived a life of servitude to Bharata. For him, his enemy was association with Rama and the beauty of Rama. Rama was very attractive, but Shatrughna resisted the temptation of serving Rama and focused on serving Bharata. He conquered this enemy. Everyone wants to have a direct connection with God, but here is a person who wanted to serve the devotee of God. Desire is the most powerful foe. Shatrughna had no desire of his own, he was happy to dedicate himself to the desires of Bharata.

[40] Lakshmana and Shatrughna were just what Sumitra had thought at the time of eating the divine dessert. The two children imbibed the mood of their mother, the desire to assist and serve in a spirit of cooperation. Lakshmana served Rama all his life and Shatrughna served Bharata all his life. Assisting the great is a far superior act of greatness than being great, because assisting requires the remarkable quality of humility.

The four brothers' names signified many things at many levels. At the devotional level, Rama led by example that whatever the situation, one should always follow the principles of truthfulness and instructions of wise superiors. Lakshmana's exemplified that the purpose of one's life must be to serve the Supreme Lord in totality, with the mind, words and actions. Bharata showed the world that one should follow the Lord's commands without questioning. And Shatrughna exemplified that serving the Lord was important, but it was just as important to serve His devotees.

At the societal level, the four brothers represented the four basic aims of human life – *dharma, artha, kaama* and *moksha*, which are righteousness, duty and morality, wealth and prosperity, worldly desires and liberation. Rama represented *dharma*, Lakshmana represented *artha*, Shatrughna represented *kaama* and Bharata *moksha*.[41]

That Lakshmana always accompanied Rama indicated that *artha* or economic pursuit were to be guided by *dharma* or higher wisdom. Wealth needed to be earned and used in accordance with Vedic wisdom. While Shatrughna's always accompanying Bharata indicated

---

[41] *Dharma* and *moksha* represent the spiritual aspects of life, while *artha* and *kaama* represent the material aspects. Most people focus on *artha* and *kaama*, conveniently neglecting and not even feeling the need for *dharma* and *moksha*. The *Ramayana* suggests that *artha* be kept close to *dharma* and *kaama* close to *moksha*, only then life can be fulfilling. If *artha* and *kaama* are kept as the exclusive goals of life, they will ruin a person. In short, *artha* and *kaama* have to be restrained within the boundary of *dharma* and *moksha*. *Dharma* refers to supreme religiosity and righteousness, which involves developing our love for God. *Artha* refers to wealth of service and *kaama* to intense desire to serve God's devotees. *Moksha* refers to liberation or freedom from the burden of worldly attachments.

that *kaama* or desires ought to be directed toward *moksha* or perfection.[42]

At the fundamental level, Rama was the Supreme Lord Himself who descended on earth. Bharata was the *sudarshan chakra* or the wheel of the Lord. Lakshmana was the snake bed or *ananta sesa* of the Lord and Shatrughna the conch or *pancajanya shankha* of the Lord. Rama was thought to be an incarnation of Vasudeva, Lakshmana of Sankarshana, Bharata of Pradyumna and Shatrughna of Anirudha, all of who were primary reincarnations of Vishnu in the spiritual world.

four reasons for the lord's manifestation

The Lord manifested as Rama for four prominent reasons – two of these reasons were known to the world, and the other two were secret desires of the Lord, unknown to the world.[43]

The first reason, as obvious from the demigods' and Brahma's request, was that Lord Rama was born to annihilate demons like

---

[42] One has to dovetail all desires and give wings to only those that help one achieve the higher purpose of loving God. A good human being balances material aspirations and spiritual goals. The important thing to bear in mind is that both these life goals should complement not contradict each other. A balanced human being is physically, mentally, intellectually and spiritually developed.

[43] There is a difference between us taking birth and the Lord taking birth. We take birth because of our past deeds or misdeeds, but the Lord takes birth because He wishes to. How much ever we may try, things don't go according to our desires; everything takes shape only if the Lord so desires.

Ravana. The second reason was an extension of the first – Lord Rama took birth to protect his devotees from the disturbances of the demons. The great demigods and sages were tortured by the demons, and Lord Rama manifested to restore peace.

The third reason for his being born as Rama was very confidential. The Lord enjoyed *rasas* or different relationships with different devotees. The Lord reciprocated according to the type of *rasa* or relationship.[44]

Lord Vishnu was lying on His snake bed and His consort, the Goddess of Fortune Lakshmi, spoke out her heart while serving Him. She in fact complained that as husband and wife, they needed to spend some quality time together. She pointed out that He was surrounded by hundreds of devotees trying to serve Him in so many different ways. And, if none else was around, the Lord's snake bed

---

[44] The five primary *rasas* between the Lord and His devotees are *Shanta Rasa, Dasya Rasa, Sakhya Rasa, Vatsalya Rasa* and *Madhurya Rasa. Shanta Rasa* devotees exchange neutral relationships with the Lord, such as trees, stones, and other inanimate objects that do not have active exchanges with the Lord but serve the Lord passively. *Dasya Rasa* devotees like Hanuman serve the Lord actively through physical, menial services. *Sakhya Rasa* devotees like Arjuna in Mahabharata serve the Lord through friendship. Their service is to be the Lord's friend, so they shed the trappings of respect and engage in true genuine friendship with the Lord. *Vatsalya Rasa* devotees like Dasaratha engage in serving the Lord through parental affection, and their awe and respect is covered by parental love. The highest and most intimate are the devotees in *Madhurya Rasa* who, like Mother Sita, serve the Lord through physical and emotional intimacy. Of course, in none of the *rasas* is there any materialism involved. These extremely pure relationships have nothing to do with our mundane experiences of material relationships.

ananta sesa was always there. She told him that while scouring for a private place, she spotted a married couple on Earth spending time talking to each other in their house with none others around. Lakshmi suggested to the Lord that both of them incarnate on Earth to experience such privacy. The Lord immediately agreed and told her that both would manifest on Earth as Sita and Rama.[45]

The fourth reason for the Lord to appear in Ayodhya had to do with His connection to the Ikshvaku dynasty. Thousands of years ago, Lord Brahma had worshipped Ranganatha, a deity of Lord Vishnu on a snake bed. Lord Vishnu had Himself given this deity to Brahma. Brahma worshipped the deity for a long time and then handed it over to King Ikshvaku, a king of the Solar dynasty. Several kings in the Ikshvaku dynasty worshipped this deity for thousands of years until it finally reached King Dasaratha. King Dasaratha worshipped Ranganatha for many long years; however, despite receiving so much worship, Ranganatha was not satisfied with the quality of worship.[46] Ranganatha had waited too long for someone who could worship Him with sufficient love and devotion. Finally, He decided that He would Himself have to descend on Earth to show the real meaning of

---

[45] Accordingly, they appeared as Sita and Rama, and waited for 12 long years to be reunited. Nevertheless, even after being united again, they were not able to spend time together. Sita's 353 mothers-in-law, who were constantly in her company, did not allow her any privacy with the Lord. Rama finally realized that if they had to get some private time together, they both would have to go to the forest under some pretext. Seen from this perspective, the whole story of the *Ramayana* took shape to facilitate one desire of the Lord.

[46] God does not need quantity in worship, but requires quality. God is hungry for our love, not the things we offer.

devotion and worship. Thus Ranganatha manifested as Lord Rama to teach the world how to worship.[47]

childhood of the four brothers

The four sons of Dasaratha became the joy of the city. Ayodhya was in love with them. The sound of the stuttering children was music to Dasaratha's ears. The chords of devotion toward these children tugged at the heartstrings of Ayodhya's citizens.

One day, the children began crying incessantly in their cradles, leaving their mothers worried. The three hassled mothers tried their best to quieten and comfort them, but all in vain. Finally, after a whole lot of futile effort, they decided to call Vasistha for help.

Vasistha studied the scenario. He saw Rama lying in the first cradle, Bharata in the next, followed by Lakshmana and Shatrughna. Vasistha shuffled the cradles to place Rama's cradle near Lakshmana's and Bharata's near Shatrughna's. Immediately, the shrieks faded; however, the crying continued. Vasistha was baffled. He then lifted Lakshmana and placed him in the same cradle as Rama. Though both children felt crammed in that little cradle, they were happy to be by each other's side. They looked at each other with

---

[47] This was a rare phenomenon since the person worshipping and the person being worshipped were the same. In fact, it is said that the facial features of Lord Ranganatha resembled Lord Rama exactly. This deity of Ranganatha is still present in a place called Sri Rangam in Tamil Nadu, South India.

affection and smiled.[48] Shatrughna and Bharata, too, felt just as happy when Vasistha put them in the same cradle. For the family, this was nothing short of a miracle! Though born of different mothers, the kind of love these children had for each other from the cradle itself was novel to human relationships. This became the mothers' magic formula whenever the children cried.[49]

As the children grew up, the pairs became inseparable. Rama could not eat or sleep without Lakshmana. Even if His mother offered Him the tastiest of sweets, He would not eat until He shared them with Lakshmana. Whenever Rama mounted a horse to go on a hunting expedition, Lakshmana madly rushed behind to assist Him.[50]

Once the children, about five years old, found an exciting little muddy patch when playing in the palace gardens. They began flinging mud balls at each other for fun. Keikeyi and Kaushalya rushed to stop them, but the boys were so carried away that they bombarded their mothers with mud balls, too. Soon the mothers were as much covered in slush as the children. Just then Rama spotted the hunchbacked Manthara, one of Keikeyi's assistants. He decided to have some fun at

---

[48] From a deeper spiritual perspective, Lakshmana represents a living entity and Rama represents God. The living entity finds satisfaction only in the loving company of God, every other means and efforts to make the living entity happy will only increase the pain of separation in its heart. Externally, the living entity may convince itself that it is happy, but internally the soul cries for connection with God.

[49] Relationships of love are beyond logic and reasoning.

[50] In *Valmiki Ramayana*, Rama's childhood is described in as few as 10 verses. But there are other sources, including Kamba Ramayana, which charm us with more sweet stories of Rama's early days.

her expense. Rama attached a mud ball to the tip of an arrow, and when the mothers weren't looking, he aimed at the Manthara's hunchback. The arrow hit its mark and the mud ball burst open, drenching Manthara in slush. Rama and His brothers began to laugh hysterically. The slush-drenched mothers had seen what had happened, but took the incident lightly and laughed along. Manthara, however, had a serious demeanor and despised pranks. Besides, she had always hated Rama. After this incident, her hatred only deepened. She snarled at Rama, and the whole scene turned grave. Keikeyi, realizing the change in mood, intervened and took Manthara aside to pacify her. Manthara harbored memories of this incident for 20 long years before finally taking her revenge.[51]

vasistha's school

Dasaratha decided to officially start training his children under the able sage Vasistha. Dasaratha approached Vasistha with the four boys, requesting that he take them under his tutelage. Vasistha gladly accepted them; in fact, he was waiting for this day from the moment they were born.

As Vasistha took charge of the boys, Dasaratha sat down to see his children learn. Rama was the apple of Dasaratha's eyes and he could not fathom why he never tired of looking at the boy for so many

---

[51] Human minds can be so complicated; one can never tell when one may offend someone. This was probably the only time in Lord Rama's life that He had played a prank, but this prank cost him 14 years of exile. Humor definitely adds value to the quality of life, but it can only be shared with those who relate to it. Else, it could change relationships forever.

hours at a stretch. Dasaratha had seen Rama through every stage of His life this far – as a newborn, as a toddler, as a small child playing around. He was now looking forward to seeing another phase of his son's childhood – His education. Vasistha interrupted Dasaratha's thoughts and requested the king to leave for his palace. Dasaratha looked distraught, almost as if Vasistha had asked him to stop breathing. Dasaratha complained to Vasistha that it was normal tradition for a father to watch his children learn. Vasistha reminded Dasaratha that normal rules applied to normal children and that his children were not normal. Realizing the futility of his request and the firmness in Vasistha's resolve, Dasaratha sadly returned to his palace.[52]

Vasistha now turned his focus on to the four boys; with folded hands, he began circumambulating them. He prayed to Lord Rama, "My dear Lord, you are the one who has blessed me with intelligence and countless capabilities and you now want me to teach you! Please empower me to teach you what I know as my offering of gratitude to you. Just as people worship Ganga by offering her own waters to her, let me worship you by offering you what you have bestowed upon me." With this, Vasistha began to teach martial arts to the boys.[53]

The four boys began learning the basics. Soon Rama could ride elephants and horses with great expertise and ride chariots dexterously. He was so good with his bow and arrows that it seemed

---

[52] Vasistha did not want Dasaratha to see him praying to Rama because as a father, he would not be able to fathom the logic behind a guru worshipping his disciple. Vasistha wanted to conceal Rama's real identity.

[53] All abilities that we possess are gifts bestowed upon us by God. When we learn to use these gifts for a higher purpose, we act like Vasistha. When we use these gifts to satisfy our selfish agendas and not to serve society, then we act like Ravana who sought selfish pleasures.

as if He breathed archery. Rama was very absorbed in everything He did. Rama and Lakshmana loved to learn from everyone they came across. They were keenly receptive and their thirst for knowledge was limitless. The brothers often visited the hermitages of great saints, sat at their feet and learnt from them. They used their skills to serve society and often looked forward to those occasions when Dasaratha wanted them for assignments so that they could serve him.[54]

Of course, learning and using their skills came along with a fair share of fun. During one lesson on archery, someone important distracted Vasistha. While Vasistha was looking away, Rama nudged Lakshmana, pointing out to a woman walking by. This woman wore a huge nose ring, which became the target of Rama's innocent mischief. Lakshmana shot an arrow, which on reaching the target's nose emitted a liquid, shrinking her ring. Her ring shrunk around her nostrils to such an extent that she began gasping for breath. She started screaming in pain. To ease her discomfort, Rama who would never even harm an ant, shot another arrow to increase the size of the nose ring. The woman was astounded; she had no clue how her nose ring became big again. She looked around and realized that the two innocent-looking boys had something to do with it all. When she asked Rama, he said that they wanted to test their archery skills by making her nose ring small, but because the ring had become too small, they had to use another arrow to increase its size. She refused to believe that human beings could do such things with a bow and arrow. To prove they were right, Lakshmana shot another arrow, which pulled the ring off her nose. She began yelling when she saw her ring fly into the sky. Instantly, Rama shot another arrow, bringing

---

[54] Humility and the eagerness to learn lead to absorption, and absorption together with praxis leads to expertise.

it back to her nose. Through this entire episode, the arrows never once touched her body. By the time Vasistha came back to teach them, they had managed to send away the shell-shocked woman.

The brothers never used their skills to harm anyone. Such fun moments were very rare, almost non-existent in their life. Rama was seriousness and maturity personified. He often traveled through Ayodhya to interact with the lay person, inquiring if they needed any help. He did all He could when it came to helping everyone. Soon, Rama became the most loved person in Ayodhya. His beauty accentuated his good qualities and made Rama very dear to the citizens of Ayodhya. Vasistha, His teacher, was particularly proud to see his student achieve such glory.[55]

---

[55] Expertise and virtuosity make for a wholesome personality.

CHAPTER 4

HAPPINESS — NOT ALWAYS SATISFACTION

dasaratha enters worryhood as rama enters boyhood

Soon Dasaratha's little toddler had become a big boy. Rama's childhood had given way to boyhood.[1] The father had soaked in every single step of his son's childhood and relished every moment of it, just as a painter would his painting - witnessing the blank canvas manifesting into a masterpiece after every stroke, swish and smudge of color. In fact, here, the masterpiece taking shape was the Creator Himself. Dasaratha was thrilled to see this masterpiece inch closer to perfection. Rama's attraction grew with each passing moment. Just when Dasaratha believed that this was the most perfect Rama could ever be, He would shine through yet again, leaving Dasaratha awestruck.

Rama and His brothers were racing toward youth, and Dasaratha

---

[1] Lord Rama's childhood is underplayed in the *Ramayana*, with the entire childhood occupying merely 10 verses. In comparison, Krishna's childhood has been elaborated extensively. Lord Rama is called *Anusthana pradhan*, meaning *the One who has descended to teach humans lessons on discipline and morality*. Lord Krishna is called *Anubhava pradhan*, meaning *the One who has descended to impart fascinating experiences*. Because Lord Rama had manifested to impart discipline, His childhood was kept low key.

began thinking that it was time he got them married. He beckoned his Big M for a discussion. Just then, a commotion broke out near the courtroom entrance, and Dasaratha spotted a dishevelled guard darting toward him, like a hen chased by a dog. Dasaratha realized the situation was crying out for immediate redressal. He rose from his throne to calm the guard's frayed nerves and address the issue at hand. The guard rambled animatedly about a seemingly important sage whose rage had left him trembling. He described the sage as impatience and anger personified. He was upset that he could not hold back this sage, who was blazing toward the throne, because his fiery eyes glared at him, threatening to reduce him to ashes. The guard begged the king to advise him on how to handle this intimidating sage Vishwamitra, the son of Gadhi.[2]

No sooner than the guard uttered the sage's name, the entire courtroom rose in reverence. The effect his name alone had on the audience was proof enough that the guard had blundered by not letting him in. To prevent matters from spinning out of control, Dasaratha immediately rushed out to receive the sage with all due honor.[3]

---

[2] Everything that happens in this world is a manifestation of our current or past desires. Here, Dasaratha wished for Rama's marriage and Vishwamitra appeared as a medium of fulfilment of that desire. Ironically, Dasaratha was unable to comprehend that connection. In fact, Dasaratha's guards saw Vishwamitra as a disturbance. How relevant this is to our lives as well! We desire so many things and to fulfil those desires, God sends multiple opportunities. But the opportunities, like Vishwamitra, do not come declaring that they are here to fulfil our desires, rather they seem to threaten or challenge our desire itself.

[3] In our daily lives, we tend to get swayed or put off by external packaging. We hardly bother to look into internal substance. Here, the guard only looked at the external appearance of the sage, but Dasaratha could see the substance within. Knowledge helps you go beyond external packaging and appreciate the value within.

an unexpected arrival

Dasaratha beamed with happiness and pride at the sight of Vishwamitra, who stood at the entrance radiating a stunning aura. He gave him a grand welcome, one that was fit for a sage of his stature. Pleased and happy with the arrangements, the sage broke into a smile, much to the relief of the browbeaten guard. Vishwamitra exchanged pleasantries with the king and every exalted sage in the courtroom, including Vasistha, his old friend (or rather his foe). Vishwamitra inquired after the well-being of the king and his relatives. Furthermore, he asked two questions – questions that had to do with the most important of a king's concerns.

The first question was whether he had conquered his enemies and whether those under his conquest were submissive to him. The second question was whether he was appropriately performing his two most important duties, that toward society and that toward God.[4]

Dasaratha ushered the sage into his palace and offered him a seat reserved for the most distinguished of guests. He showered the sage

---

[4] The enemies Vishwamitra was referring to are of two types – the external enemies of the kingdom and the internal enemies of the king, the internal enemies being vices such as lust, anger, greed, pride, illusion and envy. These internal enemies have to be conquered first (that's the easy part); the tougher part is to keep these enemies under one's submission, so that they do not raise their heads again! How does the king ensure that these internal enemies remain submissive? This can be done if the king dedicates his words, mind and body to the service of society and God. Once all this is done, he will be protected from succumbing to his internal enemies. Hence an affirmative answer to Vishwamitra's second question! How profound! Vishwamitra described a perfect model of governance in just two questions.

with praises and hailed his presence, expressing deep joy upon his arrival in the kingdom. Dasaratha allegorized his elation, comparing it to the immense joy of attaining *amrita*, the nectar of immortality; the joy of experiencing rain after years of drought; the joy of regaining long lost treasure; and the joy of fathering a son after years of longing. Dasaratha identified best with his analogy of begetting a son after ages because that was exactly how he felt upon Vishwamitra's arrival. Such effusive praise words from Dasaratha placated and appeased Vishwamitra.[5]

Dasaratha could not stop raving about how Vishwamitra's impromptu visit had made his life pure and complete, almost as if a place of pilgrimage had walked into his house.[6] Dasaratha knew that Vishwamitra did not step out of his hermitage without a reason, so he reasoned that the sage must have come to him for some kind of help. He became so carried away in his attempt to please Vishwamitra that Dasaratha decided to offer the sage *all* his help before being asked for it. Dasaratha told Vishwamitra to express what had made him step into Ayodhya, assuring him that he would do everything in his power to fulfill the great sage's desires, not knowing what he was getting into.[7]

Dasaratha's compliments and adoration won Vishwamitra over, and the sage attributed his communication skills and way with words to

---

[5] Sweet, genuine words of gratitude are the best welcome drinks!

[6] Pious saints remind one of the higher purposes of life; they represent purity, and constantly hold God in their hearts. Hence, they are like a pilgrim spot where one goes to experience closeness to God.

[7] A tiger bends its hind legs before taking a leap ahead. Similarly a thoughtful bent to the mind should be exercised before allowing words to leap out of the mouth.

his association with Vasistha.[8] Saying so, he reminded Dasaratha that it was very important for a king to keep his promises. Now, it was time to place his request before the king.[9]

vishwamitra's unusual agenda

Vishwamitra knew that Ayodhya was the only place in the world that every sage in distress rushed to because they were sure to find refuge. He remarked that just as the abodes of Shiva, Vishnu and Brahma provided shelter to everyone in need, Ayodhya, too, did the same. He reminded everyone how even great demigods like Indra had sought Dasaratha's help when he lost his abode to the demon Sambarasura.[10]

Vishwamitra, too, had traveled all the way to Ayodhya to seek help from Dasaratha. 'Vishwamitra' means friend to the entire world. His way of being a good friend was to serve the society and conduct fire sacrifices to please God to maintain peace and tranquillity in this world. His current predicament, however, came in the way of his desire to serve.

---

[8] In the *Bhagavad Gita*, Krishna speaks about five qualities that should reflect in our spoken words. The words should be truthful (*satyam*), pleasing (*priyam*), beneficial (*hitam*), and non-agitating (*anudvega-karam*) and upheld by the scriptures (*svadyaya*). Dasaratha spoke words that were pleasing, non-agitating and definitely those that were upheld by the scriptures, but now was the time to decide whether his words were truthful or just dramatic.

[9] It is easy to speak elegantly and impressively, but it requires a man of substance to stand by his words.

[10] Every living entity is created to depend on another. Dependence keeps the spirit of humility alive in the dependent and creates an opportunity for service for the one being depended upon.

There were two reasons behind Vishwamitra's hapless situation – the demons Maricha and Subahu who could transform into anything at will. The demons' favourite pastime was to disrupt a sage's ritual in its final phase by flinging all kinds of abhorrent substances like flesh and blood into the sacrificial fire to pollute it. These shape-shifting flying demons were extremely powerful and were always accompanied by hordes of followers. Vishwamitra, himself a very formidable personality, could have cursed the demons and reduced them to ashes, but he was bound by an oath of restraining his anger till sacrifice completion.[11] The two demons took advantage of Vishwamitra's helplessness and wreaked havoc during the sacrificial ceremony. The disturbances forced Vishwamitra to abandon the sacrifice each time and restart elsewhere.

Dasaratha carefully heard Vishwamitra's predicament and began thinking of how to best resolve it. Vishwamitra, however, had already identified the best possible solution. He wanted Dasaratha to allow his son Rama to accompany him to the forest to protect his sacrifice from the demons. He assured Dasaratha that Rama was completely capable of destroying the demons. To goad Dasaratha into making this tough decision, he disclosed his desire to groom Rama for universal fame. Finally, Vishwamitra reminded Dasaratha of the promise he had made. This was Vishwamitra's subtle way of helping Dasaratha supress his fatherly instincts and bring to the fore the king within him. Vishwamitra did not want to allow a father's bleeding heart to meddle with a king's responsibilities.

Vishwamitra's words tore Dasaratha apart. He felt many things at the

---

[11] Often we are thrown into situations that may allow people to take advantage of our principles. Like these two demons, they may hurl false allegations and insults akin to the unbearable substances. This is when we need to be protected by someone equipped to deal with such negativity.

same time: Dasaratha felt as if he was pierced by a spear, smacked by a burning log of timber and as if the God of Death (Yama) had asked him to part with his life. He felt like a once-blind man with new-found vision going blind again. The darkness of being "son-less" was dispelled temporarily by the brightness of Rama's birth, and now the mere thought of sending Him away was turning everything dark again. Dasaratha had gone through such severe penances for a son who was now his life, the very reason of his existence. And here was this sage wanting to take it all away from him! Dasaratha was so hurt and wounded and his heart was so heavy that he could not breathe. Dasaratha felt that his life had been sucked out of him. Unable to feel anything any longer, Dasaratha collapsed.[12]

Dasaratha had made a similar promise once before to Jatayu; however, he did not yet have to fulfil that promise. So he thought he could get away without keeping his tall promises this time, too. Little did he realize the burden of a promise![13]

dasaratha endeavors to mold destiny

Dasaratha's head started reeling; thoughts were rushing frantically inside his head, criss-crossing the crevices of his brain for ideas and

---

[12] Vishwamitra's eager eyes displayed the weight of expectation. To fulfill others' expectations is not easy.

[13] It takes a man of substance to fulfill promises. Effusive words of praise and appreciation have nothing to do with the desire to serve. Genuine desire to serve is associated with the willingness to do anything to please a person. It is better to promise less and deliver more, which will lead to elevated respect, than to promise more and deliver less, which will lead to diminished respect.

arguments to evade his promise without enraging the mighty sage. His royal clothes, adorned with priceless jewels and the perfumed garlands around his neck could not hide the agony of his aching heart. The unbearable pain made all his opulence seem unbearable and worthless.

Dasaratha analyzed the situation and figured that what Vishwamitra actually needed was protection. So he offered himself to the sage. All the poor father was trying to do was cocoon Rama, his young child, from the perils that lay ahead. The mighty sage flew into a rage, he thundered, "*Aham vedmi mahatmanam, ramam satya parakramam, vasisto api mahateja ye cha yeme tapasi sthitah.*" Translated it means, "I know who Rama is; you have *no* idea about the kind of power He has. Even Vasistha and other sages here know about it." Vishwamitra reprimanded Dasaratha for underestimating the strength of his son, the One who had the power to achieve anything He wanted.

Dasaratha's mind was filled with questions. How could Vishwamitra even begin to know about the powers of Rama without meeting Him even once when he was the one observing his son from the day He was born? Who would know Rama better? A pensive sage who had spent all his time pondering over world peace in the forest and only just stepped foot into Ayodhya? Or a pensive father who had spent all his time pondering over his son's every move and been with Him all the while since His birth? Dasaratha chose to believe that before his arrival in the city, Vishwamitra was totally unaware of his son and that he *could not* know Rama better than he did.

Dasaratha's thought process was interrupted as Vishwamitra continued to justify his demand for Rama. He pointed out that the difference between his vision and that of Dasaratha's was that his was influenced by knowledge and devotion, whereas Dasaratha's was influenced by love and attachment.

Vishwamitra went on to explain that because Dasaratha was seated high up on a throne, a crown on his head and a bow in his hand, Rama seemed like a precious crown jewel, a successor, to be protected. But to Vishwamitra who was seated at the feet of God, had dreadlocks for a crown and grass in his hands instead of a bow, Rama was the object of his devotion, adoration and a goal to be achieved.

Vishwamitra explained to Dasaratha that the one he thought was his son, nurtured in the womb of his wife, in fact held the entire universe in His stomach. He was certain that Dasaratha would not believe him; so he asked Dasaratha to verify this with his *guru*, Vasistha. Vishwamitra and Vasistha had long-standing differences of opinions, but when it came to Lord Rama, they were in complete agreement.[14]

Dasaratha pleaded with Vishwamitra to exempt his son because He was not even 16 years old – the age bar for participating in a battle. This was his first reason for exemption for the 12-year-old Rama.[15]

Next Dasaratha argued that his lotus-eyed[16] Rama's eyes automatically

---

[14] The different-colored glasses we look through influence the way we see things. Dasaratha wore red glasses of attachment and Vishwamitra wore yellow glasses of devotion. Try wearing another's glasses to see their perspective, and don't judge them by seeing through your glasses.

[15] As per numerology, the number 12 is of great significance in the *Ramayana*. Rama was born in the twelfth month; there are 6 (half of 12) sections in the *Ramayana*; the number of verses in the *Ramayana* add up to 24,000 (two times 12,000); Rama was 12 years old when Vishwamitra arrived and when He was married; Lord Rama was sent to exile 12 years after his marriage!

[16] Both Dasaratha and Vishwamitra addressed Rama as *Rajiva lochana*, meaning lotus-eyed. Dasaratha called him so because Rama's eyes closed when the sun went down just as a lotus curls its petals at sunset. When Vishwamitra called Rama lotus-eyed, he meant that Rama's eyes were similar to lotus petals that blossomed with the touch of first rays of the sun. His glance, like the glaring sun, could exterminate the existence of the nocturnal demons.

began to shut at sundown. If He could barely remain awake after sunset, how could He be expected to fight the nocturnal demons? This was Dasaratha's second reason for Rama's exemption.

Dasaratha asserted that Rama was not qualified to single-handedly fight the demons. He offered himself and his entire army to wage that war against the demons. He began to talk about his own achievements in the battlefield and lauded the abilities of his soldiers.[17]

As a doting and protective father, Dasaratha believed that sending Rama with Vishwamitra was of great risk compared to the cosy future he had planned for Rama. Dasaratha's fatherly love was so profound that it made him short-sighted. He could not envision how valuable Vishwamitra's association could be for Rama. For him, Rama was this cherished possession he could use any way he wanted, a possession that had no choice of its own and a possession no one else but he had the right to decide for.[18]

Vishwamitra's perspective, on the other hand, was entirely different. Just as Dasaratha's judgment was clouded by the subjectivity of being a parent, Vishwamitra's was empowered by the objectivity of being a

---

[17] Dasaratha emphasized on quantity, whereas Vishwamitra emphasized on quality. Dasaratha trusted his army's experience over Rama's. Vishwamitra trusted Rama's purity, which he believed could make up for lack of expertise.

[18] Dasaratha was underestimating Rama's power. Our attachments often make us undervalue the people we love. It is not unusual to come across parents who stop their children from pursuing their own dreams and force them to take up something they want them to do. These parents choose a path of least risk, ignoring the larger risk of unwittingly leaving their child dissatisfied and unhappy.

teacher.[19] Vishwamitra viewed Rama as an unpolished diamond and himself as the jeweler who had the tools to polish that diamond. Unfortunately, the jeweler did not own the diamond, and the one who owned it could not see the radiance it could emit on being polished.[20]

Vishwamitra did not know Rama as much as Dasaratha did, but he had the foresight to turn talent into success.[21] Vishwamitra had great confidence that Rama could become a role model for the society. He realized that Dasaratha's attachment was stifling his son's abilities.[22]

Vishwamitra's serious demeanor made Dasaratha aware that he was pointlessly arguing with someone he should have followed blindly. Dasaratha then decided to open up and express his helplessness. He fell at the feet of Vishwamitra and implored him to take him instead

---

[19] A father's attachment and love can smother his child, whereas a teacher's attachment and love encourages a child to prosper. Just as a father's attachment to his offspring is overpowered by the instinct to protect, the teacher's attachment to his student is overpowered by the call of duty, the duty to enrich.

[20] The father sees faults in the son, and the teacher sees good qualities in the pupil. Parents are sometimes blind to the capabilities their children possess. A good teacher highlights those capabilities, bringing out the best in the child. The role of a teacher is to find such unpolished diamonds and bring out the sparkle in them by cutting and chiselling them to perfection, by disciplining the students and enhancing their skills.

[21] Dasaratha's vision was material and peripheral, Vishwamitra's was spiritual and arcane. Material vision is a by-product of attachments and spiritual vision comes from knowledge. Dasaratha *loved* Rama, but Vishwamitra *knew* Rama.

[22] When we send out vibes of confidence, it heralds good performance. When we tie someone down with our attachments or brand someone through sheer misjudgment, the fallout can be demotivating.

of Rama. His voice trembled as he told Vishwamitra that Rama was born to him after years and years of struggle and prayer. He suggested that if Vishwamitra were to insist on taking Rama with him, then he, too, should be allowed take along his entire army to accompany the prince. Dasaratha pleaded again and again, making Vishwamitra aware of his deep attachment with Rama.[23]

vishwamitra's baffling enemies

Dasaratha wanted to know everything about the enemies that awaited his son – the power, size, shape and controller of these demons. From Vishwamitra he learned that these two demons – Maricha and Subahu, sons of Sunda and Tataka – belonged to a powerful lineage of demons. The shape-shifting, winged demons wandered far and wide around the world after sunset to hamper the sacrifices performed by sages. Dasaratha also learned that their chief was Ravana, the brother of Kubera and the son of Vishravasa *muni*. Lord Brahma's boons had rendered Ravana indestructible.

Dasaratha had closely followed the life of Sunda because he was a threat to the world. Sunda, the son of Jharjah, took great pleasure in unleashing immense destruction upon the society. Once, while on a rampage, Sunda tried to attack Agastya *rishi* during his *tapasya* but was burnt to ashes by the *rishi*'s wrath. The widowed Tataka took serious

---

[23] The nature of attachment is such that the mind justifies our attachment and hides our weakness. The nature of attachment is also that the longer you struggle to get something you are attached to, the more painful is the fear of its loss. Moreover, it evokes such sentiments that can make a serious monarch cry like a baby.

offence, so she took along her sons to resume her husband's unfinished job of wreaking havoc in the world.[24]

Dasaratha was horrified to hear the names of the demons Rama was expected to fight. Even he, an able warrior, could not successfully battle against such powerful demons, how could Rama? Dasaratha tried to convince Vishwamitra that as a well-wisher and mentor of the Ikshvaku dynasty, he ought to think of the welfare of the boys and guide them and not think of taking Rama to fight demons even great demigods, *gandharvas* and other powerful beings could not kill. Dasaratha once again reminded Vishwamitra that Rama was his first-born son, who by virtue of His piety was to bring deliverance to His father when the time came. Was he expected to sacrifice his needs at the altar of Vishwamitra's sacrifice?[25]

more anger and more agony

Just as heat takes water to its boiling point, Dasaratha's melancholic arguments pushed Vishwamitra's anger to its limits. His patience was tested further than he could tolerate. He erupted like a violent ocean. His eyes turned red like burning charcoal, his eyebrows knotted in anger, concealing his crinkled forehead. The trepidations of Vishwamitra's rage echoed through the courtroom. Dasaratha's justifications became fuel to Vishwamitra's seething anger, like

---

[24] The birth of a demon takes place first in the consciousness and then physically. Maricha and Subahu were conceived as soon as Sunda made up his mind to destroy the world. Since that was the consciousness with which he united with Tataka, the result was obviously demoniac.

[25] Most people want a mentor who will tell them exactly what they want to hear. This is the process of mentoring the mentor.

saturated butter poured into the sacrificial fire. Dasaratha had come between Vishwamitra and his desire.[26]

The sage jeered; the mocking laughter seemed to mimic the cry of death. He derided Dasaratha's tendency to make fake promises, with no desire to fulfill them. He scoffed at Dasaratha for letting down the name and glory of his dynasty and told him that it would be wiser to rethink before making a decision. Dasaratha hung his head in shame. Vishwamitra stood up to leave but not before giving a derisive look to Vasistha, implying that he was partly to blame for his pupil's ignoble behavior.[27]

vasistha saves the day

Vasistha knew it was time to step in and settle the dust.[28] He had remained silent through the entire conversation between Dasaratha

---

[26] When the desire of two people clash, the one at the losing end flares up; that's what anger is all about. Vishwamitra's rage resulted not from his selfishness but from his desire to serve.

[27] Anger is not an absolutely unwanted emotion; it can also be a wakeup call to reality for those with strong selfish desires. Vishwamitra was using his anger to awaken the slumbering Dasaratha. He wanted him to understand that Rama was not his personal property, but a ray of hope for the entire world – Dasaratha should not keep his property selfishly for his own enjoyment, but allow it to serve the world.

[28] Taking a stand at the right time is the prime duty of the Big M. Indecisiveness leads to helplessness, and helplessness is a state that makes one submissive enough to take directions. At times like these, a person like Vasistha can help one grow. Not everyone is fortunate enough to have someone like Vasistha around, but instead in the guise of Vasistha are people waiting for opportunities to sneak in their hidden agendas.

and Vishwamitra. The atmosphere was being ripped apart by opposing desires – the desires of a father trying to protect his sons and the desires of a sage trying to protect the world from evil. Realizing that the situation had worsened drastically and that balance had to be restored, Vasistha requested Vishwamitra to allow him to talk sense into the confused and indecisive Dasaratha. He reminded Dasaratha that the great dynasty he represented — the Ikshvaku dynasty – was known for ideal kings like Raghu who never faltered from their principles and vows, even if it meant overlooking personal inconveniences and desires. He reminded Dasaratha that he had earned universal respect for his ethics and that during the *ashwamedha yajna*, he had shown extreme detachment by distributing all his wealth among the *brahmanas*. He told Dasaratha that the world expected him to be righteous, ethical and a man of his words and that it would be unwise of him to sacrifice the respect he had worked so hard to earn.[29]

Vasistha told Dasaratha that time had come in the form of Vishwamitra to allow Rama to move onward to His glorious future. Just as little streams flow into big rivers, which in turn flow into massive oceans, Rama, too, had to flow from the river of Ayodhya's comfort into the ocean of Vishwamitra's knowledge.[30] Vasistha

---

[29] Dasaratha once showed detachment by giving his wealth away, but he is unable to show the same spirit again. Real detachment means detaching yourself from all the things you love the most.

[30] Life takes various unavoidable courses. One should not try to prevent a river from taking a turn nor forcibly try to stop the movement of the moon.

suggested that Dasaratha let go of Rama and allow Him to prosper; he urged him to be a reflective father not an impulsive one.[31]

Vasistha assured Dasaratha that Vishwamitra was no ordinary mortal and that he was empowered by many years of austerities and penances. He said that the great sage was intellect, power, strength and meditation all rolled into one and was capable of taking on the demons himself but that he had a higher purpose in wanting to take Rama. Just like the nectar of immortality that demigods consume is protected by a firewall in heaven, Rama was nectar personified and Vishwamitra the firewall that would do everything in his power to protect Him.[32]

Vishwamitra possessed many missiles and divine weapons of matchless power. Two sets of those divine missiles were in fact people without a concrete form. But they were made of subtle elements. These missiles were very powerful, dazzling and ever victorious. There were hundreds of missiles in each of the two sets. They were the sons of Krishaasva Prajapati and his wives Jaya and Suprabha, who were

---

[31] One's attachment can sometimes obstruct the evolution of loved ones. When great people are born, everyone connected to them has to bear the pain of separation. Because they are born to achieve great things, they have to leave the comfort of their homes and step out into the world for a larger cause. So it is up to the families of these great beings to make the sacrifice of letting them be owned by the world, because no great feat has been achieved without great sacrifices.

[32] Vasistha observed the struggle between Dasaratha and Vishwamitra from a neutral perspective; therefore, he could see the deadlock. Vasistha loved Dasaratha, but he loved Ayodhya, too. What was good for Dasaratha was not necessarily good for Ayodhya. This is the role of the big M – to look at the larger picture.

Daksha's daughters. Daksha was the demigod in charge of proliferation. The first set of missiles was known as Jayas, named in honor of their mother. The second set of missiles was known as Sambharakas or eliminator.[33] Lord Shiva, pleased with Vishwamitra's austerities, gifted him these missiles. Not only did Vishwamitra have mastery over all these missiles, but he could also create some rare ones with his power. He had the ability to use these weapons to perfection and to destroy any weapon in this world. Dasaratha was thus convinced that Rama was safer with Vishwamitra than inside the city of Ayodhya.

dasaratha's toughest decision

The words of his spiritual master Vasistha made Dasaratha finally comprehend the wisdom in Vishwamitra's plea. Realizing his mistake and feeling extremely repentant about his hostile and arrogant behavior, Dasaratha agreed to send Rama with Vishwamitra. Vasistha's intervention took Dasaratha from a state of confusion to a state of calm. He could now think clearly, be objective about the issue

---

[33] This shows us a standard where even objects (weapons) are personified; the current world standard is where persons are treated like object. When objects are treated as persons, there develops a culture of respect with refined healthy sensitivity and when persons are objectified, it leads to a culture of disrespect with gross de-sensitivity.

at hand and immediately reach the decision to allow Rama to go with Vishwamitra. [34]

Dasaratha, convinced by Vasistha's suggestion, went to fetch Rama. Rama's mother Kaushalya, too, came to bless her son and wish him a safe journey. Dasaratha blessed Him, kissed Him on His forehead and then handed Rama over to Vishwamitra. Along with Rama, Dasaratha handed over Lakshmana also. Everyone knew the two brothers were inseparable.

Dasaratha did not for once feel the need to ask Rama His desire and Rama never complained about it either. Rama's life was devoted to following the instructions of His father and other superiors. He had full faith in their choices for him.[35]

---

[34] In this entire episode, who could be considered wrong? Was Dasaratha wrong in expressing his emotions as a father? Was Vishwamitra wrong in having such an unusual expectation from Dasaratha? Both cannot be blamed because both were right in their own perspective. Apart from having different perspectives, both had flaws, too. Vishwamitra had the best of intentions but he could not convey his intentions the way Vasistha did; thus his flaw was improper communication. On the other hand, Dasaratha had immense love for his son but his attachment smothered his real love, because the nature of real love does not impede progress. Vasistha was a neutral mediator, the one who provided balance to the tipping scales, a well-wisher with an unbiased opinion of the situation and its implications. Vasistha was qualified to be the mediator because he had knowledge, maturity and a desire to help both the parties involved. The duty of a mediator is not to take decisions, but to empower both the parties to decide with calmness and objectivity.

[35] Unflinching faith and flexibility to follow the directives of superiors who not only love you but are also mature enough to select the right path are amenities in the life of a few. It is a collective test in which the follower and the superior are both equally subjected.

a tearful farewell

With tears of affection and separation streaming down his cheeks, Dasaratha told Vishwamitra that he was handing over his two boys and that from now on he was to be their mother and father. Dasaratha expected the rigidity of the sage to flex into the kindness of a mother and the protection of a father. His expectations from Vishwamitra were immense, and Dasaratha wanted those emphasized before the sage left with his beloved sons.[36]

Sage Vishwamitra and the two boys bade Ayodhya farewell and headed toward the forest. The boys were clad in royal robes, swords strapped to their waist belts and a bow and two sets of quivers each slung over their shoulders. They seemed like three-headed serpents walking down the streets of Ayodhya, with their twin quiver sets bobbing on either side of their heads. The citizens poured into the streets to catch one last glimpse of their beloved Rama and showered them with flowers as blessings and good wishes. Musical instruments played across the streets of Ayodhya to create an auspicious atmosphere for the boys' farewell. As Rama and Lakshmana blurred into the horizon and out of Dasaratha's gaze, he could feel his life walking out of him. He kept staring into the horizon long after his eyes could no longer see the sage who had walked away with his life.[37]

---

[36] The life of a sage is result-oriented, but the life of a father and mother is love-oriented. It is easier to be result-oriented than to be love-oriented because love entails accommodation of lapses. Dasaratha was appealing to Vishwamitra to be love-oriented.

[37] One man's gain is another man's loss. Life is like a game of passing the parcel, where the bundle of joy is passed from one person to another. Happiness is not guaranteed when you are doing a good deed, but satisfaction is. Dasaratha, although visibly unhappy, had the satisfaction of following his superior's instructions.

CHAPTER 5

LAWS OF PROGRESSIVE LIVING

vishwamitra empowers rama with two *mantra*s

The trio slowly made their way toward the forest, led by the wise sage Vishwamitra. The ever-obedient Rama walked behind the *muni*, and His ever-loyal brother, Lakshmana, followed Him. Before long, the smooth city streets gave way to rugged country roads flanked by flower fields and trees in full bloom, playing host to fluttering butterflies and nesting birds. The swift breeze caressed the beehives and tickled the honeycombs, so that they oozed and dripped their honey on the ground, nourishing it with sweetness. Rama and Lakshmana walked briskly behind their new teacher, awestruck by nature's wonders. As they walked, Vishwamitra described everything about each city, town, mountain and river they crossed and narrated great stories of valor to make the journey interesting for the boys. The boys had so many questions, and Vishwamitra patiently kept answering them. They walked for about eight miles and reached the southern bank of the Sarayu river. Vishwamitra was overcome with motherly compassion on seeing the tired faces of the usually energetic Rama and Lakshmana. He decided that Rama deserved to be initiated into *Bala* and *Atibala,* the two potent *mantra*s Lord Brahma had given him. He called out to Rama and asked Him take a dip in the river before accepting the *mantras* from him. Rama took to the river right away and followed instructions.[1]

Vishwamitra explained to Rama that these *mantras* were extremely powerful and that the one in possession of them would never experience fatigue or fever, would be immune to attacks from demons whether awake or asleep, would be unmatched in dexterity and strength, would be unparalleled in beauty, caliber and scholarship, would be discriminative and resourceful, would never experience hunger or thirst, would become peerlessly famous and radiant.

Rama learned the *mantras* with great dedication and focus. As soon as He had mastered the two *mantras*, He became lustrous and luminous like the sun. Even though the *mantras* had empowered Rama with

---

[1] From a devotional perspective, this story has deep connotations. Vishwamitra taught the *mantras* only to Rama and not to Lakshmana. Rama in turn, sought permission from Vishwamitra to give the *mantras* to Lakshmana. Why did Vishwamitra not impart the knowledge to Lakshmana directly? Had he done so, it would have put Lakshmana on the same plane as Rama – a status Lakshmana would never accept. Lakshmana always considered himself a servant of Rama. Had Vishwamitra initiated him into the *mantra*, he would have become a disciple of Vishwamitra, and would have been raised to the same platform as Rama. Lakshmana considered Rama a disciple of Vishwamitra and himself a disciple of Rama. Lakshmana's perspective was clear in that his position was that of Rama's servant.

From another perspective, Vishwamitra is a student and Rama the Supreme Lord, hence the Supreme Teacher. For so long, Vishwamitra carried this knowledge as a burden, assuming he was the master of it; however, after he handed it over to Lord Rama, the original master of this knowledge, he felt huge relief.

manifold power, He had deep gratitude for His teacher for imparting the *mantras* and continued to serve Vishwamitra as before.[2,3]

the trio rests by the sarayu

By sundown, the soft yet firm grass carpet by the Sarayu river seemed to beckon. It was time for the trio to take some rest. Sleeping on a grass bed did not seem to bother the princes so used to sleeping on soft downy beds.[4] Vishwamitra tried to dispel their discomfort through words of comfort and sweet talk.[5] It was for the first time in his life that the hard-hearted sage spoke softly and sweetly with children. The starlit sky, the gurgling waters and Vishwamitra's tales gradually lulled the boys to sleep.[6]

---

[2] Traditionally, the teacher blessed the student with the words *vijayi vinayi bhava*, meaning may you be victorious (*vijayi*) and humble (*vinayi*).

[3] A student should always retain a sense of gratitude. Rama was the Supreme Lord, but while playing the role of a student, He exhibited exemplary behavior. Service to the teacher dilutes the acidic pride of knowledge.

[4] A good leader is trained and happy to be flexible. Rama and Lakshmana had led a luxurious life till this point, but because they were trained to adapt, they not only adjusted to their new frugal life, but they were also visibly happy in a seemingly uncomfortable situation.

[5] Soothing words of love are more gratifying than luxuries offered without love. Of course, if both love and luxuries can be offered, it would be wonderful; however, if there were a choice between the two, the former would be preferable.

[6] Every human being has the desire to express his softer side; however, the desire to project oneself as a tough person who does not easily succumb makes expressing the softer side seem like a weakness.

_____THE LAW OF SHARING_____

The law of sharing states that sharing your knowledge multiplies loving relationships and frees one from loneliness.

The pride of being knowledgeable keeps one isolated from the rest of the world. A person who has pride of knowledge does have the strength of learning, but is also lonely.

Until now, Vishwamitra had been filled with this pride and had always been inaccessible to the world.

The law of sharing acts as a bridge across waters of frustration around the island of pride and loneliness, opening up the route to the mainland garden of love.

---

the magic of the sleeping rama

The dark night disappeared with the first rays of the morning sun just as ignorance disappears with the acquisition of knowledge. Long before the first rays of the sun touched the horizon, the austere Vishwamitra woke up for his morning oblations. Once he was through with the rituals, he went over to wake up the sleeping boys.

Vishwamitra stood mesmerized. Sleeping innocently like little angels on the green velvety mattress were the two princes, sparkling like two jewels. The rigid sage was overwhelmed by the surge of emotions in his heart, an experience that thousands of years of austerities and sacrifices could never give him. What he felt was the bare emotion of *bhakti* or loving devotion to God. He had heard that the path of devotion and surrender was superior to the path of austerities and self-denial, but he had never really believed it. Was he wrong in not trusting the power of devotion? This overpowering, sublime experience made him reconsider his basic beliefs. Rama's divinity was compelling him to surrender himself to Rama.[7]

As he observed the sleeping splendor, he began to wonder how fortunate Kaushalya, Rama's mother, was to be blessed by this poignant sight every morning. In his mind, he automatically began worshipping her and even composed a beautiful verse requesting Lord Rama to wake up.[8]

Kaushalya suprajaa raama
Poorva sandhya pravartate
Uttistha nara shaardula
Kartavyam daivamaanikam

Translated it means: "How fortunate is Kaushalya who has begotten you as her son! The sun has risen in the east, now you my dear Lord, tiger among men, please arise and perform those duties that are considered divine."

---

[7] There is a difference between the path of devotion and the path of austerities. While on the path of devotion, we are able to experience the greatness of others' love and realize the lack of our own, and this makes us humble. Humility is conducive for spiritual growth. While on the path of austerity, we are so crippled by our own feelings of greatness and achievement that we lose focus by basking in self-glory. Those on the path of devotion don't try to achieve God; they try to serve God through the medium of love and in the process, achieve Him.

[8] Great poets reveal that Vishwamitra started singing this verse much before sunrise; however, because he was so awestruck by both Kaushalya's fortune as mother and Rama's beauty, he kept repeating Kausalya's name. It was only at sunrise that he came to his senses and managed to complete the rest of the verse. This verse also means that Kaushalya had the fortunate opportunity to give birth to none other than the sun itself, Lord Rama, the One born to dispel darkness and establish divine qualities.

————THE LAW OF DEPENDENCE————

Capitalizing on mutual strengths leads to success.

The law of dependence states that one's real strength lies in realizing the strength of another. Dependence releases one from the burden of being an exclusive controller and leads one to the freedom of accepting higher powers to realize one's goal.

Taking shelter in one's own strength leads to taking pride in being the controller. By being amiable enough to depend on others' strength, one can focus on achieving the goal. Vishwamitra realized that for so long he had exclusively depended on his own strength. He learned this law of dependence from mother Kaushalya.

---

the hero's arc

A book is often based on the central hero around whom the story revolves. Who then is the central hero of Book One? In fact to make things even more confusing, *Valmiki Ramayana* refers to this book as *Bala Kanda*, which means the story of childhood. Who is the *bala* or the child in *Bala Kanda*? Whoever this child is has to be the hero of the book. Could it be Lord Rama or any of His brothers? That seems to be the most obvious conclusion. But surprisingly, the child or *bala* of *Bala Kanda* is in fact Sage Vishwamitra! So that makes him the hero of this book. Why him?

The answer lies in Vishwamitra's journey of devotion or *bhakti* toward Lord Rama – from childhood and naïveté to adulthood and maturity. Vishwamitra was a revered master and could achieve great things, but he was still in the dawn of devotion. As a child grows in maturity and his understanding of the world with age, Vishwamitra, too, while traveling with Rama, grew in maturity while understanding the process of devotion. As the sun rises slowly over the horizon and arches its way up to the top of the sky to become large and blaze bright and harsh only to settle down on the other side as this calm, soothing perfect orb of hope, understanding, maturity and warmth, Vishwamitra, too, through his close association with Rama, had risen in maturity to understand the true process of devotion.

Rise of the Sun Prince, which is basically the *Bala Kanda*, is essentially about fighting grave internal battles and overcoming great odds to emerge victorious and become exemplary. It is about swallowing pride to rise to great heights. It is about learning to let go and surrender to the Supreme One, to allow true devotion to show the path to spiritual greatness. It is about molding imperfections to achieve perfection by following the laws of progressive living. It is about rising like the sun – emotionally and spiritually – to shine brighter than ever.

By the end of *Bala Kanda*, Vishwamitra had traversed this trajectory in *bhakti*. No longer in the dawn of devotion, or in the noon of blazing rage and overbearing ego, Vishwamitra had settled in the hearts and minds of all as one of the most luminous sages of all time – warm and perfect.

rama and lakshmana tread onward

Vishwamitra recited the verse on Kaushalya to gently nudge the sleeping princes out of their sleep and let them know that great responsibility rested upon their shoulders. Calling them tigers among men, the wise sage extolled them to become leaders of human society and set examples for people to follow. Rama and Lakshmana rose and went toward to the river for a bath. They performed the rituals of worship and offered themselves to Vishwamitra.[9]

Feeling rested and rejuvenated, the trio resumed their journey. They had walked some distance, when they reached the holy River Ganga. Right at the confluence of the Sarayu and the Ganga was a picturesque hermitage. The beautiful sight made Rama curious about its history and glory. When He asked Vishwamitra about it, the sage smiled, knowing fully well that this was Rama's way of testing him. Rama was the all-knowing God and yet He innocently asked about the hermitage as if He was completely unaware. Vishwamitra did not want to fall into the trap of being all-knowing, so he decided to use this opportunity to serve Rama and narrated the story.

Long, long ago, Lord Shiva had chosen this spot for meditation. When Lord Shiva's eyes were closed in a meditative trance, a demigod named Kandarpa (aka Kaamadeva), the God of Love, came to this spot. To prove his greatness and his influence over everyone, the demigod tried to disturb Lord Shiva by darting arrows of love at him. Extremely enraged by this mischief, Lord Shiva opened his Third Eye and scorched Kaamadeva to nothingness, such that not even his ashes were visible. Since then, Kaamadeva came to be known as *Ananga*, or one who has no *anga* or body.[10] And this place came to be known as the Anga province. This hermitage belonged to Lord Shiva's disciples.

---

[9] It is natural instinct to forget one's responsibilities and become lazy. The job of a true guide is to keep the lethargic mind focused on its goal. Absolute focus is necessary for one who has to set an example for others to follow.

[10] Kaamadeva has made a place for himself in the minds of everyone. Because Kaamadeva has no body, it implies that lust is a state of mind. The lusty mind makes the prospect of pleasure seem irresistible and looks at every situation and object from the perspective of pleasure enhancement alone.

Vishwamitra decided to spend the night with the boys at the hermitage. [11] The hermitage residents welcomed them warmly and took great pleasure in serving them. That night, Vishwamitra told Rama and Lakshmana many wonderful stories, and soon the boys were fast asleep.

THE LAW OF BALANCE

The law of balance is about balancing selfish desires with selflessness, thus taking oneself from the narrow world of self-satisfaction to the broad world of self-contentment.

Selfishness leads to discontent. No matter how much one has, one hankers for evermore. The urge to take must be balanced by the wish to give. Part of fulfilling one's own needs is to fulfill the needs of others, thus creating a balance.

Selfishness stems from an egocentric perception of existence. An egocentric person is self-centered, has a small mind and lives in a small world – a world of self-satisfaction.

The owner of such a world succumbs to the pride of being an exclusive enjoyer. Vishwamitra realized the need to cap this urge.

---

[11] Vishwamitra wished to follow Lord Rama, a representative of *dharma*; to do so, he had to dovetail his desires or *kaama* in alignment with the principles of *dharma*, so that *kaama* would not be a distraction. Being a resilient sage, Vishwamitra could forcibly withdraw his mind from sensory objects; however, such artificial force can only restrain the body, not the mind. Nevertheless, the fire of devotion has the potential to transform lust to love – from the material to the spiritual.

forest of anger

The following morning, Vishwamitra, Rama and Lakshmana woke up and performed the usual rituals. Up until they reached the hermitage, the trio had traversed by foot. But this time, Vishwamitra and his pupils took a boat to ferry across the Ganga. As they were sailing, Rama heard an unusually loud noise emanating from the waters and asked Vishwamitra about it. Vishwamitra told Him that it was the sound of the confluence of the two rivers – Sarayu and Ganga. Rama and Lakshmana listened with awe as Vishwamitra told them the story of Sarayu's origin.

Lord Brahma had once created a lake with his mind and named it Manasa Lake. *Sarah* is the Sanskrit word for lake, and because the river originated from a lake was named *Sarayu*. Rama and Lakshmana paid their respects at the confluence of these two holy rivers.

They disembarked from the boat when it crossed the confluence and touched the southern bank of Ganga. The difficult part of their journey lay just ahead. The trio had to cross a dreadful and uninhabitable forest made even more menacing by dangerous wild beasts and birds with echoing roars and screeches. The forest had no trees that bore fruits or flowers, and it was blistering hot across the year, season after season. Blazing heat had charred and scarred the earth and left deep cracks along the ground. These cracks were so deep and wide that elephants would often get trapped within them. Rama and Lakshmana chanted the *Bala* and *Atibala mantras* to counter the unbearable heat and feel cool instead.

The place was so stark and harsh that Rama was curious to know how such a terrible place could possibly exist among the Lord's creations. Vishwamitra explained that the forest had not always been so horrific. In fact, at some point in the past, it was an auspicious abode.

Ages ago, Indra, the king of demigods, had killed a demon named Vritrasura, a *brahmana* trapped inside a demon's body because of past sins. Because Indra had killed a *brahmana* in the guise of a demon, he had to bear the consequences of committing the sin of killing a *brahmana*. Indra was immediately sullied and drenched by putrid substances that let off an obnoxious stench from his body. Indra, desperate to rid himself of his sin and the rancid odor, reached this forest where his assistants cleansed him of his reeking sin.

Severe hunger was another side-effect of the sin. An adjacent forest provided Indra with delectable dishes to satiate his hunger pangs. Indra was so delighted to be rid of his twin anxieties that he blessed this region with profuse prosperity. He named one of the forests Malada, meaning a place that removes *mala* or contamination, and he named the other Karusa, which means a place that removes excessive hunger. From then on, these became forests of bounty and abundance.[12]

Rama was now a little confused. How could a place so blessed be cursed to devastation? Vishwamitra continued to explain the series of incidents that ultimately led to the forest being stark, dry and dangerous. A childless *yaksha* named Suketu had performed austerities to please Lord Brahma; Brahma finally granted him the boon that he would have a beautiful daughter blessed with the strength of a thousand elephants. Suketu named her Tataka.

As mentioned earlier in this book, Tataka was the wife of the demon Sunda and the mother of two wily demons – Maricha (who had broad beefy shoulders and was very powerful) and Subahu (who was an expert wrestler). The arrogant Sunda who went about disturbing hermits, once tried to trouble sage Agastya, who was so incensed that

---

[12] Prosperity is not necessarily a result of one's boisterous efforts; it may be the result of a silent blessing. When you relieve someone of his suffering, blessing is guaranteed.

he reduce the demon to ashes. Tataka, Maricha and Subahu, aghast upon hearing the news of Sunda's death, became vengeful and pledged to destroy Agastya's hermitage. Agastya cursed the three of them into becoming ferocious human-eating demons. Having failed in her mission to harm Agastya, Tataka turned her wrath upon forests that were home to Agastya and the other sages and annihilated the Malada and Karusa forests. Her intense rage converted the once-picturesque forests into deserted thorny woodlands and she soon swamped them with demons that incessantly harassed the sages to chase them away. Tataka's sons went to Sumali, a demon who happened to be Ravana's grandfather. Sumali became fond of Maricha and Subahu and gave them shelter. Eventually, they became an integral part of Ravana's kingdom, and Ravana lovingly called them his maternal uncles because of their connection with Sumali.[13]

rama's dilemma

Vishwamitra had prepared Rama for the inevitable – to fight with Tataka. As a guru, he knew his disciple Rama's thought process. He realized that Rama's dilemma was not whether to kill an enemy but whether to kill a woman. How could Rama who could never imagine hurling abuses or glaring at a woman even think of piercing one with arrows? For Rama, a woman was a symbol of purity and was someone worthy of respect. Rama's mother had trained Him to venerate women, and He believed real education meant worshipping every woman as he would His mother. But His teacher expected Him to kill a woman, the first of His demon victims.

---

[13] Anger, as a result of frustrated desires, can transform a beautiful, prosperous heart into a parched one filled with the thorns of envy and devoid of the fruits of love.

Vishwamitra's lessons for Rama were beyond the realm of theoretical knowledge. Vishwamitra reminded Rama of the multiple responsibilities and roles that He was playing and that waited for Him. He told Him that His main role was that of the prince of Ikshwaku Dynasty, a dynasty expected to protect society. Sacrifice was expected of a king, even sacrificing one's principles at times. On the one hand, was Rama's sacred principle of respect and worship for a woman, but on the other hand was the higher principle of protecting citizens from torture and trauma. Rama had to weigh His principles.

To diffuse Rama's dilemma and mould His mind toward killing Tataka, Vishwamitra explained to Him how Tataka was everything a woman should not be and narrated several instances from the past when gods and demigods had been required to kill women.

Vishwamitra justified that Tataka possessed no womanly virtues to command His respect and veneration. She was evil; her actions were atrocious and behaviour deplorable; she had such malefic valor that she spread terror across the universe. He said that only if a woman with good qualities were mistreated would the aggressor lose all virtue and be destined to a horrendous future. He assured Rama that killing Tataka was necessary and that in doing so, He would not violate His *dharma*.

Vishwamitra told Rama about an instance when the demigod Indra had to kill an outrageous woman. He told Rama about Sumati, who had acquired such unlimited powers that it had blinded her with arrogance. Drunk with power and strength, she began killing and torturing every living thing that came her way. She had gone so far into evil that her name was changed to Kumati, meaning one with crooked intelligence. Indra realized that she was causing too much damage and killed her. Indra also had to kill Manthara, the daughter of Virochana, because she was attempting to destroy the entire earth.

Vishwamitra also told Him about Khyati, the extremely beautiful, fish-eyed wife of sage Bhrigu. Although she was the wife of such an exalted sage, she had a soft spot for demons, pitied them and let them in on the secrets of demigods. Worried that it might cause uncontrollable troubles later, Lord Vishnu had to kill her. At one point in time, the demons were becoming weaker than the demigods. So Sukracharya, their *guru*, performed *tapasya* to appease Lord Shiva. When the guru was away meditating, the demigods tried to attack the demons. They ran for shelter to Khyati, the step-mother of Sukracharya and the wife of Bhrigu. To protect the demons, Khyati used her power of penance to freeze the demigods. The frozen demigods would have become easy prey for the demons had it not been for Lord Vishnu who absorbed all of them into His own body. Khyati realized that Lord Vishnu had thwarted her plans; she was about to curse Him when He released His *sudarshan chakra*, severing her head. When Bhrigu learned of his wife's death, he cursed Lord Vishnu to appear on Earth 10 times. The result of Bhrigu's curse was Lord Vishnu's 10 incarnations, famously known as the *dasavatar*.[14]

Vishwamitra gently reminded Rama that as a prince He had to shoulder the responsibility of protecting the innocent from destructive individuals. He told Rama that to prove His commitment to His people, He was expected to come out victorious at the end of many such difficult missions, even if these appeared ruthless, sinful, or against His principles.[15]

Rama contemplated the words of His teacher while also being reminded of His father's instructions: to always abide by the words of

---

[14] Interestingly, Lord Rama was one of the 10 incarnations of Lord Vishnu, and Vishwamitra was explaining His own story to Him!

[15] Leading is not just about action, but about thinking and weighing the diverse possibilities before acting. Guided intelligence thinks in the right direction. Personal choices have to be sacrificed at the altar of the good of the whole.

Vishwamitra. Keeping both in mind, He spent some time on deliberation. Rama decided that His primary task was the welfare of this world, so He expressed His eagerness to execute His teacher's orders.[16]

Rama held His bow with one hand, pulled back the string with the other. The twang of the bow was so powerful and resounding that it shook the entire forest. The thunderous sound forced the birds to fly out of every tree for fear that the forest would be destroyed. At the far end of the forest, the monstrous Tataka who was relaxing in a cave heard the reverberating twang of the bow string. Although she was so used to torturing others, she found the thunderous sound of Rama's bow unbearable. Infuriated, she hollered out of her cave and ran toward the source of the sound. She wanted to kill the one who had caused her such torment.

Rama and Lakshmana saw Tataka running toward them from a distance; her ghastly and monstrous features becoming clearer as she inched closer. She had shoulders as strong as the Mandara Mountains, feet so huge and heavy that her earth-carving footsteps left behind a trail of lakes. As Tataka avalanched toward Rama, He was convinced that this couldn't be a woman, because trapped and mauled under each of her footsteps were hundreds of living beings. She wore golden anklets, elephant head–studded earrings and a blood-oozing garland of elephants strung tail to trunk. Her teeth were

---

[16] Dasaratha advised Rama to follow all of Vishwamitra's instructions without questioning, but Rama gave the instructions a thought before following them. Why? Different authorities instruct us at different times. Vishwamitra was one authority in Rama's life, Dasaratha was another. Before taking action, Rama thought about what advice yet another authority – the scriptures – would give Him in such a situation. Only when He was convinced that Dasaratha's and Vishwamitra's instructions were in complete alignment with the scriptures did He execute them.

like the trident of Yama, the God of death. The sight of such a ghastly being did not arouse any respect or veneration in Rama.

As she hurtled closer to Rama, she seemed like a tornado running into a mountain. Rama stood still, aiming an arrow at her. Suddenly, He was overwhelmed by compassion. It dawned upon Him that the first person He had to kill in this incarnation was a woman. Instead of killing her, He decided to get rid of her impudence. As Rama was pondering, Tataka went wild and hurled a storm of stones toward the brothers. Rama, while evading the stones, swiftly released arrows that chopped off her arms, whereas Lakshmana's arrows struck off her nose and ears. Tataka realized she was now courting defeat, so she swirled up dust and disappeared and tried to trick the princes by pelting stones at them from different directions simultaneously.

Vishwamitra immediately understood that although Rama had agreed to kill Tataka, compassion and righteousness were holding Him from killing a woman. Vishwamitra urged Rama to relinquish His misplaced compassion as this was no innocent woman who had to be protected but a sinister evil that had to be destroyed. He reminded Rama that her powers would multiply with the setting sun and that there were only few minutes to sunset, after which it would be difficult to destroy her.

Rama realized then that Vishwamitra was right; His compassion was coming in the way of the larger cause. Tataka was still invisible and hurling stones from different directions. She laughed out loud at Rama's plight. No sooner than she laughed, she realized her fatal mistake. Rama immediately released an arrow toward the source of the sound. The arrow was as effective as the curse of a sage; it pierced through her heart and tore out of her back and flew into the sky.[17]

---

[17] The arrow whizzed out through Tataka like advice given by noble people whizzes past foolish people, swiftly disappearing after entering their minds!

Tataka was dead in an instant; her monstrous dismembered body slumped to the ground.

Rama begged Vishwamitra for forgiveness for momentarily having disregarded his instructions and allowed His principles to cloud His judgment. Rama felt that He was an offender in the eyes of His spiritual master and His father, Dasaratha. Vishwamitra was thoroughly impressed with Rama's sincerity in admitting to His faults and begging forgiveness.[18] He was also impressed with Rama's ability to think independently, a crucial quality in a leader.[19]

Tataka's death brought much-wanted relief and thawed the whole universe. The demigods, led by Indra, assembled and applauded Rama for eliminating her and rained celestial flowers on the brothers. Indra instructed Vishwamitra to give Rama the rest of the missiles in his possession because He indeed deserved to have them.

With Tataka's death, the beauty and abundance of the forest was immediately restored, just as festivities resume on the homecoming of a long-lost son. A proud and beaming Vishwamitra kissed Rama on His forehead because the destruction of Tataka meant another level of personal victory for Him.

---

[18] Rama was able to see His own faults and sincerely repent because of them, whereas Vishwamitra was trying to only see the good qualities in Rama. This combination is what makes relationships last during potential misunderstandings.

[19] Rama was in a catch 22 situation, because, for a leader, sensitivity and discipline are of equal importance. Showing sensitivity during a situation that demands disciplinary action is bad governance. A leader needs to seek advice but at the same use his discretion to decide which advice to take. The ability to use discretion is a sign that a leader can be given more responsibility and power.

THE LAW OF AWARENESS

The law of awareness states that access to knowledge can help an insensitive person become sensitive by allowing the light of true knowledge to exterminate the darkness of ignorance.

Tataka represents ignorance or avidya. *Ignorance stems from lack of knowledge and results in a life without a conscience. Like a person in a dark room, a person under the influence of ignorance may not realize the effects of being insensitive to others and may actually take pleasure in tormenting the innocent and terrorizing the helpless.*

The solution to darkness is light; similarly, the solution to ignorance is knowledge. The light of knowledge illuminates dark hearts, which leads to the development of a conscience.

The following day at dawn, Vishwamitra told Rama that He was qualified to receive more mystic missiles because of the great level of discretion He had displayed when killing Tataka. He gave Rama, four types of wheels – a wheel that punishes, a wheel that establishes virtue, a wheel that controls time and the wheel of Vishnu. He also gave Rama the thunderbolt weapon of Indra, trident missiles of Shiva, the *brahma sirsha* missile of Brahma, two maces named *modaki* and *shikari*, three nooses called *dharma pasa*, *kaala pasa* and *varuna pasa*. In addition to these, he gave Him innumerable weapons of various shapes and powers. All weapons appeared in front of Rama in person, requesting that He use them at His will. Each weapon expressed its desire and eagerness to serve Him. Rama accepted all of them and instructed the missiles to leave and appear whenever He called for them. Rama bowed to Vishwamitra in gratitude.

vishwamitra's river sister

After handing over to Rama all the celestial weapons he had in his possession, Vishwamitra told them that it was about time they continued onward to their destination. From the banks of the Ganga, they reached the banks of another river named Kaushiki. Rama wanted to know the story of this river that was adored by the demigods as well. Vishwamitra began describing the ancient tale about the river's formation. Brahma had given birth to a son named Kusa, whose wonderful qualities led him to become the emperor of the world. His wife Vaidharbhi and he had four sons, Kusa (his first son was also named Kusa), Kusanabha, Adhurta and Vasu. Of these sons, Kusanabha had a hundred beautiful daughters. Once, in the peak of their youth, when they were playing in a garden, Vayu, the wind God, happened to see them. He fell madly in love with all of them and asked them to marry him. He gloated about his power, position and influence over the world. The girls bowed to him in respect but said that they would have to take the father's consent, and only if he, the great Kusanabha, allowed would they marry him. Vayu did not expect to be snubbed by the girls; he lost his temper. To teach them a lesson, he broke their backbones, leaving them writhing in extreme pain. Kusanabha was immensely agonized by Vayu's arrogance and his daughters' pain. He was also proud that they had not compromised on the prestige of the family and knew how to uphold its glory.

Kusanabha arranged for his daughters to be married to a great sage named Brahmadatta. Soon after the wedding, one touch by Brahmadatta healed the girls' backs.[20] Kusanabha now wanted a son so he performed a sacrifice in the hope of fathering one. He was eventually blessed with an effulgent son named Gadhi whom he crowned king before leaving in pursuit of spiritual aspirations. Gadhi had two children – Kaushiki, a beautiful girl, and Vishwamitra, the sage himself.

Vishwamitra's sister Kaushiki was married to sage Richika, the son of the great sage Bhrigu. Richika spent some time with Kaushiki and then left for Brahmaloka. Kaushiki could not bear the separation from her husband. Through austerities and penances, she took the form of a river to be able to follow him to heaven. When Richika saw his wife transform into a river to follow him, he encouraged her to remain on Earth as a river and continue to serve humanity. Richika then returned to Brahmaloka never to return again. Vishwamitra touched the waters of the Kaushiki river; the river was his own sister. Rama and Lakshmana were spellbound on hearing a story so close to their teacher's life.[21] They were grateful to him for sharing a piece of his own life, and bowed to the holy river – the holy sister of their teacher.

---

[20] The inability to realize personal agenda drives us to break others' backs and also their hearts. A selfless heart is not interested in pleasantries, but in the opportunity to serve; such a selfless heart can restore real beauty. The selfish Vayu broke the back of the hundred daughters of Kusanabha, whereas the mere touch of a selfless Brahmadatta restored their real beauty.

[21] The way children behave reflects the values and culture of their families. Gadhi, an ideal king, lived a life of servitude toward his citizens; his children Vishwamitra and Kaushiki adopted the culture of service and lived to serve the society. While Kaushiki became a river to serve people through her waters, quenching their thirst and purifying them, Vishwamitra became a sage to serve people through his knowledge, purifying the world through his sacrifices. Such selfless lives attracted the appreciation of Lord Rama.

a hermitage of perfection

In the distance, Rama and Lakshmana spotted a hermitage surrounded by a beautiful, lush forest. As always, they turned to Vishwamitra for answers to questions buzzing in their heads.

Vishwamitra told them about the purity and significance of the hermitage. This heritage hermitage was thousands of years old, dating back to the time of Lord Vishnu. Even Lord Vishnu had performed austerities here for thousands of years. Vishwamitra narrated the story of Bali.

Led by a king named Bali, the demons attacked the heavens and displaced the demigods from their kingdom. The distressed demigods took refuge under Vishnu and asked Him to help them regain their lost glory. Lord Vishnu agreed.

At that same time, somewhere nearby, a couple was performing austerities. They were Kasyapa and his wife Aditi, the mother of the demigods. Pleased with their sincerity and devotion, Lord Vishnu appeared before them and granted them a boon of their choice. Kasyapa in fact had two wishes. One that Lord Vishnu be born as his son and become the younger brother of Indra, the king of the demigods. The other that the place be named Siddhashram or 'Hermitage of Perfection' because it was in this hermitage that he had attained perfection by finding a personal audience with the Lord. Lord Vishnu granted him both his wishes. Soon Lord Vishnu manifested as Vaamana, the dwarf son of Kasyapa. Vaamana also resided in this hermitage and performed austerities.

One day while traversing the forest, Vaamana reached the place the demon Bali was performing an elaborate fire sacrifice. He went there as a *brahmana,* begging for alms. The extremely charitable Bali asked the *brahmana* to wish for anything. Bali's spiritual master, Shukaracharya, who could see through the entire trick, warned his pupil about making the promise to Vaamana because the dwarf was none other than Vishnu, the protector of demigods. Bali, however, ignored the pleas of his spiritual master. To him, being granted the opportunity to serve the Supreme Lord was more important than paying heed to his spiritual master who was in fact trying to disconnect him from God. Bali extended his promise to Vaamana, who promptly asked him for three steps of land. Bali was surprised by the "tiny" request. Three steps, is that all the Lord wanted? As soon as Bali granted Vaamana the wish, the tiny dwarf grew in size to become Trivikrama, and with just two steps, covered the entire universe - by extending His body, He covered the entire sky, and with His hands, He covered all directions; with His second step, He covered the heavens; for His third footstep, there was no place. So He turned to Bali to ask him where He was to place the third step. Bali now understood what had happened and placed his own head under the feet of Vaamana, allowing himself to be pushed out of this world. Vaamana was so pleased with Bali's offer of his head for His third step that He decided to shower him with rewards for such genuine devotion and sincerity.

Vaamana offered Bali the entire Sutalaloka to rule over and promised to personally become the guard at the gates of Bali *maharaja*'s palace and protect him. That was not all. Vaamana knew of Bali's intense desire to become king of the heavens, so he assured him that he would be king after Indra's reign.

Bali was extremely happy with these gifts for he realized that Vaamana had given him more than He had taken from him. Before departing for Sutalaloka, though, Bali had one last request: that he be allowed to return to his earthly kingdom once a year to visit his citizens.

Vaamana granted him that wish.[22] Bali thus surrendered his ego to Vaamana and became a great devotee of the Lord. Vishwamitra explained to the princes that after granting deliverance to Bali and returning the kingdom to the demigods, Vaamana came to this very hermitage to rest.

And after thousands of years, the *ashram* had fallen under the care of Vishwamitra and his disciples. Vishwamitra told Rama that this hermitage was as much Rama's as it was his, indicating that the hermitage actually belonged to Rama and that he was just a caretaker. Rama had previously appeared here as Vishnu to perform austerities and later as Vaamana to deliver Bali. Now Rama had come back to His own abode following Vishwamitra.[23]

---

[22] In accordance to the desire of Bali, Vaamana permitted him to visit his kingdom, which is considered to be modern day Kerala, India. This return of Bali to his kingdom is celebrated every year as Onam. The only reason Bali wanted to come to his kingdom was to see if his citizens were prosperous and lived a life of purity and devotion to the Lord.

[23] The story of Vishwamitra and Bali are similar in the sense that they both surrendered to the Supreme Lord. But the manner in which they surrendered was different. Bali was forced by Vaamana to surrender by rendering him helpless. Lord Vishnu had to go through so much trouble to get Bali to surrender. He had to incarnate, He had to beg from Bali and He had to extend His feet all over the universe. But Vishwamitra voluntarily went to Ayodhya and requested Dasaratha to allow Rama to accompany him. During the course of the journey, Vishwamitra surrendered each of his possessions, one by one, to Lord Rama. Either one takes shelter of the Lord voluntarily to become glorious or one waits for the Lord's powers to create a situation of helplessness to ensure the outcome of surrender.

THE LAW OF TRUSTEESHIP

The law of trusteeship teaches us that ownership does not imply control (Rama owned but did not control) and control does not imply ownership (Vishwamitra controlled but did not claim ownership).

Proprietorship is actually illusory and at best temporary. When one is not permanent in this world, how can one claim permanent proprietorship? Things of this world do not really belong to anyone; merely one can consider himself a trustee.

Vishwamitra realized that though he was in possession of the Siddhashram, the real proprietor was Lord Rama. Vishwamitra was at best, a trustee; thus, he decided to relinquish his claim of proprietorship over the ashram that really did not belong to him.

The law of trusteeship helps you handle any property (everything including life itself) that comes your way with respect (because it belongs to God) and at the same time with detachment (because, ultimately, it does not belong to you).

---

vishwamitra's sacrifice begins

Vishwamitra told Rama and Lakshmana that Siddhashram was where he desired to complete his long-pending sacrifice for the welfare of the world for which he needed their help. Rama requested Vishwamitra to immediately start preparing for the sacrifice. He assured Vishwamitra that He would protect the sacrifice from the demons.

Vishwamitra took a vow of silence till the completion of the sacrifice. As the sage began making arrangements, Rama began preparing for the battle ahead. He asked other sages about the demons and the source, location and time of the attacks. The sages warned Rama and Lakshmana that the demons could attack anytime of the day and from anywhere. They advised them to stay focused and not let even a moment of inattention interrupt them for the next six days. A tiny gap in alertness was all the demons needed to create havoc and destroy the sacrifice.

Rama and Lakshmana kept their eyes peeled on the sacrificial arena. Their job of protecting the sacrifice was akin to the function of eyelids protecting eyeballs. The boys guarded the sacrificial arena just as the eyelids are ever watchful and do not let anything enter the eyes. Lakshmana was stationed at the gate, while Rama walked the flanks. Every time Rama reached the gate, He would alert Lakshmana by gently touching him. Lakshmana was like the stationary lower lid and Rama the constantly blinking upper lid. Just as the upper lid travels all the way up to the top of the eye and then comes all the way down to touch the lower lid, Rama walked from one end of the arena right up to the gate to nudge Lakshmana. The sacrificial altar was the constantly protected eyeball.[24]

---

[24] From another perspective, this is a metaphor – good advisors (sages), when pouring good advice (clarified butter) into a mind (sacrificial arena), are harassed by faultfinders (demons) who try to corrupt the mind (sacrificial arena) by filling it with contaminated thoughts (blood) and filthy words (flesh). Rama and Lakshmana considered the sacrifice very valuable for the welfare of society – just as the eyelids know how valuable the eyes are for the overall welfare of the body. When the value is immense, it is imperative that alertness, too, be continuous. The guard positions of Rama and Lakshmana symbolize alert intelligence that constantly watches out for faultfinders and prevents the mind from being contaminated by them and allows the mind to become purified by the good advisors. A moment of inattention on the part of the intelligence can allow a contaminated thought to pollute the mind.

Six long days and nights passed under the alert vigil of Rama and Lakshmana. Nothing seemed to occur, and it seemed that the sages had worried needlessly. As the last day approached, the flames in the sacrificial altar blazed ferociously right up to the sky as Vishwamitra poured in the last oblation of clarified butter. And as the flames erupted vigorously, they infused a new energy into the sacrificial arena. Everyone's face shone with brilliance and filled with anticipation like that of a calf on seeing its mother's udders.

Just when everyone was basking in the brilliance of the fire, a sudden shriek ripped the atmosphere.[25] Rama, also known as *Rajivalochana*, had lotus-like ability to spot the sun from a distance. Now He could see the fierce demons sweeping down from a distance. The moment He spotted Maricha and Subahu, He warned Lakshmana to be on guard. The much-awaited assault began. Rama and Lakshmana had been waiting eagerly for six continuous days; they could at last use their mystic weapons.

All hell broke loose, and the ascetics scrambled toward Rama for protection. The cool and composed Rama raised His right hand, His pinkish palms facing the sages in the unmistakable *abhaya mudra* (an indication of protection). Lord Rama's protective palm evoked smiles of triumph in the sages.[26]

---

[25] The most vulnerable time for mistakes is when victory is close at hand. Intelligence is required to stop the mind from getting carried away by the proximity to success.

[26] This was the first instance of Rama showing this sign in this incarnation. Body language gives away the state of mind. The sages went with folded hands in a state of fear and Rama stood with open palms in a state of confidence. Rama's pose gave the sages much-needed assurance.

Maricha and Subahu, the avenging sons of Tataka, were leading hoards of demons to swoop down and destroy the sacrifice. The demons had four fangs, two of which covered their lower lips, their hair was coppery red and their eyes rolled, emitting fire. They covered the sacrificial arena with pseudo fires and false black clouds and created an artificial rain of blood. With blood came a shower of arrows, spears and battle-axes. Water, too, began to pour along with huge chunks of mountain peaks. The demons used their hands and mouths to sully the sacrificial fire. They hurled stones, rocks and dirt at the arena with their hands and abuses with their foul mouths. Interestingly, the demons could not descend over the sacrificial arena because of the power and purity of the sages' *mantras*; hence they continued attacking suspended in air. [27]

The demons became even more spiteful because of their helplessness in being able to descend on Earth. But when they started throwing huge quantities of blood and flesh toward the sacrificial fire, Rama created a floating canopy of arrows to protect it.

This incensed the demons even more, and they began hurling more things. Finally, having had enough, Rama decided to end the war. He chose a missile known as *manavastra*, empowered it and released it

---

[27] The power of sound vibrations is evident here. All believed in the power of their own sound vibrations. While the demons were confident their foul words and curses would make the intensely spiritual atmosphere impure, the sages believed their *mantras* would keep the demons away. The sages had one advantage though – their purity was enhanced by the presence of the source of their purity, the pure Lord Rama. Because the faith and purity of the sages were very high, the demons did not dare descend on the sacrificial arena.

at Maricha.[28] The arrow hit his chest, but instead of penetrating him, it hurled him to a distance of 100 *yojanas* (about 800 miles) and threw him into the ocean.

THE LAW OF DISCRIMINATION

You take unwarranted risks when you become arrogant about your powers. You become overconfident about your safety, undermine the dangers of the task you undertake and over-rely on fallible people for direction.

The danger in taking unguided risks is like jumping off a building, hoping Superman will save you. The risk-taker, in fact, gambles away his life assuming he is safe.

Maricha represents the risk-taking person who depends on his own strengths and illusory powers and takes guidance from wrong mentors like Ravana. He undermines the strength of his opponent and takes reckless risks and faces definite failures.

The law of discrimination appeals to such risk-takers to make an honest self-assessment about their strengths and weaknesses, keep in mind the challenge ahead and abstain from masked friends. Else, the risk one takes may whisk one away from one's goal.

---

[28] The word Maricha means mirage or optical illusions. Just as the sun creates the illusion of the existence of water in a desert, Maricha was adept at creating illusory effects and showing what did not exist. He represented those wrongs committed in this birth that would result in sufferings in the next. Rama flung him very far away. This indicated that when one takes refuge in God, the suffering awaiting him is sent far away. Yet another interpretation suggests that Maricha represented accumulated knowledge; there are unlimited books and resources available to gain knowledge, but such knowledge is only information. Unless knowledge leads to tangible transformation, it is useless.

the battle continues

With Maricha gone, Rama chose yet another missile named *agneyastra*, endowed by Agni, the fire God. He released it at Subahu, who instantly burst into flames and turned into a heap of ashes. With their leaders dead, the other demons began to run pell-mell. Not wanting to leave even a single source of negative power alive, Rama pulled out the *vayavastra*, the missile empowered by Vayu. The missile decimated every single one of the demons. The war was finally over!

The death of the demons dispelled the black mystical clouds of illusion and the sun's rays filled the atmosphere with brightness. The sages of Siddhashram gathered around Rama, Lakshmana and Vishwamitra. The uninterrupted sacrifice was now complete and it was a grand success. The demigods who had been watching the destruction of the demons rained celestial flowers on Rama and Lakshmana. Even the trees in Siddhashram rained flowers on the boys. A relieved and proud Vishwamitra praised Rama for His valor and appreciated Him for keeping His father Dasaratha's promise by protecting the sacrifice.

Vishwamitra knew in his heart that this war was but a small accomplishment in the life of the great Lord Rama. His purpose of bringing Rama all the way from Ayodhya was finally served. The hermitage had regained its original glory and after Vishwamitra's massive sacrifice, become Siddhashram, the place of perfection, yet again.

After six exhausting days of unrest and turmoil, every one retired to peace and tranquility.

THE LAW OF SELF-CONTROL

The law of self-control inspires one to discipline the untamed animalistic mind through the whip of focused intelligence, keeping it within the protective fence of a regulated lifestyle.

When the untamed mind escapes the protective fence and the ever-cracking whip, it instinctively resorts to animalistic behavior with unruly desires. An uncontrolled mind loses focus and commits gross and subtle errors, mistaking the powerful to be weak and the unattractive to be attractive.

Subahu represents the disruptive person who makes the mistake of considering the powerful Rama to be weak. A whim-driven reckless and fenceless lifestyle leads such a person to disregard the intelligence of discipline.

The law of self-control helps discipline the unregulated mind through resolute intelligence. A regulated lifestyle based on spiritual principles acts as a fence that keeps unlawful tendencies at bay.

CHAPTER 6

A River of Tales

departure from siddhashram

The next morning, the now-peaceful Siddhashram was buzzing with activity. Basking in the light of regained freedom, the sages and their students went about their daily chores with great gusto. Rama and Lakshmana, after their morning prayers, went and bowed to Vishwamitra and urged for more opportunities to serve him. His disciples' eagerness to serve stoked him and his face glowed with happiness.

Much of the hectic activity at the *ashram* had to do with the sages preparing to go to Mithila. King Janaka, the king of Mithila, had planned a special *yajna*. The sages urged Rama and Lakshmana to accompany them because they wanted the boys to have a glimpse of the biggest attraction of this *yajna* – Saivachapa, the legendary and much-talked-about marvellous bow of Lord Shiva. The mere mention of such a powerful bow captivated the two boys, just like butterflies captivate a toddler. Every sage had something or the other to say about the glorious and extraordinary bow. It was extremely heavy and was unstrung at one end, as if imperfect and incomplete; it almost seemed as if it lay there awaiting a worthy archer to string it and make it perfect and whole again.

Lord Shiva had handed over the bow to the celestial beings after his fight with Daksha. The celestial beings in turn had handed it down to King Devavrata (ancestor of King Janaka) as a reward for successfully performing a *yajna*. Since then, the bow had adorned the court of Mithila. People from everywhere visited Mithila to catch a glimpse of the famed bow. Demigods, *gandharvas*, *yaksas*, *rakshasas* and innumerable princes all tried to lift the bow and string it, all in vain. The bow story excited Rama and Lakshmana, and they were only too eager to undertake the long trip to Mithila.

Vishwamitra began preparing to leave; he called the presiding deities of the forest and bade them farewell, knowing he would never return to the forest. He paid his respects to them and expressed deep gratitude for being allowed to its unlimited resources and being made to feel at home. Vishwamitra's mind was brimming with all the wonderful memories and enchanting chronicles attached with Siddhashram. No matter how deep his affection was for the *ashram*, he had to leave because a larger purpose awaited him; he decided to head northward toward the boundless Himalayan mountains.[1]

Vishwamitra's disciples arranged hundred cart-loads full of worship equipment and ingredients for the onward journey. The great sage walked ahead of the entire caravan. Every animal and every bird of the forest kept following them to bid them adieu. As the boundary neared, Vishwamitra turned around and asked them to return to their homes.[2] The heavy-hearted animals and birds returned to their homes, as the sages continued onward to the northern banks of Ganga.

---

[1] Respect is natural when one sees divinity in everything and everyone. The outcome of such respect is gratitude.

[2] It appeared as if these animals were giving a loving send-off to their dear relatives. To love God, we must love everything that God loves to the same degree as we love God. When one lives a genuine life of love toward every living entity, the reciprocation one experiences is also genuine.

With no halts in between, the caravan traveled on until they reached the banks of river Sona that evening. Rama was enthralled by the beauty of the place and turned to Vishwamitra for details. Vishwamitra recounted stories about his own ancestors and told Rama that the land was his ancestors', all of whom were pious kings. The sages accompanying Vishwamitra praised him and his lineage for their service to humanity. Rama, too, bowed in reverence of His teacher's lineage. As night fell, everyone went off to sleep as birds would in their nests with the setting sun.

lessons on crossing a river

As the rising sun heralded dawn over the Sona river, the entourage woke up and prepared to continue with their journey. While crossing the river, Rama noticed that it was shallow at some places and deep at others. He assumed that a boat was not necessary to cross a river that was full of so many sand dunes at the shallow points. He took his suggestion to Vishwamitra whose prompt reply was: "Follow the path laid down by the great sages of the past."[3]

---

[3] Profound insight lay within Vishwamitra's spontaneous reply. A spiritual aspirant does not need to invent newer ways of perfecting his life but needs only follow the path established by great spiritual authorities. Some paths may seem easy, but they may in fact conceal quicksands that suck away the enthusiasm to practice spiritual life. Furthermore, some paths may seem tough initially, but they may in fact be safe and secure because they have already been trod upon by great authorities, who had left clues to crossing arduous paths with relative ease. Hence, always ask an authority before treading on any path, and you may find valuable clues of experience!

lessons in ganga's story

The entourage traveled for half a day more since crossing the Sona river, when suddenly, the most profound vision unfolded before them – it was Ganga, the holiest of all rivers. The sages were immensely delighted to have a glimpse of this holy river.[4]

The sages, along with Vishwamitra and Rama and Lakshmana, stopped to enter the pristine waters of Ganga to take a holy dip. Each cupped a palm full of water from the holy river and in obeisance offered it back to the river.[5]

As the day gave way to dusk, Rama sat at Vishwamitra's feet, eager to hear the story of Ganga's appearance on earth.[6] Vishwamitra was aware that Rama already knew the story; nonetheless, he began narrating the tale of Ganga with great enthusiasm to impart a lesson in eagerness to others through this story.

Himavan, the king of the mountains, was married to Manorama, the daughter of Mount Meru. They were blessed with two beautiful and virtuous daughters, Ganga and Uma. Impressed by Ganga's purity,

---

[4] The ambience of holy places invariably fills a human with delight because these places are reservoirs of spiritual vibrations emitted by thousands of spiritual personalities from the past.

[5] To gain favor from a person, you should offer something in return with love and devotion. There cannot be a more appropriate gift to offer Ganga than its own waters, implying these thoughts: "I do not possess anything that maybe a worthy gift to give you, the one who has given me so much. So let me offer your own waters to you, added with my love and devotion. Please accept it and purify me."

[6] Eagerness to gain knowledge is the prerequisite to becoming knowledgeable.

the celestial beings requested Himavan to send his daughter to serve the heavenly planets. Ganga then became a holy river in the world of demigods. Meanwhile, Uma performed austerities to become the wife of Lord Shiva. Soon they had a son named Kartikeya.

On Earth, King Sagara, an ancestor of Lord Rama, ruled Ayodhya. Sagara and his wives, Keshini and Sumati, went to the Himalayas to perform austerities. After long years of penance, Sage Brighu appeared before them and blessed them with a boon – a son named Asmanja for Kesini and 60,000 sons for Sumati.

Asmanja grew up to be a very destructive and violent child, and his greatest pleasure came from killing innocent children by flinging them into running waters. Exasperated and disgusted with the incurable hostility in Asmanja, Sagara cast him out of the kingdom.[7] On the contrary, Asmanja's son, Anshuman, was very good and obedient.

Sagara wanted to conduct a horse sacrifice for the welfare of the world. Because of Indra's vicious conspiracy[8], the horse meant for the sacrifice suddenly disappeared. Sagara ordered his 60,000 sons to find the horse; his sons searched every nook and corner of Earth without much success. So, hoping to find it in the nether world, they began digging the earth, creating huge craters in the process. They finally

---

[7] A leader determines right and wrong based on the greater good his actions can do for the welfare of society.

[8] Sagara's sacrifice was for world peace, but Indra had to disrupt it, as was Indra's habit with any such ceremony anyone else conducted. Whenever huge sacrifices were conducted across the world, Indra felt the person conducting it would be empowered and would eventually usurp him. Always assuming his reign was at stake, Indra did everything in his power to sabotage every sacrifice he thought threatening.

found the horse in the nether world. Seated next to the horse in peaceful meditation was sage Kapila. Mistaking him to be the horse thief, they attacked him. But this hasty attack cost them their lives, and they were reduced to ashes.[9]

Up above on Earth, Sagara began worrying about the prolonged absence of his sons. He asked his grandson, Anshuman, to go in search of them. When Anshuman found the truth, he was deeply pained by the unfortunate death of his uncles. A distraught Anshuman wanted to purify the souls of his dead uncles and needed water for that. As a downcast Anshuman searched the nether world for water, Garuda, the bird carrier of Lord Vishnu and, incidentally, his grandmother Sumati's brother, came to his aid. He told Anshuman to take the horse back to complete the sacrifice. The completion of the sacrifice was important because his uncles had sacrificed their lives for it. Garuda also told Anshuman that because his uncles had been too violent and mauled Earth, no water other than Ganga's could wash off their sins. And for that, the heavenly Ganga would have to be made to flow on Earth.

Sagara completed the sacrifice successfully but he was too deeply hurt to think of another penance to bring Ganga down to Earth. He left the kingdom to Anshuman when he came of age. Anshuman was constantly driven by the anxiety of getting Ganga to flow on Earth so his uncles, lying as heaps of ashes for so many years, could be purified by the touch of the holy water. But he, too, could not convince Ganga to wash off his uncles' sins, so his son, Dileepa, inherited his father's unmet desire. Dileepa, too, failed to bring peace to his grand uncles' souls and bequeathed the "Ganga task" to his son, Bhagiratha. By

---

[9] Hasty decisions as a result of frustration and lack of clarity can turn even a king into ashes.

now, this unfinished task had become a curse because of the aching and trapped souls of Sagara's sons. Bhagiratha took it upon himself to complete the task his ancestors could not. He reached Mount Gokarna in the Himalayas and performed years of austerities in the severest of conditions. He succeeded in pleasing Brahma, who appeared before him and acceded to his request of letting Ganga descend on Earth, but on one condition: Bhagiratha would also have to perform austerities to please Lord Shiva, so that the Lord would bear Ganga on his head to withstand the impact of her descent, the force of which would be too much for Earth to bear.

Bhagiratha then channelized his time and energy in appeasing Lord Shiva, and finally, the Lord agreed to absorb Ganga's ravaging flow. Lord Shiva held Ganga in his knotted dreadlocks and released her into the Bindu lake, distributing her as six streams. The seventh stream of Ganga followed Bhagiratha's chariot to where his ancestors' ashes lay. Along the way, the chariot traversed through plains, mountain ranges, forests and rocky terrain. Flowing rapidly and unhindered, Ganga unintentionally destroyed Jahnu *muni's* hermitage. The sage became furious and drank up the entire river.[10] Bhagiratha pleaded repeatedly for the release of Ganga. After constant apologies, the sage consented, releasing her through his ears. This rebirth from Jahnu *muni's* ears gave Ganga another name – Jahnavi! After years of effort and a long arduous trail, Bhagiratha

---

[10] Focusing on the goal while on the path of success could lead you to ignore minor details. These minor details could end up swallowing the pride of achieving your goal.

•———▶

managed to bring Ganga to flow upon the ashes of his ancestors who were finally free from their offense against Kapila.[11]

As on all nights before this, Vishwamitra narrated enchanting stories from the past and lulled the boys to sleep.

the glorious mithila

The next morning, the entourage woke up early for they had to cross the wide Ganga to reach a beautiful city called Vishala. The king of Vishala, Sumati, stepped out of his palace to greet the venerable sage Vishwamitra and his fellow travellers. The king was charmed by the amazing personas of Rama and Lakshmana. From the *rishis* traveling with Vishwamitra he heard of their brave conquests at Siddhashram. Impressed, he requested the entourage to spend the night in his kingdom and accept his hospitality.

At daybreak, the caravan trail made its way toward the glorious city of Mithila. As Mithila became visible in the horizon, the sages broke into a broad smile. Destination, at last! The glistening temple domes, the fluttering flags, the immaculate pathways all exemplified the greatness of the king ruling the city. The name Mithila evoked immediate reverence because it was a famous temple town, the town

---

[11] Bhagiratha is the epitome of determination, as seen in the way he achieved his goal. The path to perfection is filled with unlimited impediments. Success, more than contemplation, requires determined action. Bhagiratha made every effort to wash away his ancestors' sins, but the act itself was purely self-centered. Yet he had this genuine desire to serve the people, like all his ancestors before him. This resulted in his effort to serve humanity through a gift named Ganga.

that housed Saivachapa. Hordes flocked to the city every day to pay homage to the majestic bow.

Mithila's outskirts were equally captivating - picturesque gardens, lush fields, glistening lakes carpeted with blue and pink water lillies, flocks of magnificent birds and disciplined row after row of *ashoka* trees lining the pathways. Trees were filled with nectar-oozing flowers that lured black wasps and bees to hover over them and take some of their nectar to make honey. When the buffaloes stepped into Mithila's rivers, their milk mingled with the pristine waters. Golden mangoes on the banks spewed sweet nectarine juice into the flowing waters as did sugarcane juice and honey from honeycombs. It seemed as if the river had milk and juice and honey and not water!

the stone damsel

Along the way were many mango orchards and groves of fruits trees. Vishwamitra took Rama and Lakshmana on a detour into one such thicket, just at the edge of the city of Mithila. Nestled in it was a dilapidated and deserted hermitage. The hermitage seemed like it had seen better and glorious days. But just as old age envelops the beauty of a living being, uneasy crinkles and furrows had swamped the hermitage of its glory. This pit stop seemed uncalled for, but Vishwamitra had taken Rama there for a purpose.

As always, Rama wanted to know about the history of the hermitage, and Vishwamitra embarked upon an old, related story. Years ago, Lord Brahma had created through his imagination the extremely beautiful Ahalya. She was natural beauty personified - each of her features seemed exquisitely carved, her appearance most astounding. In fact, she was Lord Brahma's most fascinating creation.

Lord Brahma wanted only the most qualified groom for his dearest daughter Ahalya. All the demigods, including Indra wanted to marry her and were willing to go to any extent to become her husband. Lord Brahma thought it wiser to hold a competition to assess the suitor's worth and choose the right groom. He declared that the one to circumambulate the world fastest would receive his daughter's hand in marriage.

All the demigods jumped into the fray; they mounted their divine vehicles and set off with hopes of victory in the race. Gautama *rishi*, a sage of divine origin, was one such competitor. Wise that he was, he had a different "time-saving" interpretation of the task. Gautama *rishi* circled a cow instead! His logic: Mother cow represents the entire universe. Lord Brahma was floored by Gautama *rishi*'s knowledge and comprehension of the scriptures as well as his wisdom.[12] Lord Brahma gave his daughter's hand to the ideal groom, Gautama, much to Indra's consternation.

Gautama *rishi* took his new bride, Ahalya, to this very hermitage and began his spiritual pursuits with her by his side. Indra, however, was so besotted by the beauty of Ahalya that he could not get her out of his mind. He was still nursing his wounds and did not want to give up on Ahalya so easily and was waiting for the opportune moment to exploit her.

The impatient Indra could wait no longer. He "forced" an opportune moment instead. One day, in the wee hours, Indra imitated cock-crowing to announce daybreak.[13] Gautama *rishi* responded to the call,

---

[12] Wisdom is the application of the deeper truths of life in a way that is practical. The demigods were trying to be technically correct, but Gautama rishi was practically correct. It requires wisdom to match expectations.

[13] The more you ponder over things that your mind is obsessed with, the more the mind churns out ways to acquire that thing.

woke up and proceeded to the river for his ritual bath. The moment Indra was waiting for had finally arrived. He morphed into Gautama *rishi*, entered the hermitage and expressed his desire to make love to Ahalya.

Ahalya, immediately realized that it was an imposter because her husband was too disciplined and focused to make such a request at such an untimely hour. She at once knew it was Indra. She felt flattered that Indra, the king of the demigods, was smitten by her. Besides, she found Indra's charms irresistible. Although in her head, she battled hard to fend off the raging passion, she eventually succumbed to temptation unable to curb her uncontrollable lust for Indra or resist his ardent advances.[14]

When all passion was spent, Ahalya realized the horrible reality of her actions; she knew she had sinned. Soon the burden of guilt weighed down on her lust for Indra. She tore herself away from the demigod and urged him to leave right away, lest her husband came and destroyed them both. As she pushed Indra away from her, she implored him to keep their transgression a secret.[15]

Hard as he tried to avoid any repercussions, Indra knew he would have to bear the consequences of his actions. He was suddenly aware of the dangerous predicament he was in and could not ignore the possibility of Gautama *rishi* returning home any moment. No sooner than this thought ran through Indra's mind, Gautama *rishi* had stepped into the hermitage to the sight of an imposter and his wife in

---

[14] Justification is the mind's way of overpowering the discretion of intelligence; however, justification when combined with lust for enjoyment makes the operation irreversible.

[15] Shamelessness hides the tricks of the mind. The mind tricks you into an impulsive moment of weakness. It is only after the trick is executed that guilt creeps in disgracefully.

embrace. The wise sage knew what had transpired and he could sense intense anger building up inside him. An extremely embarrassed Indra tried to dodge Gautama's fiery eyes. Indra even tried to slip out in the form of a cat but in vain. Indra could not move; the guilt of immorality froze him.[16]

The incensed Gautama *rishi* hissed like a trampled snake. It might have been possible for Indra to dodge an arrow, but not Gautama's curse; Indra was cursed to become a eunuch. Gautama then turned to his mortified wife and cursed her into an inert stone.[17]

Ahalya begged and pleaded for forgiveness and was sincerely remorseful of her gross mistake. Gautama *rishi* was moved by her sincerity and justified her act as momentary weakness. But the curse had been pronounced and could not be undone. Gautama was angry but felt compassionate toward Ahalya. He told her that at some point in future Lord Rama would visit the hermitage to redeem her from the curse and help her reunite with him. Ahalya then turned into a stone instantly and Gautama *rishi* left the hermitage for the Himalayas.

---

[16] It was an encounter of the Pure with the Impure. The persona of Gautama *rishi* reflected innocence while that of Indra reflected guilt and fear. Gautama *rishi*, radiated purity having just bathed in the Ganga, while Indra's face reflected the dark shame of immorality. Compromising on integrity for cheap worldly thrills leads to fear and guilt. Guilt engulfs the mind like spreading ink on blotting paper.

[17] Ahalya's actions reflected the hard-heartedness of a stone; she deservedly became one. A stone-hearted person is selfish and is concerned with self-enjoyment. Gautama *rishi* realized that she was afflicted by the attention-seeking disease and false sense of pride. Because no one pays attention to a stone, cursing her into a stone was to cure her of her "illness." Gautama *rishi* simply saw her as a patient with a disease. The cure for her disease was a tonic called repentance, which she had already started consuming. Soon the disease would vanish.

Vishwamitra had been narrating the entire story standing near the very stone that was Ahalya. He pointed toward the stone that had been waiting for ages, praying every moment for the touch of Rama's lotus feet. Vishwamitra urged Rama to place His feet on her and exonerate her. As soon as Lord Rama placed His feet slowly upon the stone, Ahalya stirred back to life, her beauty restored. Ahalya had tears of gratitude as she thanked Lord Rama for having freed her despite her heinous sin.[18] For her, Rama was a father who gave her a fresh lease of life, a new birth. She rushed into the hermitage to arrange for a ceremonial welcome for Rama. Ahalya's glorious husband, Gautama *rishi*, also returned and was happy to be reunited with her.[19]

---

[18] Continuous repentance for her mistake and incessant reminiscence of Lord Rama's name purified Ahalya of all her corrupt proclivities.

[19] Tataka's slaying demonstrated the power of Lord Rama's arms, whereas Ahalya's deliverance demonstrated the power of His feet. Both women who had committed mistakes, but Lord Rama's treatment toward both differed. Repentance was what made the difference: Tataka never repented for her mistakes, Ahalya did. This episode instills hope in us that even a sinner has a future, provided he is sincerely repentant.

In terms of practical application, one can learn to be vigilant against the whims of the mind. Indra is compared to the mind and Gautama to intelligence associated with wisdom that helps one differentiate. Ahalya is compared to an individual. If an individual uses his intelligence, he can transform this world; but if the connection with mind is strong then there can only be a strong exhibition of selfishness. The moment an individual connects with the mind too strongly, the intellect abandons him, and he becomes inert like a stone. It is only a momentary impulse under whose influence the individual turns away from the shelter of intelligence to accept the whims of the mind. When the inert individual comes in constant connection with spiritual sound vibrations, the desire to serve God arises and the opportunity to do so follows.

love takes a bow

Once the glory of Gautama's hermitage was restored, Sage Vishwamitra's entourage walked onward in the northeastern direction into the city of Mithila. Their destination was the ritual hall of King Janaka's fire sacrifice.

The city was soaking in splendor. Mithila's towering buildings, fluttering flags, chiming bells, decked walls, all seemed as if they had all been waiting to welcome Rama into the city. It seemed that the city, too, had been waiting for Rama. The city had been in possession of a priceless jewel that needed an owner. Rama was the only one qualified to possess that precious jewel.

Rama and Lakshmana went sightseeing with Vishwamitra; they were enraptured by the beauty of the city and its festive fervor. They soon reached what appeared to be the most beautiful section of the city. It was the palace of princess Sita, the daughter of King Janaka. The princess was the epitome of beauty and was indeed the most priceless jewel of the city. All who saw Her were so struck and mesmerized by Her beauty that they could not tear their eyes away from Her. Instead they regretted blinking because it disrupted uninterrupted vision of Sita's beauty. Demigods with unblinking eyes, too, complained because they felt that two eyes were insufficient to behold Sita's infinite beauty!

When Rama was walking down the streets, Sita was on the palace rooftop. Rama looked up and spotted the beautiful Sita. Exactly at the same time, Sita's gaze fell on Rama, and their eyes met and locked. A flutter escaped their hearts and everything became silent; it seemed the world passing by had come to a standstill. They just kept staring at each other for the longest time. Their hearts leaped out and touched each other through their eyes. The lips were shut, but the eyes were talking. The deepest of emotions were exchanged through that one long glance. Sita, for the first time, understood what real beauty was. Rama soaked in the image of the doe-eyed Sita within His heart, and Sita soaked in that of Rama with a bow and quiver slung across His strong shoulders. For the first time, Rama had no questions for Vishwamitra.

The moment passed, and Rama and Lakshmana returned to the city center. The center was bustling with people. Thousands of *rishis* and *munis* and huge crowds had gathered to witness Janaka's *yajna*. Rama, however, had left his mind with Sita. His thoughts kept returning to the beautiful Sita, and in her palace, Sita was feeling feverish with thoughts of Rama.

The moment King Janaka heard of the arrival of Vishwamitra's entourage, he darted toward the resting place of the sage. Vishwamitra and his people had chosen as their resting place the shade of a pipal tree near a water tank in the heart of Mithila. Janaka took with him his most prominent ministers and his head priest, Satananda. He paid his respects to Vishwamitra and expressed his happiness at his arrival. The sage asked Janaka about his welfare and that of his kingdom. Janaka considered Vishwamitra's arrival during the final stages of his sacrifice a sure sign of the ritual's success.[20]

Janaka urged Vishwamitra to extend his stay for 12 more days until the completion of the ritual. As he spoke, Janaka's eyes strayed toward the two young boys accompanying Vishwamitra and wanted to know who they were. Vishwamitra introduced them as the sons of the great King Dasaratha. Janaka recalled Dasaratha's invitation to the

---

[20] Any sacrifice becomes successful if Lord Vishnu is pleased. In the case of Janaka, Lord Rama was Vishnu Himself, and He was not just pleased, but had also made it auspicious by His presence.

putrakamesti yajna and realized that these children were the auspicious gifts of the *yajna*. Vishwamitra beamed with pride when he narrated how Rama killed Tataka with only a single arrow from His bow and how He protected his fire sacrifice by destroying Maricha and Subahu. Janaka and Satananda *rishi* listened with rapt attention. When Vishwamitra came to the part where Rama had redeemed Ahalya, the wife of Gautama *rishi* with the touch of His feet, Satananda *rishi* jumped up in joy. He was the son of the same Ahalya and Gautama *rishi*. Satananda *rishi* was filled with immense gratitude and respect toward Rama for freeing his mother from the long curse.[21]

Janaka noticed that even though Vishwamitra was singing praises about Rama, the prince was sitting with His head lowered in humility.[22] He was humbled that His own spiritual master was glorifying Him in front of so many exalted sages.

---

[21] Heroic acts may attract a common person, but acts of compassion and kindness attract the heart of great souls.

[22] A fruit-laden tree bends low because of the weight. Humility is a natural outcome of a person laden with good qualities.

CHAPTER 7

YOU RISE WHEN YOUR PRIDE FALLS

a king's journey to spiritual supremacy

Rama had brought Satananda good fortune, but had it not been for
Vishwamitra, Rama would never have stepped into Gautama *rishi's*
hermitage and redeemed his mother, Ahalya. As his way of expressing
gratitude to Vishwamitra, Satananda narrated the story behind the
epic rise of Vishwamitra. Rama and Lakshmana had never heard their
master talk about himself because great sages like him were too
humble to gloat about their achievements. They had never known this
very personal facet of their guru.[1]

---

[1] Self-praise almost always leads to the dilution of one's achievements,
wise personalities make it a point let their actions speak for themselves.
Just as it is not wont of a great sage to blow his own trumpet, it is no
mean task either for one great sage to appreciate another. Satananda and
Vishwamitra were equals by virtue of being mentors to great rulers. Here
is a lesson on how equals ought to behave with each other in front of
their subordinates. Vishwamitra's disciples, including Rama and
Lakshmana, as well as Satananda's, including King Janaka and his
ministers, were all present at the time of the narration. Satananda had the
opportunity to paint a very sordid picture of Vishwamitra to prove
himself superior, but he did not do so. Instead, he glorified Vishwamitra,
highlighting only his good qualities and talking about the negative aspects
very diplomatically to avoid making the great sage appear bad. It is
difficult to narrate the tale of someone when he is right in front of you.
One has to maintain a delicate balance between unwarranted praise and
overcriticism. At the same time, no compromise should be made in the
narration for the mere purpose of pleasing the person being talked about.

Satananda began at the beginning: the origin of Vishwamitra's dynasty of great kings. Vishwamitra came from a long line of great rulers who were in fact descendants of the Moon God itself. The lineage started with the son of Chandra (Moon God), Pururava, whose great-great-great grandson was Jahnu who had swallowed Ganga. Jahnu's great-grandson was Kusa, whose grandson was Gadhi. Kaushika, or Vishwamitra as he was famously known, was Gadhi's son. Following in the footsteps of his illustrious father, Vishwamitra became a revered king.

He spent his time traversing his kingdom, meeting his subjects, discussing and solving their problems and every so often going on hunting expeditions into deep forests as does every king. On one such hunting expedition, a tired Vishwamitra spotted a quaint little hermitage. As was wont, the king strolled into the hermitage to offer customary venerations to the sage in charge.

the poor rich hermitage

Vishwamitra was a little surprised to find very few hermits in the hermitage. It was sparse unlike his impression of hermitages, especially of revered sages. Now that he learned that the hermitage belonged to the great sage Vasistha, a brahmarishi (a sage of the greatest order), its frugality astounded Vishwamitra even more. Vasistha, he learned, was a very humble sage, with little or no need or desire for material possessions, totally focused on supreme meditation. An eager Vishwamitra raced to the great sage's seat and offered his respects.

Vasistha immediately rose upon seeing the king. When the king bowed to him, Vasistha blessed him and warmly welcomed him to his hermitage. He wished to serve the king's entourage. Vishwamitra looked around the impoverished hermitage and did not think it appropriate to accept anything, so he gently declined the offer saying that the sage's kindness and sweet words more than made up for everything and were satisfactory enough. Vasistha, however, persisted with his request, so the king had no choice but to invite his entire entourage consisting of his hundred sons and thousands of followers.

Vishwamitra had no expectations of a grand feast or even a small one. But Vasistha had no such doubts. He brought out a dappled cow, much to Vishwamitra's surprise. He then instructed his cow, Shabala, to lay feast fit for the king and his entourage. Shabala laid out a grand feast in front of them within moments! An ordinary cow had presented before the king and his men an extraordinary meal! Vishwamitra was dumbfounded.

He had no inkling that Shabala was no ordinary cow, or that she had emerged from the churning of the milk ocean or that she was *kaamadhenu* herself! Shabala was the wish-fulfilling cow who could grant anything expressed to her. Lord Vishnu, pleased with Vasistha's penances, had personally gifted Shabala to him.

This was by far the most sumptuous meal the king and his entourage had ever consumed. Each dish was rich in taste, flavour, color and texture. There were hundreds of dishes par excellence and the food served had all the six flavours – sweet, sour, salty, pungent, astringent and bitter – and touched every corner of the palate. The perplexed king ate in silence, astounded by the miracle food he and his men had had the chance to eat. All the while that he enjoyed his meal, he could not tear his gaze from Shabala, the cow that had produced it all. Vishwamitra's men were beaming, feeling more than content with the meal.

the clash for a cow

Vishwamitra was king, and everything in his kingdom, in fact, belonged to him. Shabala had caught his fancy, and he thought Vasistha's home was no place for such a special cow. He wanted Shabala and nothing could come between him and the cow. So, he approached the exalted Vasistha and offered him a lakh of milch cows of the most excellent breed in exchange for the prized cow. Vasistha strictly refused to part with Shabala as she was like his mother. He told an agitated Vishwamitra that Shabala was priceless and that he would never barter her for anything in this world, no matter how precious that offering. Vasistha insisted that he and Shabala were as eternally inseparable as is the respectability of a self-respecting person. But the king was not one to give up. He assumed these words were Vasishta's way of bargaining for more. So he raised his offer to 14,000 elephants, 800 golden chariots, 11,000 horses and 10 million milch cows. Vasistha emphatically put an end to the bargaining by saying that no offer would make him give away Shabala. His life was centered on worshipping and pleasing God, and Shabala was integral to that goal because she helped him fulfill all his needs to serve God and his guests. Nothing that Vishwamitra had could fulfill this desire of his.[2]

Vishwamitra took offence at this refusal. He was so furious that he began to snarl wildly. How dare anybody refuse him? After all, he was the king of that region. And everything, everything under the purview of the kingdom was rightfully his. This cow was part of his kingdom,

---

[2] Vasistha treated the cow as a person who deserved the highest respect. Vishwamitra treated her as an object that could be bartered. When people are treated as commodities, then they are given price tags.

hence he had a natural right over it.[3] It was then that Vasistha gently pointed out to Vishwamitra that Shabala was in fact not "standing" on his ground at all. She was hovering an inch above the ground! Vasistha explained that because she was not standing on anyone's ground, no one had a right over her.

Vishwamitra realized the pointlessness of his argument with Vasistha. Vasistha's words were like those etched in stone. His strength lay in his words. So Vishwamitra decided to use his might and decided that if Vasistha was not going to hand Shabala over to him at any cost, he would use force to take her away from the great sage. Vishwamitra then began to drag a reluctant and resisting Shabala away from Vasistha.[4]

Vasistha watched helplessly as the powerful king and his men dragged Shabala away from the hermitage. Shabala, on the other hand, felt sad assuming that Vasistha had abandoned her. She could not understand what made him allow her to be weaned away from him and began wondering if she had failed him in any way. She just could not go with Vishwamitra. At least, not before Vasistha gave her a

---

[3] A façade falls apart at the first sight of temptation. Toward the beginning when Vishwamitra was under the impression that Vasistha was impoverished, he behaved like the ideal king, compassionate toward his subjects. The moment he realized that Vasistha was in fact the one with more, he turned coercive and wanted to grab everything. His craving blinded his role as a king. An ideal leader never considers himself the proprietor of those in his charge, rather he thinks of himself as a trustee responsible for satisfying the needs, interests and concerns of those he is privileged to serve.

[4] Shabala represents prosperity. Prosperity is a reward for the deserving, those with past good deeds. Prosperity can be neither forcefully dragged into anyone's life nor dragged out of anyone's life.

reason for letting go of her. Shabala wrested off Vishwamitra's clutches and ran back to her master who claimed to love her as much as his own life but was allowing her to be taken. Tears streaming down her large eyes, she demanded an answer from Vasistha for refusing to protect her or fighting to keep her. Saddened as he was to let Shabala go, Vasistha said he was helpless because he was the king's subject and had to bow to his wishes no matter how unreasonable and unjust. As king, he was God's representative on Earth and he could never go against him. Besides, Vishwamitra was a guest. How could he humiliate a guest?

Shabala was angry and unhappy with Vasistha's meek reply. She shook her head in anger and disagreement. Didn't Vasistha know that a sage was far more powerful than a king? A sage's role is to provide vision and direction to a king, and the king's role is to use his strength and follow the sage's directions. Everything goes haywire and topsy-turvy if the king decides to follow his own vision and the sage has to use his strength to defend his rights. Shabala wanted permission to defend herself from exploitation. Vasistha relented. Shabala then turned to face a shocked and aghast Vishwamitra and unleashed a blitzkrieg he had never imagined possible.[5]

---

[5] History has repeated itself on numerous occasions when exploitative leaders have harassed genuine followers. Every time, the concern is the same – should one keep quiet and tolerate the shame or stand up and exert one's rights? Shabala has the answer to this question. If you are strong like Shabala, stand up and oppose the exploitation. If you are weak like Vasistha, empower someone with your wisdom to do the task. The cow's advice to us is simple: Follow when a leader is good and defend yourself when the leader is bad.

will shabala cow down?

One loud holler from Shabala was enough to emit a hoard of *Pahlava* soldiers from her body. These soldiers charged toward Vishwamitra's army. Vishwamitra jumped in and obliterated the *Pahlavas* in no time. Shabala then manifested multiple armies of terrible forces. From her tail, *Palhavas*; from her udders, *Dravidas* and *Shakas*; from her womb, *Yavanas*; from her dung, *Savaras*; from her urine, *Kanchis*; from her sides, *Savaras*; from her cud *Paundras, Haritas, Kiratas, Yavanas, Sinhalas, Khasas, Chivukas, Pulindas, Chinas, Hunas, Keralas,* and numerous other Mleccha tribes.[6] They wreaked havoc and soon annihilated Vishwamitra's army, leaving no trace of them. Once his army was erased, Vishwamitra's hundred sons targeted Vasistha, the root of all trouble. As they raced toward Vasistha, with weapons in their hands and destruction in their minds, the sage let out a blaring, earth-shattering *hum* (the powerful *humakara mantra*) which burned them to a pile of ashes. Vishwamitra's was now a one-man army – the king alone.

Vishwamitra had never been this helpless in his life. He felt like an ocean without waves, a serpent without fangs, a bird without wings and the eclipsed sun with no sparkle.[7]

---

[6] It is believed that the Pahlavas were actually Pallava from South India, whereas the Yavanas or Yonas were actually the Ionians, or Greeks. Kambojas were apparently Indo-Iranian Mleccha or barbarous tribes who spoke Avestan or old Persian. Shakas were Scythian tribes of East Iranian origin and were *soma* (the divine psychedelic drink) drinkers and somehow related to the *devas* and *apsaras*. Haritas were descendants of the Suryavanshi king, Harita.

[7] Situations of helplessness create the most fertile environment for the plant of realization to grow. If we deposit seeds of good guidance and prayer to God, flowers of humility and maturity will grow. But if we deposit seeds of revenge, thorns of arrogance and discontent will grow.

the desire for revenge

A heavy-hearted Vishwamitra returned home, disgruntled and disappointed. He had never lost before, not to anything not to anyone. This battle had left him with nothing but a battered ego. Vishwamitra took the most important decisions of his life that day, a decision that changed the course of his life. Revenge! That was all he knew now, and that was all that was left. Vasistha's superpowers were far superior to his, and this fact gnawed away at his ego. He could not bear to think of a person in possession of such extreme prowess. The only way out, Vishwamitra decided, was to please Lord Shiva to acquire unlimited powers and weapons through penance and austerities. This became his mission. He crowned his surviving son the king and then walked away into the forest in pursuit of his goal.

Vishwamitra was born in luxury, yet he chose a life of hardship and penury. He left behind the opulence of his palace and embraced the starkness of the wild. He was no more king; he was now an ascetic with the goal to become the greatest of them all. He sat in meditation, he forsook all pleasures known to man, he undertook austerities and he pushed himself beyond limits only to invoke Lord Shiva. After many years of fervent worship, Lord Shiva stood before him and asked him what could have forced him to such severe meditation and what was it that he wanted from him. Vishwamitra had waited for this moment all this while. He asked Lord Shiva to make him master and possessor of all military sciences and missiles in the world. Smiling, the all-knowing Lord Shiva granted this desire. No sooner than Lord Shiva disappeared, Vishwamitra was back where he started: blistering with the burning memory of his dead sons. Revenge was all he wanted now. Armed with powerful weapons and refreshed rage, Vishwamitra headed straight toward Vasistha's ashram:

a journey he had been taking in his mind every moment since he was humiliated and hurt.[8]

Vishwamitra had infinite powers and owned every weapon anyone ever aspired for. He was brimming with arrogance like an ocean heavy with tide on a full moon night. Vishwamitra barged into Vasistha's hermitage with a haughty grin. All he wanted was Vasistha's destruction – his hermitage, his pride and everything he stood for. Vishwamitra hurled a powerful missile that immediately demolished the serene hermitage. In place of the beautiful huts and trees was a smoking cemetery, ashes strewn all over. Vasistha's disciples panicked and began running helter-skelter. The great sage, upon hearing the commotion, came out of the blazing fire unscathed and stepped out into the remains of his hermitage. Vasistha tried to calm his disciples but to no avail. Looming over it all was the freshly empowered Vishwamitra. Just like the fires that raged outside, the fires within Vishwamitra raged even more at the sight of Vasistha. He could not swallow the fact that the very person he wished to destroy was standing right in front of him.

A livid Vasistha raised his *Brahma danda*[9] (a celestial seven-knotted bamboo staff carried by great *brahmarishis*) and chastized Vishwamitra. Vasistha told him that he was foolish to have misused his powers and burned down the hermitage because it served no purpose.

---

[8] A past incident is not what agitates the mind at times of distress and pain; it is the amount of attention we give to the memory of that incident that unsettles us. The more the attention, the bigger the incident appears. Without attention, it would merely be irrelevant history.

[9] The *Brahma danda* was an ever-blazing seven-knotted staff that held within it the power of years and years of Vasistha's meditation and it could withstand the onslaught of any weapon and swallow all the weapons hurled at it. It kept blazing because it held the sacred fires by which a sage attained eternal knowledge and became free from the yoke of Yama.

———▶

Vishwamitra hissed like a trampled serpent, deriding the great sage and boasting about his newfound powers. He threw a challenge at Vasistha: "Outdo me." Vasistha planted his staff in front of him and was ready for everything that Vishwamitra had to throw at him. He incited Vishwamitra to exhaust every missile in his arsenal.

Vishwamitra hurled missile after extraordinary missile at Vasistha, but the calm sage merely stood glued to the ground, *Brahma danda* in hand. Vishwamitra was befuddled by the *Brahma danda*'s power to withstand all his powerful weapons – the staff swallowed every single missile hurled at it! Before long, Vishwamitra exhausted every power missile he possessed, all except the most powerful one – the *Brahma astra*. He could not go wrong with this, surely. It was *the* most powerful weapon in the universe. It could cause destruction like no other. Surely, Vasistha's staff could not withstand that, Vishwamitra thought. He picked up the *Brahma astra* with complete belief in its supernatural powers and flung it at Vasistha. The blazing *astra* charged toward the potent *danda*, which had been waiting for the assault. The moment the *astra* touched the *danda*, it fizzled out and disappeared. The *danda* had swallowed the *Brahma astra* too. The now-powerful *Brahma danda* shone like the bright sun, and the owner of the staff, Vasistha, too, looked resplendent in victory, resembling the Sun God himself. Vasistha stood unscathed, unharmed and glowing in glory.

Vishwamitra felt charred; his ego wounded more than ever. Stunned and defeated, he ran over everything in his head again and again: first a cow and now a bamboo staff? What could be more humiliating than to have a cow annihilate his entire army and a frail old man with a staff nullify all his celestial weapons?[10]

---

[10] The degree of insult is inversely proportional to the size of the entity causing it.

Vishwamitra finally acceded to the undeniable truth that a *brahmana's* (visionary) power was far more superior to a *kshatriya's* (administrator). Vishwamitra had a clearer goal this time: He would become a *brahmarishi* just like Vasistha. No matter how many years of austerities it took, how many years of penance, how many years of living in the wilderness, how many years of meditating ... no matter what it took, he was willing to do everything to achieve his goal.

the man who wished for the impossible

With a clearer vision of what path he must take, Vishwamitra headed south to perform intense austerities. This time the object of his invocation was the god of gods, Lord Brahma himself. Years went by, spent in meditating with rigour and surviving on fruits and roots alone till Lord Brahma appeared before him one day. Vishwamitra, ears perked in joyful anticipation, yearned to hear the magic words he had toiled so hard for - that he was now a *brahmarishi*. Instead, Brahma blessed him and told him that he was extremely happy to confer on him the title *rajarishi* (a sage among kings). Brahma said he had a long way to go to before he could attain *brahmarishi* status. A *rajarishi*? After so many years of penance? His hopes were dashed and he felt like a deserving child handed a rotten apple. Disappointed and disillusioned, he began the process of austerities all over again.[11]

As one king was spending years in the forest meditating to become a *brahmarishi*, another was ruling Ayodhya, with dreams of spending his

---

[11] A desired qualification must be preceded with the endeavor to prove that it is deserved. If you want to be a source of light to the world, be ready to burn, too.

afterlife in a body he loved so much that he hated parting with it. Trishanku, the king from the Ikshvaku Dynasty, was extremely handsome and charismatic. The heady combination of beauty and splendor made him arrogant and vain. He was so in love with himself and his beauty that he spent hours preening in front of the mirror. During one narcissistic moment, an unusual desire entered his inflated head. He would have to die some day and give up this beautiful body. Was there any way he could inhabit forever this body that he loved so much? Was it possible to go to the death-free heavens in this same body? The unheard-of conceited idea was bizarre no doubt, but the more he pondered, the more it became a craving he was certain could be satisfied. Just as Vishwamitra was determined to become a *brahmarishi*, Trishanku was "heaven-bent" on becoming the one to ascend to the world of the gods in a human body. Little did they know that their paths would cross during their quest for their goals.

To guide him through to achieving his desire, Trishanku could think of none better than Vasistha, the spiritual master of the Ikshvaku dynasty. The moment he voiced his wish, however, Vasistha was repelled and disgusted as much by the very idea as with Trishanku's arrogance and attachment to his perishable body. He reprimanded Trishanku for having such an improbable wish. Only the deserving found a place in heaven. Besides, no human body ever made it there. Trishanku's craving began to dissolve in the face of Vasistha's anger, just as the Himalayan snow melts helplessly with the rising sun. He returned to his palace knowing well that it was futile trying to convince Vasistha.[12]

---

[12] Looking for shortcuts is a symptom for the diseases of intolerance and impatience. Here, the hard work toward seeking qualification is replaced by the hard work toward finding a shortcut.

Stubborn that he was, Trishanku had no intention of giving up on his unique and novel desire. An old man's rejection of the idea did not mean that it was unattainable. He thought Vasistha was too old and conventional and too fixed in his ways to bend a few rules here and there to explore new ideas and possibilities. Perhaps his hundred young and dynamic sons would be more forthcoming and show him how to reach the heavens in the same body.

"Impossible," shouted Vasistha's one hundred sons in unison. They were appalled that Trishanku had rejected the sane advice of his mentor and their father, Vasistha. If Vasistha were the tree, they were the branches. So how could they go against their father and grant Trishanku his silly wish. He shamelessly replied that indeed their father had rejected him, but that did not mean they should also reject him. Not one to give up easily, he tried to provoke them. They were fresh-blooded and aspiring, and what better way to prove their worth to the world than setting a precedent. If they still had no intention of helping him, he would surely find someone bold enough who would.[13]

Vasistha's sons were incensed that not only did this man have no reverence for his spiritual *guru*, he was also trying to play with them and use them as a means to achieve his desire, like a child who toys with a rare diamond without understanding its worth. As Trishanku turned to leave, they cursed him to a life bereft of beauty and wealth.[14]

---

[13] Trishanku believed every human was naturally predisposed to outdoing his seniors. He assumed Vasistha's sons would definitely be eager to become trendsetters and outgrow their father's shadow. His intention was to play on that eagerness.

[14] Pride in education, vanity in personal beauty, intoxication of wealth and influence over people are four chemicals that, when combined together with the catalyst of disrespect, create an amalgam of arrogance.

→

At the crack of dawn, deep darkness befell Trishanku. The morning breeze swept away every trace of beauty and wealth from the honey-skinned handsome king. He had transformed into an unsightly man with rough and mottled skin. His repulsive dull, drab rags and the garland of faded flowers around his neck made him seem so ordinary and lacklustre. Trishanku walked the streets of his own kingdom unrecognized and unacknowledged. All his implorations about his identity to his ministers and subjects were ignored. Instead, his people began chasing out this repulsive-looking vagrant who was pestering them. This was no king; this was just an irritating beggar. Trishanku, the king, had been abandoned by his kingdom!

vishwamitra dreams big

Trishanku was suffering no doubt, but that did not stop him from seeking his goal. Then it struck him: If Vasistha refused to fulfil his wishes for him, his arch enemy definitely would. This time, Trishanku was sure his desire would be met. He dragged his bruised and deformed body to Vishwamitra. The meditating *rajarishi* opened his eyes to the shuffling sound. Standing with folded hands before him was bedraggled Trishanku. He wanted to know what befell the handsome king. Trishanku narrated his sorry tale. He felt that he had been wronged and was being punished for vocalizing an honest desire. He meant no one any harm nor did he ask for something that would rob someone else of anything. He was not adopting the wrong or dishonest path to achieve his goal either. Was a sincere attempt to achieve what most people desire such a crime?[15]

---

[15] Trishanku offered justifications to shield his weakness. It is human to see good in oneself and faults in others. Trishanku was arrogant and disrespectful, but claimed to be honest and sincere.

Trishanku fervently pleaded with Vishwamitra to help him reach his goal. He was confident that the merciful and powerful Vishwamitra would succeed where Vasistha and his sons could not. Trishanku had deliberately touched a raw nerve. Yet again, Vishwamitra was filled with a desire to outperform Vasistha. This was the right opportunity to display his superiority, and he jumped at it. He decided that he would get Trishanku what he wanted.[16]

Vishwamitra wanted to lose no time, so he swung into action. He ordered his sons to invite all the great sages and their disciples to witness and assist him in this unusual ritual to send Trishanku to the heavens. He also told his sons to mark the sages unwilling to cooperate either by words or through actions. The news of the ritual spread rapidly, and sages from far and wide began arriving at the scene of the event. They were not convinced about the efficacy or even the intention of the ritual, but they arrived nonetheless, in fear. Yes, they were afraid of what the powerful Vishwamitra would do to them if they refused to partake in the ritual.

All sages but Vasistha and his hundred sons had agreed to witness the ritual. Vasistha's sons refused to comply with Vishwamitra and condemned the performance of this ritual. Going ahead with anything rejected by their illustrious father was vain. Vishwamitra did not take kindly to the refusal. His eyes turned blood red with anger and shot forth sparks as his mouth spewed fire. He cursed that Vasistha's sons take 700 births in uncultured and disregarded

---

[16] Trishanku used flattery and Vishwamitra's weakness as baits to convince him for help. He blandished Vishwamitra by placing him above Vasistha and tickled his weakness of wanting to be superior to Vasistha. Flattered and itching to prove his superiority over Vasistha, Vishwamitra had fallen prey to Trishanku's proposal.

families. Vishwamitra then glanced menacingly at the sages present. Thank God, they had been wiser and escaped limitless fury.[17]

Vishwamitra headed the unique ritual. He was organized and detailed through the ceremony. Although not sure of its success, the sages meekly cooperated in silence, not wanting to sacrifice their lives. As the ceremony ended, Vishwamitra invited the demigods to descend and accept their share of the oblations. But none obliged. This was an unacceptable Vedic ritual. Vishwamitra waited a little while longer. Perhaps they would come around. But no one was in sight. Vishwamitra was beginning to lose patience and was unwilling to let his reputation slip. His word was now at stake, the statements he made in the presence of the most prominent sages of the world seemed empty and boastful. He could visualize Vasistha's chuckling face staring right at him just as clearly as he could see Trishanku's hopeful eyes pinned on him.

Something had to be done. He could not let go. Not now when he had ventured this far. Vishwamitra invoked his *tapobala* (power that he earned through his austerities) to send Trishanku to the heavens. He lifted the ladle he was performing the ritual with and empowered it with all the intensity of his meditation. As the ladle rose toward the skies, so did Trishanku. He actually began flying toward the heavens. The sages gaped at the flying Trishanku. Never had they witnessed such sheer power and such wonder - a live human flying up to the heavens in his material body! Was it all really happening? How could

---

[17] The easiest way to get people to cooperate is by showing might. A better way is to offer a benefit. But the best way is to influence them through character and vision. If you show them might, you gain their physical presence (numbers increase); if you offer a benefit, you gain their intelligence (ideas increase); but if you show them love, you will gain their hearts (commitment increases).

they deny it now that it was unbelievably true? Vishwamitra had made the impossible possible! Trishanku had flown so high up that he was a mere speck in the sky now. Jaws hanging, they continued to gawk till Trishanku had disappeared. Finally, they turned to Vishwamitra.[18] Lotus-postured with an erect back, the great sage sat entranced and radiating energy. Eyes closed and eyebrows knotted in absolute concentration, Vishwamitra's arms were raised in the air still holding the ladle. Their admiration for Vishwamitra suddenly multiplied manifold. This was no mean feat for a human. A mere mortal could challenge and overcome the laws of nature after all!

impossible is possible

Trishanku began to fly, and he was euphoric. He immediately felt thankful to Vishwamitra for making this journey come true. He was heaven bound. But Trishanku had not expected the journey to be so painful. As he floated higher and higher, his body began to crush and tear, his blood vessels started throbbing and his skin began to tear. The body he so loved was not made to handle such intense air pressure. But Trishanku had no control over it anymore; in fact, he had nothing under his control. He could communicate with none nor could he tell anyone of his predicament. His head was ripping with pain and driving him insane. Just as he was about to lose consciousness, he saw his dreamland. Ah, the heavens! His

---

[18] Trishanku represents those who take credit for others' efforts without putting in any of their own. Here, Vishwamitra put in all the effort, and Trishanku was the one on his way to gain the advantage of the heavenly abode.

eager mind pushed aside all that pain. Focus, great pleasures lie ahead, he thought.[19]

Indra and the demigods were amid joyous recreation and revellery when a guard came running to warn them of an inflated and deformed, undeserving intruder flying up toward the heavens. Indra went to the flying human and said, "Trishanku, you do not deserve entry into the heavens, because you have offended your mentor Vasistha and have been rejected by him." Indra pushed him down and Trishanku fell back, his head turned down. Oh no! He was now hurtling down toward Earth.[20]

Back on Earth, soaked by Vishwamitra's intoxicating power, the sages were heading home assuming the ritual was over and its goal achieved when a sudden shriek tore the skies. Vishwamitra's trance was broken. "Save me! Save me!" It was Trishanku. Helpless and heading earthward. With hands pressed against his ears in pain, eyes bulging in their sockets, hair disheveled and clothes in disarray, Trishanku awaited the impact of the fall and imminent death. Vishwamitra could not let that happen. Now it was a matter of his prestige and not that of fulfilling Trishanku's bizarre desire anymore.

Vishwamitra once again waved his ladle in the air, instantly turning Trishanku's body face up, toward the heavens yet again. One more

---

[19] Any shortcut seems a pleasure in the beginning because it gives one a feeling of being ahead of many, but each shortcut has hidden sources of pain. The man who has reached the quintessence of success through shortcuts will have some pain to conceal from the world, pain that is too embarrassing to accept.

[20] Obsession makes one shameless. Trishanku was obsessed with entering a zone he was neither qualified nor welcome to enter.

swish of the ladle and Trishanku was accelerating through the sky toward the heavens. Trishanku no longer wanted to make this trip. He had had enough. He pleaded with Vishwamitra to bring him back to Earth and let him return to his kingdom. But Vishwamitra would hear none of it; this had become personal. He had to send Trishanku to heaven in his human body.[21]

a dream turns into a nightmare

So Trishanku began his aerial journey toward heaven once again. Once again Indra pushed him back to Earth.[22] When Vishwamitra saw the returning Trishanku, he realized that sending him to heaven again would be futile. But that was not going to stop him from keeping his word. He could not let Trishanku ever return to Earth. So he decided to create a parallel heaven just to accommodate Trishanku. Using up every bit of superpower left in him, Vishwamitra created a replica of the heavenly kingdom complete with clones of Indra and the demigods. He redirected Trishanku to this artificial heaven. Trishanku was in agony, but he had no choice. Anything seemed better than being shuttled back and forth between

---

[21] Heaven was no longer Trishanku's personal ambition, it had become Vishwamitra's acquired ambition.

[22] Here is a fight for superiority between Indra and Vishwamitra with Trishanku as a pawn between the two kings. It is difficult to empathize with the suffering of others when you are absorbed fully in self-establishment.

heaven and Earth. If only he had appreciated his well-wisher Vasistha's wisdom.[23]

Vishwamitra had exhausted his celestial powers to create Trishanku's heaven, but maintaining it was proving difficult. It was eroding his vital forces. His head was splitting and he realized that if he did not gain access to any higher power, he would soon perish. In this helpless state, he began calling out the names of Lord Vishnu, earnestly requesting for His mercy. No sooner than Vishwamitra began chanting, Lord Vishnu appeared and told him that creating or destroying anything was easy, but maintaining it was the hardest part. It was no wonder then that creation was Lord Brahma's task, destruction Lord Shiva's, and the most difficult – the task of maintenance – fell on the Lord Himself. Lord Vishnu assured Vishwamitra that now that he had created a heaven, it would remain as one of the stars and He would maintain it, but Trishanku would have to dangle upside down just as Indra had wished. Lord Vishnu then disappeared.

Trishanku got what he wanted, only not exactly as he had envisaged! He now had a heaven of his own for eternity, but he would have to remain upside down in his deformed body, something he loathed. Every moment spent in that horrible state reminded him of

---

[23] From Trishanku's perspective, wise words make sense in hindsight only when one falls into trouble. He could not appreciate Vasistha's wisdom earlier, but now his words seem prophetic. Earlier Vasistha had seemed like an obstacle in the path of his desire, but now Trishanku realized that he was a well-wisher.

his arrogance. He repented his misbehavior toward his spiritual master Vasistha.[24]

Trishanku's embarrassment was small compared to Vishwamitra's. All that penance and meditation ended up with nothing. Vishwamitra had succumbed to yet another pitfall - pride in his abilities. Yet again, his pride had robbed him of all the superpowers he had gained after years of austerities. He had been waylaid from the path of his goal.[25]

The southern direction had failed Vishwamitra. He reasoned that the south represented ignorance and, possibly, it was the influence of this ignorance that led him to believe that he could create and maintain heavens easily. To renew his efforts, he now decided to head westward.[26]

---

[24] If one cannot achieve success, one creates a model of success and redefines the standard of real success. Vishwamitra could not send Trishanku to the heavens, so he created a replica of the heavens and sent him there instead. To the rest of world, it may have seemed like a new model of success. But in their hearts, Trishanku and Vishwamitra knew this was not success after all, instead it was unlimited suffering. Trying to imitate God can be costly.

[25] In this episode, Trishanku represents inertia or laziness that prevents one from working hard to achieve one's goals. Vishwamitra represents too much activity or overenergetic endeavor to achieve a goal even though unqualified. Such overconfidence leads to anguish. Vasistha represents a balance between the two, which is harmony. After sufficient endeavor, one must wait for grace to decide whether one is qualified or not.

[26] Vishwamitra was constantly looking for external reasons to pin his failures on. He blamed either the place or the situation for his failure. Blaming external factors is a consistent defect in one who does not strengthen his internal faculties.

the dogtail

Vishwamitra sat in penance and meditation yet again. Yet again he survived on fruits and water droplets whenever needed. Not far from where Vishwamitra sat, another king, Ambarisha, was performing an elaborate Vedic sacrifice, which would culminate with the offering of a sacrificial animal. When time for the final sacrifice came, the king noticed that the animal was missing. Indra the king of demigods, as always, had become insecure of King Ambarisha's rising popularity and decided to sabotage the sacrifice by stealing the animal. The official priest was furious at the king's negligence in protecting the animal and ordered him to bring a willing human for the sacrifice instead. King Ambarisha was in a dilemma; where would he find a human willing to give up his life for someone else's sacrifice? The priest was adamant; forced by circumstances, King Ambarisha set forth to look for a willing person.

He travelled far to reach the house of Richika *rishi*, who also happened to be the husband of Kaushiki and hence the brother-in-law of Vishwamitra. Richika had three sons, and Ambarisha asked him to part with one of them in exchange for 100,000 cows. Richika was attached to his first son and refused to part with him for anything in this world. Kaushiki said that she could not bear separation from her youngest as he was extremely dear to her. Listening in on this conversation, the middle son, Sunashepa, felt extremely forsaken and unwanted. Yet he was grateful that even though they disliked him, his parents had raised him with care and attention. He wanted to repay this debt and considered this as an opportunity. At this moment in his life, the only one who desperately wanted him was Ambarisha and the least he could do was be useful to this one man. In exchange for

Sunashepa, King Ambarisha gave his parents many cows, heaps of gold and numerous valuable things.[27]

Ambarisha and Sunashepa rode all day on their chariot and at noon, they decided to take a break for lunch and rest for a while on the banks of a scenic lake. Death was knocking, and suddenly Sunashepa was not so sure he had made the right decision. While Ambarisha was slumbering, he decided to find ways to evade death.

Sunashepa set out to explore his possibilities. Along the way, he heard villagers talk of a great sage performing intense austerities nearby. Perhaps there was hope. He rushed to the spot as a sick man would to a doctor. He gaped at the sight in front of him. How was it possible? It was not just any sage, it was sage Vishwamitra, his own uncle. He was now convinced that Ambarisha's choosing to rest near this lake and his uncle's proximity to it was not mere coincidence but providence. It was God's design to save him from imminent death. He fell at his meditating uncle's feet and pleaded that he save his life. Vishwamitra opened his eyes to see who was pleading so piteously: his own nephew, his sister's son. What trouble had befallen his nephew? Sunashepa said that he wanted his life saved but at the same time, he wanted Ambarisha's ritual completed.

The compassionate Vishwamitra beckoned his sons and asked one of them to sacrifice his life and replace this boy. What had gotten into their father? How could their father be so foolish and consider giving up one his own sons to save someone else's life? Vishwamitra's sons refused to sacrifice their lives for their cousin's. The great sage realized

---

[27] Sunashepa never considered himself worthy, so people around him also never valued him. A diamond begins as an ordinary stone but with pressure and time, shines with self-worth. Suneshepa was a diamond in the making.

that his boys did not know that a sage had to dedicate his life to serve others. And here they were – all looking to live for themselves rather than being happy for being offered a chance to serve others through their own lives. Disappointed, Vishwamitra cursed his unworthy sons to a life of selfishness in fringe communities.[28]

Vishwamitra then taught Sunashepa two Vedic hymns to chant just before being flung into the sacrificial fire. Sunashepa learnt these mantras with the same focus and attention that a lion puts into hunting down its prey, be it a rabbit or an elephant![29]

Now equipped with two life-saving mantras, Sunashepa was brimming with life. He sprinted back to Ambarisha and woke him up, reminding him about the ritual. Soon they were at the sacrificial arena. Sunashepa was ready to be offered to the flames. Clad in a red cloth, adorned with blood-red garlands and tied to the sacrificial post, Sunashepa began chanting the two hymns his uncle had taught him with greatest fervor. The rumbling sound of his intense chant brought the chief demigod Indra and Lord Brahma before the assembly of sages. They bestowed longevity upon Sunashepa and also declared the

---

[28] The three characters in this story represent three different lifestyles. Ambarisha represents a life of competition. Competition demands that you die in order for me to prosper. Ambarisha was willing to sacrifice Sunashepa for the prosperity of his kingdom. Sunashepa represents a life of cooperation. Cooperation implies that both you and I prosper. Sunashepa desired that his life be saved but also wanted Ambarisha's desire fulfilled. Vishwamitra represents a life of service, meaning I live for you to prosper. Vishwamitra told his sons to sacrifice their lives for the prosperity of Ambarisha and Sunashepa.

[29] Learning with attention comes naturally when you know the practical application and the powerful effect that learning is going to have in your life.

ritual successful and offered its fruit to Ambarisha, much to the delight of both.

Sunashepa had thus far never really lived up to his name.[30] He realized it was time to do something with his life. His experience had left him with two very valuable life lessons.

First, no one in this world is your true well-wisher; everyone has an ulterior motive. His parents abandoned him, but King Ambarisha accepted him. The rejection and acceptance were both driven by an ulterior purpose. Second, there is no greater strength than the refuge of higher powers. Vishwamitra had nothing to gain from helping Sunashepa, yet he gave him the life-saving *mantras* to take shelter in higher powers. Sunashepa realized that if taking refuge in the Gods helped him in his calamitous situation, how much more benefit would he find if he were to do it on a regular basis.

Sunashepa's future now lay before him, and he had to make a choice. As far as his parents were concerned, he no longer existed. So he decided never to return home and instead tread the path set by his uncle: sagehood. That way he would become an asset to the society and serve the Sunashepas of this world who needed guidance at

---

[30] The word *suna* means dog and *shepa* refers to the tail of a dog. Which parent would name their child tail of a dog? Although the name seems ridiculous, deep meaning is embedded within it. There is a dog in the heavens called Deva Suna. When one reads the scriptures in a hurry and goes ahead without understanding the deep meaning, this dog barks and stops one from going ahead. This unique dog helps one understand the essence of the scriptures. When Sunashepa's father named him thus, he expected his son to be like the dog who understands the essence of the scriptures and lives a life based on lessons from these.

different levels. Sunashepa eventually went on to become a great *maharishi* who wrote many scriptures, thereby living up to his name.[31]

the beautiful distraction

Vishwamitra continued with his intense austerities on the banks of that lake. Sunashepa's interruption not only cost him his sons but also precious time and energy. Vishwamitra coaxed his mind back to his goal and went back to meditation. His meditation was getting more intense by the day and Indra was squirming in his throne. Insecurity began to set in. Not too long ago he had stolen Ambarisha's sacrificial animal, and now Vishwamitra's austerities were worrying. The powerful sage had created parallel heaven, what would stop him from usurping his throne in the heavens someday? Indra decided he had to stop him now; else, it would be too late. He called upon one of his most beautiful heavenly damsels, Meneka, to distract Vishwamitra.

Meneka, although worried about Vishwamitra's wrath, followed orders and descended upon Earth. Vishwamitra was focusing on his spiritual practices in a lake when Meneka entered the waters and began swimming around, singing softly. With her soft fragrance wafting into his nose, her melodious voice ringing in his ears, Vishwamitra opened his eyes and was bedazzled by such ethereal beauty. Her dazzling body was like a flash of lightning in the crystal

---

[31] Sunashepa emerged as a valuable diamond because of the situations he experienced and by observing the behavior of various people in his life. Life itself is a school campus - each day is a different classroom and every experience a different subject. It is called a school of hard knocks.

clear waters of the dark lake. As she sashayed gracefully up to him, Vishwamitra's harsh penances and austerities succumbed to her tender love. Forgotten was his goal in the ten years that he spent in Meneka's intimate embraces. Life with her was bliss.

Suddenly one fine day, it dawned on him that he had completely deviated from his path. As he snapped out of his bliss and took off the blinkers of sensuality, everything became crystal clear: Meneka was no ordinary woman. Indra must have sent her to distract him. All those years of penance sacrificed at the altar of lusty love. Vishwamitra had failed yet again.

Meneka realized that he had regained his senses and began to tremble in fear. By now Vishwamitra knew cursing her was futile. He had lost his path because of his own irresponsibility. Remorse engulfed him. He had to start all over. Slowly, he regained composure and took to the path he had forsaken a decade ago.[32]

the downside of anger

Vishwamitra now headed northward, toward the mighty Himalayas. He performed *tapasya* for several more years till Lord Brahma appeared before him. At least now he could be declared a *brahmarishi*. Lord Brahma pointed out to Vishwamitra that he was yet to be master of his senses and bring them under his control totally. There was still some distance to cover before being pronounced a *brahmarishi*.

---

[32] The curious mind convinces you to blindly follow its lusty proposals, promising joys that in actuality may be beautiful packages of sorrow.

----->

Lord Brahma was so blunt about his weaknesses that Vishwamitra intensified his austerities with a vengeance. He meditated for many more years; he sat burning inside raging flames in summers and stood submerged neck deep in ice-cold water in winters.

Indra could not bear to have Vishwamitra become so powerful. So this time he sent Rambha, another pretty damsel, to sidetrack him. Rambha was not so sure she should disturb the powerful *rishi*; however, Indra assured her that he would personally assist her along with Kaamadeva (Cupid). A reluctant Rambha appeared before the meditating Vishwamitra. Indra took the form of a cuckoo and began singing sweetly even as Kaamadeva created a romantic atmosphere with fragrant breeze and flower showers. A wiser Vishwamitra, fresh from Meneka's interruption, knew that this was just another attempt to sabotage his penance. He could not allow Indra to get his way this time. Livid, he cursed that Rambha would remain a rock until a great *brahmarishi* rescued her. Rambha turned into a rock right away. Indra and Kaamadeva disappeared immediately to avoid a similar fate.

Not again, thought Vishwamitra. Not again. His curse had taken everything down with it. Those hardships, those penances, those austerities had come to naught. He had let everything slip away yet again. He had resisted temptation and controlled lust. But anger? Vishwamitra was remorseful that he had yet to tame his wrath.[33]

---

[33] Any exhibition of anger is preceded by self-destruction. The vessel that holds poison becomes equally poisonous. When you are angry at someone, remember, you suffer the most.

success at last — a *brahmarishi*

This time, Vishwamitra went eastward to meditate. He had failed thrice before; he had to succeed this time. He took a vow of silence, and with fierce determination, began practicing austerities for many, many years, without eating or even breathing. After a long period of intense austerities, he was about to have his first meal when Indra came disguised as a *brahmana*. He asked Vishwamitra for something to eat. The sage promptly gave him all he had and resumed his *tapasya*. Over time, Vishwamitra began simmering with the flames of meditation. His penance reached such a peak that fumes began emanating from his head, creating a disturbance in the entire world. The demigods were perplexed. Together with Lord Brahma, they approached Vishwamitra. They agreed that he was now indeed a *brahmarishi*. Lord Brahma was willing to bestow any benediction upon him.

Vishwamitra wished for knowledge of all the Vedas. He also wanted that all the sages, including Vasistha, recognize him as a *brahmarishi*. Vasistha came and acknowledged Vishwamitra as a *brahmarishi*. At long last, such relief!

Then Vishwamitra did something that came as a pleasant surprise to everyone. Even Vasistha had not seen this coming. The *brahmarishi* placed Vasistha's feet on his lap. He washed the feet of the great sage with water and began worshipping them with a lot of love and respect. Vishwamitra had seen enough and struggled enough to understand that to become a *brahmarishi* was not child's play. Enmity with such an exalted person for so long a time had been such a grave mistake. He now wanted to redeem that mistake by begging forgiveness and taking refuge under the great sage. Vasistha helped Vishwamitra up and embraced him. Envy had turned into love![34]

Satananda *rishi* concluded Vishwamitra's story by glorifying the determination and relentless pursuit and focus of the great sage. Rama and Lakshmana were spellbound by the adventures and struggles of their teacher. Their respect toward him increased a thousand fold, realizing now that he had gone through so much to achieve perfection. King Janaka was amazed and humbled that a sage of his caliber was now in his kingdom. He showered Vishwamitra with profuse praise and begged him to visit his palace the next day with the illustrious Rama and Lakshmana to see Lord Shiva's bow.

vishwamitra's diary

That night, as Rama and Lakshmana lay next to him, Vishwamitra reflected upon his life. The story might have seemed fascinating to an outsider, but he knew more was to come. One particular event from the past struck him as he lay on the grass staring at the starlit sky.

He remembered the time he had felt his head splitting because he could not maintain the heaven he had created. He had screamed aloud in agony and chanted the names of Lord Vishnu. It was the first time he had felt so vulnerable; it was also the first time he had cried out so helplessly. What he remembered most about that event was not the helplessness but the soothing effect the presence of Lord

---

[34] Sheer determination made the ordinary Vishwamitra extraordinary. Vishwamitra began with envy toward Vasistha, but now as he matured in his culmination of knowledge and practice of spirituality, envy had transformed into genuine humility and love.

Vishnu had on him; his burden had been lifted off his head the moment Lord Vishnu assured him protection and took over his responsibility.

Vishwamitra had always tried to prove himself worthier than Vasistha and was willing to put in so much effort to that end – years of nonstop austerity. He had pushed himself beyond his capabilities and continued to move at a great pace to achieve his goal, never stopping to think where he was headed. Meeting Lord Vishnu had been like standing in front of a door that he should have opened. The door had been right in front of him but he was too preoccupied to open it. He had to become a *brahmarishi* first.[35]

When he became a *brahmarishi*, he realized it was time he explored what was behind that door. He knew all his efforts were in vain. Had it occurred to him back then to completely submit to Lord Vishnu, he would not have had to go through such trouble. Besides, he would have actually reached a higher destination. He now began wondering why his friend Vasistha who detested opulence and was always travelling had decided to become a mentor to the king of Ayodhya.

Vasistha was no fool. He would not do anything without a higher cause. From greatly exalted sages and demigods, Vishwamitra learned that the same Lord Vishnu he met earlier had manifested in the Ikshvaku Dynasty as Rama, the son of Dasaratha. He felt the same

---

[35] Often in life, like Vishwamitra, we are so busy pursuing our short-term goals that we do not find any time to pause and reflect on the direction we are heading toward. Life gives us many hidden doors, which become visible only if we pause. Most people live their lives by the clock, running at a frantic pace. A balanced individual needs to use a compass from time to time to check if one is running in the right direction. Else, the faster you run in the wrong direction, the farther you stray from your goal.

door opening up for him again. This time around, he did not want to miss the opportunity and felt the urge to enter that door.

Vishwamitra recalled every effort he had made to convince Dasaratha to send Rama along with him. Under the pretext of training Him and protecting his sacrifice, he had really wanted some private moments with Lord Rama, to hand over every power he had acquired over the years to Him and ultimately, take shelter under His lotus feet.

As he gazed at the serene face of Lord Rama, his heart swelled with immense happiness, the kind he had never known before, not even when he was declared a *brahmarishi*. He had surrendered everything to Lord Rama. Only one last service remained. Once done with it the next day, he would head to the Himalayas to live in remembrance of Lord Rama, walking through that open door toward perfection.

CHAPTER 8

VIRTUES AND THE VIRTUOUS

rama's emotional turmoil

As Vishwamitra lay there drowned in Rama's gratitude, Rama lay lost in His own world. His thoughts transported Him to that window in Mithila behind which had stood the most beautiful damsel He had ever seen. The window framed Her like a painter's flawless masterpiece. He was so captivated and awestruck by this mystic beauty that He turned around for a second glimpse. It was magical; He could not fathom what force drew Him toward Her. He had never felt this way before.

He thought that all the human virtues were battling it out for the honor of being able to reside within Her. Beauty seemed to have performed unlimited austerities to have the fortune of being associated with Her. Since Her birth, no woman could boast of being the most beautiful, proclaimed Rama.

As Rama lay on the grass thinking about Her, deep in the innermost chambers of the palace, Sita was tossing and turning in her soft, downy bed. The restlessness in Her heart made Her bed feel like thorns. She could not take Her mind off the boy She had seen on the street from Her window. She remembered every inch of His handsome physique - the broad shoulders, the strong feet, the pinkish palms and the deep, intense eyes through which He consumed Her beauty completely. When Rama had walked out of Her sight, Sita's mind, resolve and beauty had shamelessly followed Him. She had never felt this way before. When He walked away, She had felt like a thirsty person who could not find the way to the water tank even after having spotted it. Here, the water tank had just walked away from a thirsty Sita!

Rama was not sure if He was sinning by thinking about that girl. What if She were married? No, it couldn't be. In His heart and mind He knew that She was the One. If His mind had settled on Her, surely She must be the divine bride in waiting. Rama's faith in His mind was restored. Such was his confidence that He knew He couldn't sin.[1] Rama, Lord Vishnu Himself, the one who slept in an ocean of milk, was now sleeping in an ocean of agony. The night was as restless as His mind.

the story of the bow

In the wee hours, Vishwamitra proceeded with Rama and Lakshmana to King Janaka's palace.

At the palace, however, everyone was awaiting the arrival of the king. Janaka, after performing his morning oblations, headed straight to the courtroom. His elephant gait seemed to match the rhythm of the drum beats ushering him into the courtroom. As he inched closer to

---

[1] Confidence in one's mind can be achieved if one's thoughts, words and actions are centered on higher principles. A trained mind as this can be relied upon. On the contrary, a frivolous mind hunts for opportunities to drag one down to compromise, and it must be dealt with carefully.

his throne, the beats rose to a crescendo filling the palace up with a thunderous sound. The palace rumbled as King Janaka slowly walked up to his throne to take his seat.

As Vishwamitra, Rama and Lakshmana were about to enter the palace, they lifted their heads to take a look at the sky-kissing dome of the structure. The palace stood so tall that its dome peak seemed to touch the slow-fading moon from the previous night.

As the glowing Vishwamitra stepped into his courtroom, his mentor Satananda's narration of the previous evening came flooding back to Janaka. He could visualize the sage going through the severe austerities to become the effulgent *brahmarishi* he now was. He was so proud to have the great Vishwamitra in his palace. He requested Vishwamitra to express his desire.

Vishwamitra asked King Janaka to show the bow to the two brothers. Janaka agreed, but first he wanted them to know the story behind the bow and how it reached Mithila.[2]

Long ago, Vishwakarma, the celestial architect of the demigods, had used all his creative powers to construct two bows of unlimited strength and fortitude. He presented one each to Lord Vishnu and Lord Shiva. Lord Shiva had used his to kill the demon Tripurasura. The idle demigods wished to test which of the two was stronger. They approached Lord Brahma to arrange a duel between Lord Shiva and Lord Vishnu.

Lord Brahma could foresee a calamitous future were this duel to go

---

[2] Assessing the value of anything based on external appearance is like equating a crow with a cuckoo. Assessing the value based on hearing the greatness of the object is akin to appreciating a cuckoo over a crow.

on till the end. He warned the demigods of dire consequences were the fight to ensue, but the demigods disregarded the warning. He manifested a difference of opinion between Lord Shiva and Lord Vishnu so that they enter into a fight. Lord Vishnu and Lord Shiva did not want to fight, but they relented at the demigods' persistence. But when the fight began, neither wanted to be the one to lose. The hair-raising duel took such a devastating universe-threatening turn that the demigods began to worry. The demigods had not foreseen this. During the duel, Lord Vishnu let out a menacing war cry that deafened the demigods to semi-unconsciousness. Now extremely apprehensive about the existence of the universe, they rushed to the two warring Lords and prayed that they stop the contest. The Lords agreed.[3] Both Lord Vishnu and Lord Shiva had their bows with them till each gave it away to someone else for safekeeping.

Daksha was the demigod responsible for the creation of living beings in the universe. He was also the father of Sati, wife of Lord Shiva. Sati loved Shiva, but Daksha did not really like him because he did not think the ash-smeared Shiva who wore skulls and snakes and visited graveyards was the right match for his daughter. Sati spurned him to marry the ascetic God. His pride was so wounded that he performed a *yajna* where he invited everyone except Lord Shiva and Sati. Sati went nonetheless and wanted an explanation for not being invited. Her father insulted her husband and said the *yajna* was no place for an ascetic such as him. Humiliated, Sati burnt herself to ashes. Lord Shiva was so hurt and angry that he went to Daksha and in the presence of all the demigods at the *yajna*, he threatened to sever

---

[3] Too much curiosity to intervene in matters where one has neither authority nor control is guaranteed to bring personal embarrassment and public disturbance. The curiosity of the demigods could have resulted in universal destruction.

Daksha's head with the bow Vishwakarma had gifted him. The demigods begged for forgiveness and pleaded with Lord Shiva to hand his bow over to them. The kind-hearted Lord Shiva was quick to anger yet quick to forgive too. So, he handed over his bow to them, who in turn gave it to King Devavrata, the sixth descendent of King Nimi, the founder of King Janaka's dynasty.

Meanwhile, Lord Vishnu, too, handed His bow over to Richika *rishi*, who in turn gave it to his son Jamadagni, who passed it on to his son Parashurama.

the astonishing might of the bow

By the time Janaka finished narrating the breathtaking tale of the bow, the two princes were aching to see it. The crowd, too, waited in anticipation. Janaka shifted his attention from the boys and Vishwamitra to the job at hand. Everyone understood that the moment had arrived. They would all get to see the magnificent longbow in full splendor. Janaka ordered his soldiers to wheel in the bow to the assembly. His army marched out to the adjacent building where the bow was kept. Was an army needed to get the bow? The bow was extremely heavy and wheeling it in to the courtroom was a back-breaking task. It took nearly 5000 able-bodied Maithil men, with elephant-like bodies and rock-solid arms, to push a cart pulled by 500 mighty bulls to bring it into the court. Perhaps, the place where the bow was kept for so long felt relieved. At long last a huge weight was off its aching back! Alas, the ache shifted to a new place, Janaka's court.

The backs of these strong, gigantic men seemed to curl under the weight of the bow as they tried to lift it and place it at the center of the courtroom. An anxious buzz spread through the courtroom. Some Maithils began speculating that the bow was Mount Meru itself; some others thought it was Mount Mandara, which was used to churn the ocean. Yet others thought it was a rainbow that had fallen from the sky. The rainbow analogy did not seem very far from the truth as the bow became visible. Bright colors reflected off its surface and it radiated a beautiful aura. The elephant skin and tiger skin covers along the bow curves added to the exotic charm of the wonderful bow. Everyone was mesmerized by its grandeur.

Janaka's faith and appreciation for the formidable bow was renewed when he witnessed the herculean effort it took to wheel it in. He told Vishwamitra how the bow was worshipped everyday in Mithila, adorned with the most fragrant sandalwood pastes and flower garlands. Because no one in Mithila was qualified enough to use the bow, all they could do was worship it.[4]

the nagging pain in janaka's heart

Never once taking his eyes off the bow, Janaka told his guests that no one had been able to lift this bow since it was brought to Mithila, not even the great demigods, *gandharvas* and *kinnaras*. Janaka fought back his tears at the thought of no one being capable of lifting the bow. He

---

[4] Most people develop eagerness to possess something valuable rather than develop the ability to make everything in their possession valuable. Lord Shiva knew how to use the bow, but for the demigods and the kings of Mithila it remained the valuable object they owned but could not use. Brief connection with Lord Shiva made the bow worship-worthy just like a brief connection with flowers in a garland makes the thread that holds them fragrant.

became emotional because he was a father in pain, bearing the agony of being unable to give away his daughter in marriage. Only the one who could lift the bow could marry Sita. It had been years and no worthy suitor had come by to Mithila to claim his daughter. Many Maithils began whispering about Janaka's foolhardy decision to keep such an impossible condition for his daughter's hand. Though old, Janaka heard those comments and began doubting if he had any intelligence at all.

Perhaps he was not that foolish. Now that Rama was here and so was Vishwamitra, Janaka had become optimistic. He decided to reveal the tumultuous secret that beat within his throbbing heart to Vishwamitra - something he had kept from even his dearest friends.[5]

Janaka began narrating to Vishwamitra about his decision to marry Sita off to only the one who could lift and string Lord Shiva's bow. At the back of his mind, Janaka had his hopes pinned on Vishwamitra to encourage Rama to lift the bow, and he hoped narrating this story about the precondition to Sita's marriage would actually make his desire come true.

Janaka went on to narrate that the moment he had made the announcement, hundreds of kings, princes and even extraterrestrial personalities lined up to try their hand at lifting the bow in the hope of marrying the lotus-eyed princess. Every single one of them failed. The suitors, unable to even budge the bow, began to accuse Janaka of cheating them and trying to insult them by exposing them to ridicule. They were convinced none could lift that bow, not even Lord Shiva,

---

[5] Revealing the heart in confidence is an act performed only after verifying the detachment, maturity, wisdom and unbiased spirit of the one in whom you want to confide.

and this was merely Janaka's attempt to run them down. Some of the kings were so offended that they banded together and decided to attack Mithila city.[6]

Mithila was now under siege from all corners; Janaka's soldiers tried all they could to protect the city from the attack. Unfortunately, Janaka was rapidly losing men and wealth in this suitors' battle. He had very few options left, so he requested the demigods for help. They were only too happy to oblige and hence sent their armies to Mithila and helped defeat the attacking suitors.

This victory over the suitors was not enough to convince the Maithils of Janaka's wisdom. Sita was their dear princess, the most beautiful and able girl in the entire world. Yet here She was languishing without a groom because of Her father's insane precondition. Each time they saw Her, they could not help but discuss Janaka's folly.

the inside story

Was he really a fool? Janaka would often ask himself the same question. But the self-doubt would last only until the recollection of this startling incident from the past.

A young Sita had been playing ball with her friends. The flower ball She was playing with rolled into the room where the bow was kept. She ran into the room in search of her ball. Searching frantically for it around and under the bow, She finally located it under the bow.

---

[6] Friendship formed to achieve a selfish common agenda is a relationship with an egocentric base. The building of the relationship founded on such a hollow base collapses with the first tremor that demands sacrifice.

Almost as if it was as light as a feather, with Her left hand, She lifted the bow and with Her other hand, She picked up the ball. Then She put it back in place as if She had just lifted paper off the floor! Sita then went back to Her gaping friends who had been watching everything all the while. The friends, still astounded by what had transpired, rushed to King Janaka with the news.[7]

Stunned as he was, Janaka decided that if his girl was so miraculously strong, there was no doubt in his mind that the one to marry Her must match Her strength. Even if he were unable to lift the bow as effortlessly, he should at least be able to lift it anyway and string it. A precondition thus took birth - a precondition that, with time, had begun tightening like a noose around Janaka's neck.

Not everyone knew of Sita's bow-room feat, especially those who ridiculed him. The king was mute through the mockery. He knew better. At least he hoped he knew better. Through countless silent prayers and countless mental battles to continue backing his

---

[7] There are two versions of the same story. These stories are presented neither in the *Valmiki Ramayana* nor in the *Kamba Ramayana*, but they do portray very effectively Janaka's situation in graphic detail. Since they neither contradict the flow of the *Ramayana* nor create any dent in any of the characters, we can safely assume them to be compatible with the rendition of the epic. While this is one version, the other version held that Sita was plucking flowers in Her gardens when She saw some really beautiful flowers hanging high up on a tree. She tried Her best to reach out to them, but in vain. She began looking for a stick to pluck the flowers. She could not find one in the garden, so She ventured into the palace and found Lord Shiva's bow. She quickly picked it up and ran to the garden. Seeing Her run effortlessly with the bow in Her left hand, every guard and maid along the way fell unconscious. Once they regained their consciousness, they ran to Janaka and narrated this amazing feat to him.

judgment and decision, Janaka just wished he was not wrong – for the sake of his daughter and for the sake of his citizens.[8]

lord rama – a ray of hope

Janaka looked hopefully at Rama. He then turned to Vishwamitra and suggested that *if* Rama were to lift the bow and string it, He could win the hand of the beautiful Sita.[9] Or, would it be wiser to just hand Sita over to Rama without making Him go through the bow-lifting exercise considering He was the most eligible by far and had come from such a distant land? Of course, there lay this possibility that Rama would fail to lift the bow and Sita would remain a spinster all Her life. But there was also this strong possibility that He would be victorious and Janaka's precondition would be a success in that it would have helped find the right man for Sita. Either way, Janaka was willing to take this calculated risk. Vishwamitra's presence encouraged him to take a leap of faith.

Lord Rama courted challenges. Besides, He, too, wanted to win Sita's

---

[8] Life often puts us through tricky and sticky situations, where we cannot share our struggles and frustrations even with those we love. At times such as these, we look for an alternative to find hope; prayer is one such alternative.

[9] The word 'if' indicates Janaka's state of mind – doubt in the ability of Rama. Constantly witnessing failures often converts one to a doubting Janaka. The antidote to such a doubting Janaka is associating with a confident Rama. The citizens of Mithila kept on passing negative comments. It seemed that Mithila's environment was filled with the disease of doubt and failures. In such an environment, Rama came as a gust of confidence.

hand, although he was not yet quite sure if She was the one He had spotted in the balcony and lost His heart to. If this was the only way to have the girl He could not stop thinking about, then He was not going to give up without trying. After a long, hard look at the bow, He turned toward Vishwamitra. He wanted His master's approval to take a closer look at the bow. With Dasaratha absent, Vishwamitra took on the mantle of father. The *brahmarishi* had been waiting for this moment for quite a while now. He promptly agreed, showered his blessings and gave Rama permission to assess the bow. Rama then walked up to Vishwamitra, touched his feet and sought empowerment and began walking toward the bow.

Silence fell over the courtroom. The audience skipped a beat with every step He took toward the bow. Rama was confidence personified. His gait had the power of a lion (*simha gathi*), the rage of a tiger (*vyagra gathi*), the pride of a bull (*rishabha gathi*), the majesty of an elephant (*gaja gathi*) and the latent energy of a snake (*sarpa gathi*). It seemed as if Rama embodied the spirit of each of these wild creatures. For the first time in all these years, everyone present in the courtroom was convinced that Rama would accomplish the impossible.[10]

As Rama stood near the bow, He imagined it to be Sita's necklace. Once again His mind raced back to that balcony. Surely, the girl He was to marry now after lifting the bow *was* the same girl He had seen on the balcony and fallen so deeply in love with. Rama shook Himself back to the present and the task at hand. He gazed at the bow one last time, reminisced about its greatness and its association with Lord Shiva and circumambulated it thrice, hands folded, head lowered with respect.

---

[10] Blessings from well-wishers exude from every pore and gesture of one's body as confidence. Confidence is not a solo undertaking.

→

Back in position, He looked to Vishwamitra and asked for permission to touch it. Vishwamitra nodded. Rama was ready. He extended His arms, gripped the middle of the bow and again turned toward His teacher for permission to lift it.[11] By this time, everyone had their hearts in their mouths. Excitement, anticipation and hopes had peaked. Anything was possible now. They soaked in every single moment through their eyes like a drunk would eye the last drop in the pitcher. Not for anything did they want to miss any part of the action. They all sat immobile, unblinking in rapt attention. Everyone's breath was held, their lungs constricted, their heads throbbing. Ah, the suffocation of anticipation!

Lord Rama was all focus; the bow being the only thing on His mind now, He tightened His grip on it. A chorus of gasps filled the air as he lifted it off the casket as elegantly, gently and effortlessly as an elephant lifts a lotus from a lake. The bow had been lifted! Even before everyone could absorb the shock of what they saw, Rama had erected the bow on the ground with His right hand, held down the bulbous tip with His left big toe, pulled down its top with His left hand and strung it. The entire task was completed in crackling speed. All of it happened so fast that none could understand how He lifted the bow or when He strung it. Even as they wondered how everything happened so fleetingly, a deafening sound rent the air. The majestic bow of Lord Shiva, the pride of Mithila, had snapped right in the middle. Everyone barring Rama, Lakshmana, Janaka and Vishwamitra, dropped unconscious unable to bear the thundering sound. It was almost as if the mighty bow was letting out a cry, a cry that

---

[11] Respect is the antiseptic that does not allow confidence to degenerate into arrogance. Rama was definitely confident of His abilities, but His confidence was exhibited very carefully within the confines of respect. He obediently sought permission at every step, not assuming sanction arrogantly. Continued respect assures continued blessings.

reverberated through the entire universe. Across the universe, everyone dropped everything trying to trace the source of the ripping sound. Rama, with two broken pieces of the bow in His mighty hands, stood there innocently, as if He had done nothing extraordinary.[12]

"Bravo!" jumped up a beaming Janaka. Thank God! What a proud moment for Janaka: Rama had saved his face, prestige and fame. He was so overwhelmed with emotion that he could not find the right words to express his joy. Bursting at the seams with happiness, he brought forth his wealth and donated generously to the needy,[13]

---

[12] Lord Shiva, his father-in-law Daksha and Lord Vishnu symbolize three of nature's energy forces: destructive energy, constructive or creative energy and conservation or maintenance energy. If this world were a huge construction company with two departments – Shiva's (destruction) and Daksha's (construction) – the departments would have to stay apart yet work in tandem, else balance in this world would be disturbed by competing and not complementing forces. Maintaining a sensitive balance between these departments is Vishnu – the liaison between the two.

In Mithila, the bow (Lord Shiva's department) lay unused and construction (Dasksha's department) was in a limbo because of the constant wars the rejected suitors waged against Mithila; hence, there was no construction and only constant destruction. It became imperative for Lord Vishnu – in the form of Lord Rama – to destroy the bow and end the one-sided destruction and bring harmony to the land. Rama's act of destroying the bow can also be compared to the havoc-wreaking tilling process that facilitates the growth of beautiful crops in a land that seemed leveled before being tilled. Rama's destruction of the bow was necessary to herald a new eon of positivity and construction, in a world that seemed razed to the ground by the intense negative energies in the form of the bow on one side and the demons on the other.

[13] Janaka spontaneously shared the joy of his heart by giving joy to others. When you become the harbinger of joy to others' hearts, your own joy multiplies; thus, in giving, you receive.

who were like white clouds absorbing water from a sea full of surging waves.

janaka invites sita

It was a happy moment for Janaka. His daughter was finally going to be a bride. He had waited so long for this moment. He called out for Sita to appear in the assembly. Sita's friends rushed to her room with the exhilarating news; Sita was sitting right there, yet not quite. She seemed oblivious to the tumultuous events in the courtroom. She lay on her bed in a world of Her own, lost in thought. Her mind still replaying the moment She spotted that handsome boy from Her balcony. She was so entranced by thoughts of Him that She did not even hear Him break the bow. It baffled Her friends that She had missed such an earth-shattering sound.[14]

Sita's chuckling friends rattled off everything·that had occurred in the courtroom. They told Her that Her groom was a handsome prince named Rama who was in Mithila along with his equally charming brother Lakshmana and wise teacher Vishwamitra. Sita stood up in amazement, and then doubt crept in. Was Rama the same boy She had seen from Her balcony the previous day? None knew the answer. Was it Him? Was it not? Would She marry the one She so loved? Was it someone She had never known? She was pacing the room, restless and inquisitive. She *had* to go and see for Herself. Her friends dressed

---

[14] Sita represents us, Rama represents changelessness and the world represents constant change. When one is absorbed in the internal constant aspects of life, one remains unaffected by unlimited external changes.

Her up, adorning Her with the most exquisite jewelry and flowers and anointing Her with the most fragrant of perfumes and walked Her to the courtroom.

Sita's veil of modesty was drawn over Her head and reached Her chin. In Her hand was the wedding garland woven with the best of flowers in the land. She walked up to Rama. She wanted to lift Her veil and catch a quick glance of Her husband to be, but was torn apart by Her bashfulness and Her curiosity. She checked Her zeal. Voila! She needn't break norms. She could recognize Him by His feet, too! So She glanced at His feet. Indeed, they were the same feet She had noticed from her balcony. Her heart racing at recognizing the same strong feet now standing right in front of Her, She lifted the corner of Her veil and stole a glance at His handsome face.

rama shocks janaka

Everything was moving so fast. The bow was broken, the city was celebrating and Rama was standing in front of a girl and was about to be married. The magnanimity of the situation suddenly dawned upon Him. He had been in turmoil, fighting His own inner battle. He was just as unsure as Sita about His spouse to be. Was Sita the girl He had given His heart to? He knew She was the one the moment She entered the room. But his battle had not ended there. Now a fiercer war waged in His mind: that of a son versus a lover. As lover, He was fulfilling His duty by standing there waiting to be garlanded, but as son had He done His duty? He was duty bound to abide by His father's wishes, so how could He marry without His father's approval?

Rama's life was etched by principles. It was meant to set an ideal example for the world to follow. So Rama decided that at this point in time, it was more important to be the ideal son than to be the ideal lover. So He set aside His desires and announced: "My father sent Me with Vishwamitra to assist him. I came here to see the bow because My spiritual master instructed me to. Marriage was not at all on My agenda. I cannot marry Her without My father's approval."

It would be a grave insult to His father if He were to marry Sita without His father's permission. He was taught to respect His superiors. It was a prime value, and He could not forgo it for anything in this world.

Rama's words pricked Janaka like thorns and he fainted in disappointment. This was not what he expected the perfect match for his daughter to say. A No? Is that what his daughter deserved after so many years of waiting? The man most qualified to marry his much-sought-after daughter was not eager to jump into matrimony? Janaka thought his world was falling apart. He quickly turned to Vishwamitra with hope in his eyes, looking much like the helpless mother of a sick child imploring a doctor. Vishwamitra was calm and not worried at all. He instructed Janaka to immediately dispatch his most trusted and eloquent couriers to Ayodhya with a personal invitation and proposal to Dasaratha. He assured Janaka that Dasaratha would be more than happy to accept this proposal. To Janaka, Vishwamitra's words were like soothing balm on a searing wound.[15]

---

[15] Rama was the only person who could marry Sita, but He desisted. This was a paradox for Janaka. But for Vishwamitra, the paradox would cease to exist with Dasaratha's approval. Reconciling paradoxes requires prudence. Janaka here was trying to solve a problem that hadn't yet surfaced, whereas Vishwamitra was used to handling a problem only at its onset.

sita's delight amid the drama

Sita was the one person most delighted with Rama's pause. She blushed and smiled to the Herself, much to the astonishment of Her friends. They had feared the worst and assumed She would be heartbroken. But seeing Her happy made them wonder if something were terribly wrong with Her. But Sita was a very intelligent girl; She understood the deeper nature of humans. Rama's response to the marriage proposal made Her realize His true worth. She was now sure that Rama was the most suitable husband.

For Sita, a man had to have three very special attributes for a woman to be able to submit her life to him. First, he must be valiant or have the ability to protect; second, he should be prudent and have the ability and wisdom to say the right things; and third, he must have self-control or the ability to resist temptation and control emotions. She could tick Rama on all three qualities. Rama was valiant because He took up a challenge everyone had failed at. Besides, how could She ever forget His confidence-exuding stately gait that had impressed Her so much even as He was walking away from below Her balcony? She knew He was prudent and articulate because she heard Him speak to Her father with respect.[16] He had self-control because He curbed His desire to marry Her.

Wars had been fought over Her beauty and none of those kings had impressed Sita as much as Rama did. Rama's denial was invaluable to her. It proved to Her that Rama was a man of principles, a man who placed principles above desires.[17]

---

[16] Why did Sita want to judge Rama's speech? Every wife expects her husband to spend some time speaking with her. This is as important as physical protection because this is emotional nourishment.

[17] An ideal man can be an ideal husband if he follows the principles of marriage with honor and respect.

THE PRINCIPLES OF MARRIAGE

Till the wedding, Rama was a student focused only on studies and self-development. His focus was "me" – a state of healthy selfishness. Marrying Sita made Him think beyond His own needs. His focus shifted to "us" – a state of selflessness.

Student life thrives on guided competition, whereas marriage works best with happy cooperation. Records can be broken when students compete, but only hearts are broken when couples compete. To avoid heartbreak, a couple must cooperate with and complement each other.

Rama's marriage with Sita exemplifies two essential principles that sustain a marriage – genuine love and effective communication. Rama loved Sita but that did not destroy His communication with His father. Self-focus can push communication to the backburner and hurt sentiments. As a grafted tree accommodates hundreds of varieties of fruits, a genuine and empathic individual can accommodate different personalities within a family. By reaching out to His family despite being so in love with Sita, Rama reinforced that marriage is not merely a husband–wife relationship but the coming-together of two families and legacies. Just as the confluence of two rivers is auspicious because it denotes yoga (Sanskrit for connection), the coming together of two families creates kalyana (Sanskrit for marriage and auspiciousness).

Because a wedding brings two craving hearts together, the principle of marriage is companionship. It aims to end loneliness; hence, to avoid re-experiencing loneliness, a couple must treat the institution of marriage as a vehicle that must be expertly maneuvered through differences, disagreements, disappointments and disturbances. Like a good driver behind the wheel guarantees a smooth journey, a couple that uses the clutch of empathy, the accelerator of encouragement and always pulls the brakes on misjudgment successfully steers the union with effective communication to guarantee a happy marriage.

dasaratha's dreams come true

Janaka sent his most articulate couriers to apprise Dasaratha about the latest developments. Just as a greedy-for-pleasure mind flits rapidly from one corner to another, the desire to please Janaka inspired his couriers to hold their breath and rush from Mithila to Ayodhya at breakneck speed. They inhaled only after reaching King Dasaratha's courtroom.

Once in the courtroom, the couriers handed Janaka's invitation to Dasaratha. They took turns to narrate the events that led to the big moment. They described the glorious adventures and achievements of Rama and Lakshmana through their voyage with Vishwamitra – how they killed the indestructible Tataka, how they hurled the demons away and saved Vishwamitra's world-saving *yajna*, and how Rama redeemed Ahalya from her stony existence. They then told Dasaratha about how Vishwamitra and the boys accidentally walked into their city, Mithila.[18]

They then came to the most exciting part of their narration. Dasaratha listened with amazement as they described how Rama took Vishwamitra's permission and not only lifted the famed bow of Lord Shiva but also broke it as simply as an elephant would rip sugarcane. They could not contain their excitement when narrating how the reverberation of the bow-breaking could be heard across Mithila and the entire world. A beaming Dasaratha told the messenger that he too had heard a tumultuous sound and assumed it was lightning striking

---

[18] Janaka had a reason for terming their entry into his city accidental. He did not want Dasaratha's decision on the marriage proposal to be hampered by the suspicion that taking the boys to Mithila was Vishwamitra's preconceived idea.

somewhere. Dasaratha's chest swelled up with pride. This was exactly what he had expected from his sons!

Now was the time to tell Dasaratha the actual purpose of their visit. The king was floating with joy and he could be safely told the real implication of breaking the bow: Lord Rama had won the hand of Sita, the most beautiful and virtuous daughter of Janaka. An overjoyed Dasaratha rose from his seat. What did he just hear? A marriage proposal for his beloved Rama? How did his dream come true? He had wanted this a while now.

Dasaratha turned to his Big M for their opinion. One glance at Vasistha and Vamadeva and he knew their answer. He had known them for so long that he just needed to see their expression to understand them. A jubilant Vasistha rose and declared that this alliance would be most beneficial for Rama and for Ayodhya. Dasaratha's ministers unanimously seconded Vasistha.

"Celebrations!" declared Dasaratha. He showered Janaka's couriers with valuable jewels. He even donated profusely across his kingdom to share his joy. He invited every citizen to the wedding of Rama with Sita and welcomed them to join him on his voyage to Mithila.

ayodhya proceeds to mithila

Zealous citizens began packing right away. They loved Rama so much that they did not want to miss this big event in their prince's life. Dasaratha realized their immense love for Rama when he saw almost the entire city of Ayodhya heading toward Mithila. Everyone was very excited and chatted away, but the most enthusiastic of them all was the very old Dasaratha. He was so energized by this news that he kept a pace ahead of the entire entourage, almost as if he was growing younger with each step toward Mithila. Equally, if not more, enthusiastic were the three queens. As the entourage walked faster toward Mithila, the jeweled palanquins of the queens swung vigorously, reflecting the cadence in their hearts. For Bharata and Shatrughna this was the most joyous moment in years: They would get to see their brothers. They had no idea how they survived without their beloved brothers Rama and Lakshmana all this while.

Dasaratha's ministers carried with them limitless riches to share as gifts with King Janaka, who was soon to be the kingdom's most important relative. The caskets were filled with gems of every kind; every possible jewel ever seen or imagined was there. Then there were different types of vehicles, palanquins, horses, elephants and cows – all of these in mind-boggling quantities.

Dasaratha's procession was so vast that when Dasaratha, the leader of the troupe, reached the gates of Mithila city, the last person was yet to start from Ayodhya! The procession seemed like an endless human sea from Ayodhya to Mithila – the elephants seemed like waves, the umbrellas and fans like sea foam, the palanquins were like little boats floating on that sea and the multihued turbans like multicolored fishes.

It took the procession four days to cover the distance between Ayodhya and Mithila. When they finally rested on the banks of the Ganga river, it seemed as if the sea of Ayodhya's citizens merged with the river, as opposed to the usual river meeting the sea.

mithila welcomes ayodhya

Janaka's alert soldiers realized that the happy procession at Mithila's borders were the king of Ayodhya, Dasaratha and his retinue. They ran to inform King Janaka about their much-awaited arrival. Janaka was ecstatic as he walked from his palace to the banks of the Ganga. He was relieved when he saw Dasaratha, his friend, and soon-to-be relative. The friends embraced each other; the embrace seemed to last till eternity. There was so much love and so much respect in that embrace. Janaka belonged to the Lunar dynasty and Dasaratha to the Solar dynasty, and this was truly a celestial event – the sun and moon embracing each other!

Ayodhya's citizens entered Mithila to a warm, elaborate welcome. Janaka instructed his ministers to take care of every guest as they would have received their own family. He instructed that every guest irrespective of his or her position and qualification be cared for and their every need addressed. Janaka personally took care of the royal family's needs at Mithila.

Janaka talked and talked about the feats of Rama and Lakshmana and about their incomparable achievements. He was euphoric and felt truly blessed to have Rama as his son-in-law. He could not thank Dasaratha enough for having agreed to this marriage proposal and transforming their long-lasting friendship to an eternal relationship. Janaka then asked Dasaratha to share his expectations from this marriage. Because Rama had already fulfilled Janaka's conditions, it was now his turn to fulfill Dasaratha's. Janaka's humility made Dasaratha misty-eyed. What was Janaka talking about? How could he, Dasaratha, have preconditions on the marriage? Instead, he was a receiver who was willing to accept everything his donor gave him. Janaka bowed further and embraced Dasaratha, pleased with his humble and kind words.[19]

---

[19] Conditions and satisfaction are inversely proportional to each other. The more conditions you put down to guarantee your satisfaction, the more dissatisfied you become. Unconditional love definitely guarantees infinite satisfaction.

The moment the boys heard of their family's arrival they rushed to their father and gave him a joyous and warm hug. After so many days of separation, it was as if the sun had met the horizon. The mothers, too, hugged their long-separated sons with streaming eyes, shedding copious tears of joy and reunion.

the glory of rama's dynasty

Everyone was out to witness the greatest event of their time. Janaka's court that day seemed to herald an exclusive sight – the confluence of the two most powerful kingdoms, the Lunar and Solar dynasties. To get the celebrations rolling, the stage was set for each dynasty to highlight the achievements of their significant kings.

Vasistha took on the mantle of eulogizing the Solar dynasty. He narrated how Rama's extraordinary qualities carried on the tradition of glory founded by the numerous luminaries of His dynasty. If the luminaries were so glorious, could anyone imagine the glory of the sun itself, Lord Rama, the king of all luminaries? Vasistha touched upon the lives and greatness of some of the great kings in that dynasty, starting with Ikshvaku, empowered ruler of the entire planet Earth and a king very dear to Lord Brahma. Next was the glorious King Prithu, who was a partial manifestation of Lord Vishnu and the most ideal leader the world had ever seen. Then there was King Kakustha, who was so valorous that the demigods sought his help during their fights with demons. In fact, during one such fight, Lord Indra took the form of a bull and carried Kakustha on his shoulders to fight the demons. Then there was the celebrity king, the most virtuous King Mandhata, during whose reign there was parity among the strong and the weak; such was the parity that tigers and deer would fearlessly drink water off the same lake!

Vasistha then talked of King Muchukunda who, too, helped the demigods during troubled times. King Shibi offered his own flesh to an eagle to protect a pigeon, both of whom were his needy citizens. He then talked of Sagara and Dileepa who were great kings, and also about Bhagiratha, who helped bring Ganga to Earth. No description of the Solar dynasty could begin or end without the mention of the charitable and principled King Raghu. And Dasaratha was like the effulgent rays of the Solar dynasty. Finally, Lord Rama, his son was the sun itself. It is very interesting that this sun, Lord Rama, was not of ordinary birth but was a fruit of a *yajna* performed by Dasaratha. Vasistha congratulated King Janaka and said that it was his good fortune to become connected with this glorious dynasty.[20]

the glory of sita's dynasty

Janaka spoke on behalf of his own Lunar dynasty. He began with King Nimi, who had once invited Vasistha as the officiating priest for a sacrifice he was conducting. But Vasistha was also invited by the demigods to perform a *yajna* in the heavens. The great sage decided to go to the heavens, reasoning that by virtue of being his disciple, Nimi would wait for him and that the remuneration of the heavens were always more attractive. Nimi waited till he lost patience and invited another priest to perform the sacrifice. By the time Vasistha returned, Nimi's *yajna* was complete. Offended and humiliated, he cursed Nimi to death. But there was a twist. Nimi counter-cursed his master to

---

[20] The natural expectation from a swan is to have the pure heart of a swan so as to maintain the glory of its dynasty. When a swan associates with a crow, its body remains white, but its heart turns black. Who you are is definitely influenced by who you connect with!

death. Despite being a *brahmana*, Vasistha had followed greed. As Nimi's spiritual master, Vasistha was duty bound to his disciple and was expected to not be motivated by wealth.[21]

King Nimi died of the curse. He did not wish for another body nor was he too attached to it to regain it. Vasistha died, too, but he wanted to return to life, so he kept his soul in a water pot till he got another body. After giving up his body, Nimi chose higher realms. When the sages realized that there was no king to rule, they churned Nimi's body from which was born another king, Mithi Janaka.[22] It was Mithi Janaka who established the kingdom of Mithila. Since then, every king in this dynasty took on the hereditary name Janaka as a reminder of their ancestor Nimi who had no attachment toward his body but toward higher spiritual goals. Because of this selfless pursuit, the kingdom was known by another self-explanatory name Vaideha, meaning one without a material body or without attachment to it. All Maithils embodied this virtue and it was ingrained in them and earned them the name Vaidehas, and Mithila was called Vaidehapur.[23]

---

[21] In a desire for higher prospects, we tend to sacrifice people who love us. Vasistha took the love of his disciple Nimi for granted. Vasistha tries to please everybody by being available for everyone. The quality of your contribution is more important than the quantity of your availability, a lesson human beings are yet to learn.

[22] *Ja* refers to birth, and *Mithi Janaka* means one who is born out of churning another's body.

[23] When the focus is on the body, the heart remains underdeveloped. Beginning from King Nimi to Sita and to every citizen of Mithila who possessed beautiful bodies, everyone focused on their inner beauty. The name Vaidehapur indicates that every person in this city focused on inner beauty.

Sixth after Nimi was King Devavrata Janaka, the one who received the bow of Lord Shiva from the demigods. Fifteen generations after Devavrata Janaka was Shiradvaja Janaka – incumbent ruler of Mithila, Sita's father and Dasaratha's friend. His brother Kusadvaja was the king of the adjacent kingdom of Samkasya. Each king along this line of exemplary rulers was as glorious as the previous one. Ensconced on this treasure trove of glory was Shiradvaja Janaka with two valuable possessions – the bow of Lord Shiva and the exceptionally beautiful and virtuous Sita. Rama had broken the bow and it was no longer Janaka's. The king was to give away to Rama the one last treasure he had left with him – his beloved daughter Sita.

story of the birth of sita

Tears swelled up as Janaka's mind raced back to the joyous moment he had found his beautiful daughter. Gathering himself, Janaka continued with his narration and related the truth about the birth of Sita. Janaka remembered that he had once organized a great sacrifice. At the onset of the sacrifice, rituals required him to till the soil up to the sacrificial arena. The sacrifice could commence only after the tilling. The real reason behind the sacrifice was the prosperity of his dear citizens. Janaka was like an overflowing lake, complete and full in itself and yet interested in sharing its fortune.[24]

Janaka had promised to make massive donations to the *brahmanas* every single time his plough got stuck. It so happened that the plough

---

[24] The word sacrifice means sharing what you have with those who don't. If the purpose of any sacrifice were to accumulate, then it should be called Gratifice.

did get stuck every few steps. After ploughing through a considerable distance and making countless donations, there came a point when the plough seemed permanently stuck. Intrigued by this "plough-jam", Janaka ordered his workers to dig up the spot. As they dug, they felt their tools hit something. A beautiful, intricately carved golden box too big and opulent lay there glistening in the sun. Thousands gathered around the radiating box. Everyone wanted to know what was inside it. Janaka, curious and bewildered, held up the box with his left hand and with his right hand he touched the lid. He was not sure what was within. Was it priceless treasure buried long ago? Was it a key to some secret? Trembling with anticipation, Janaka opened the box. Good heavens! A beautiful little bright face beamed like the bright sun from within that box!

"This is impossible!" Janaka screamed inside his head. But his heart was melting at the cherubic sweet-smiling baby girl that lay staring at him. She was life Herself. She was the Moon. She was the brightest of jewels he had ever laid hands on. The golden-skinned innocent little baby astounded him. She was the most delicate and most radiant baby he had ever seen. Her soft dark downy hair complimented her lustrous dark eyes and her bright red delicate lips seemed to set everything on her angelic face so beautifully. This girl was surely God's gift and Janaka accepted her with open arms. He named Her Sita because She was found at the tip of a plough. Some also called Her Bhumisuta, daughter of *Bhumi* or Earth, yet others called her Vaidehi, the one mistress of Vaidehapur or Mithila.[25]

---

[25] Every individual, like Janak, is trying to dig for his fortune. For Janaka, his fortune came wrapped in a golden box. Had the box been wooden, would he still have opened it? The content is more important than the packaging. Our fortunes may come in a golden box, but what's important is to recognize every gift sent by God, no matter how trivial or priceless, as our fortune and to be grateful for it.

Janaka once again became nostalgic and teary-eyed; however, this time streaming down his eyes were tears of joy. Standing before him was the same girl, the most beautiful creation ever manifested, on the verge of marriage. Soon She would be gone to another city, another family. Janaka felt as though She was disappearing back into that box he had opened so many years ago.

joy quadruples for ayodhya and mithila

The wonderful and awe-inspiring stories about the two dynasties made their citizens feel lucky to have been born in these glorious kingdoms. They felt this union of Rama and Sita, Dasaratha and Janaka, Ayodhya and Mithila, the sun and the moon, strength and compassion, valor and beauty, was for the good of the world.[26]

Vasistha then took Vishwamitra aside for a discussion on something very important that had dawned upon him. Why did the two sages walk away *together* to a corner? What could be wrong? Janaka wondered. Not too long ago, they could not see eye to eye. And now they were sharing a secret? Janaka was delighted to see them engrossed in conversation, but he could not fathom the reason behind this collaboration. He had no idea that they were in fact talking about him and his family, making plans to quadruple the joy of the two families. As Janaka was trying to comprehend their secret meeting, the now-

---

[26] No two humans have the same forte and frailties. Triumph comes when one honestly recognizes and comes to terms with one's forte and frailties, simultaneously endeavoring to connect with those inversely endowed. When humans harmonize with each other, their success is imminent.

smiling sages returned, casting knowing glances at each other, almost as if holding an idea that was struggling to burst forth.[27]

Janaka and Dasaratha tried to read the faces of the two sages but without much success. What were they up to? Certainly something good, but how much better could things get? Vasistha smiled and made the most exhilarating revelation thus far: "We have pondered on this subject for some time and feel it apt to propose it to you for your consideration and action. Janaka, we feel that since your daughter Sita is being wedded to Rama, it would be perfect for your second daughter, the beautiful Urmila, to marry Lakshmana, the one inseparable from Rama. We also suggest to your younger brother Kusadhvaja, king of Samkasya, who has two exquisitely beautiful daughters Maandavi and Srutakirti that they be married to Bharata and Shatrughna."

Kusadhvaja was stumped. He was in Mithila to be part of his niece's wedding. Not even in his wildest dreams had he imagined that this trip to Mithila would be such a windfall. Janaka, Dasaratha and Kusadhvaja all embraced each other, their hearts thumping with joy. It was an offer they could not and did not want to refuse. How could they! This was like all their dreams coming true at one go. Joy to one and all! The couples, all began darting loving glances at their spouses to be and beamed like the sun and the moon.

---

[27] Two bricks when held together by a layer of cement remain bonded under all circumstances. Similarly, when two independent and thoughtful men are cemented together by love for the same divine object, they not only remain bonded but they actively cooperate to please the object of their love. Rama was that connection between Vasistha and Vishwamitra.

the perfect weddings

Mithila now had to prepare for not just one, but four grand weddings. Arrangements for ceremonies began with much gusto. Vasistha personally presided over the marriage ceremonies with Vishwamitra and Satananda *rishi* for support.

The rituals were about to begin when Yuthajit, Keikeyi's brother and Bharata's maternal uncle, arrived from Kekeya. He walked to Dasaratha and came straight to the reason of his unexpected visit. Bharata's grandfather had suddenly expressed a desire to see him. Yuthajit had traveled all the way from Kekeya to Ayodhya to fetch Bharata only to learn that everyone in the city had ventured toward Mithila to partake in the wedding. Yuthajit followed the people of Ayodhya to Mithila. Dasaratha considered it his great fortune that providence had led Yuthajit to this city, so he invited him to witness these four divine weddings. Yuthajit accepted the invitation, glad to participate in the elaborate preparations.

Yuthajit looked around and noticed that Rama and Sita were the talk of the town. Every discussion in every home revolved around the two. The eyes of Ayodhya's citizens who had made this journey to Mithila were like two cups filling up with the nectar of Rama's and Sita's beauty. The eyes battled with each other over whom to focus on, Rama or Sita. Soon they would become so confused and cockeyed because they could not manage to look at two mesmerizing attractions simultaneously. Tired, they would shut their eyes and see both Rama and Sita within their heart, but their eyes would then fight to open again to have their fill of Rama and Sita.

Some felt that Sita would need at least a thousand pair of eyes to appreciate her husband's beauty. Some said that Rama was the one who needed that many eyes to appreciate Sita's beauty. They realized that the earth had never experienced the touch of Sita's feet because She had never ventured out of Her palace without her golden sandals. The sun and the moon could never steal a glance at Her face because She never left Her palace without a palanquin. Her gait was so graceful that swans tried to imitate Her and would get frustrated when they failed. Her molten gold complexion constantly radiated the fragrance of exotic flowers. So some of the citizens reasoned that not only would Rama need a thousand pair of eyes, He would also need an equal number of eyes added every minute to appreciate Sita's ever-increasing beauty.

Vasistha went through the marriage rituals with utmost care and sincerity. The rituals were to culminate with Janaka placing the hands of his daughters in the hands of their husbands. A proud father Janaka stepped forward and placed the hand of Sita in the hands of Rama.

janaka's touching advice

Janaka was choking on his tears, his heart unable to handle the mixed emotions of gratitude and separation. He placed Sita's hands over Rama's, implying that Rama was now under Sita's care.[28]

---

[28] From a spiritual perspective, Rama represented the Supreme Lord and Sita the Energy of God, the Eternal Mother. For a spiritual aspirant, the role of the mother is more important than that of the father. While the father sees everything from the perspective of the law, the mother sees everything from the perspective of love. There would be no hope for a spiritual aspirant if his actions were to be judged by law. But the mother is kind enough to hide the defects because of her love; therefore, by placing Sita's hands over Rama's, Janaka indicated a lot of hope for a spiritual aspirant despite his lapses. Janaka's act symbolized that in the family, the

As he handed Sita over to Rama, he recounted his daughter's special attributes to Rama. One of Sita's many names was Ayonija, meaning, one not born as an ordinary human being, which made Her the best match for Rama because His, too, was not an ordinary birth.

Janaka then turned to Sita and told Rama, "This is *your* Sita. Don't garland anyone else mistaking her for Sita. Your Sita is standing right here."[29]

Janaka then said that Sita was virtuous and rule-abiding and because She was raised in a royal family She knew everything that was expected of Her as an ideal queen. The gushing father guaranteed that his daughter would be a model wife, who would respect Her husband, take a backseat when He chose the right path, but unhesitatingly correct Him and take over from Him if He deviated.

Janaka assured Rama that Sita would be His shadow.[30] Sita would be

---

[28] *contd.* role of a woman was more important than that of the male. To the world, the male may seem powerful, but his strength actually comes from the warmth, love and encouragement he receives at home from his wife and mother. Janaka placing Sita's hands over Rama's is a symbolic indication to Him that Sita would always be there by His side and protect Him from succumbing to weaknesses.

[29] It surprised everyone that Janaka was pointing out the obvious. Why did he do that? He had two reasons. First, till now, Rama had never looked at anyone because He felt that His own beauty was unmatched. By pointing out to Sita, Janaka directed him to look at Sita because His match had been found. With the exceptional beauty that She possessed, Rama did not need to look elsewhere. Second, Janaka was aware that Sita's beauty had enamored Rama to such an extent that he saw Her everywhere.

[30] Sita is compared to the shadow that is connected to the person at the feet. In the morning when one is facing the sun, the shadow falls behind and toward the end of the day, the shadow lies ahead. In all situations, the sun and the shadow are never separated from each other.

in sync with Rama from head to toe. She would follow Rama in His time of prosperity and in times of distress, She would take the lead and help Her husband. Like the shadow, Sita would never separate Herself from Rama. Janaka implored Rama to treat Sita as a precious stone valued enough to be protected with life. Janaka's role as a caretaker was now complete. He had given his daughter over to Her eternal companion.

Once Janaka was done praising Sita, Rama took a vow that struck a chord with all women. Rama bequeathed Himself to Sita all His life. He called it the *eka-patni-vrata* – a vow of monogamy, to have only one wife and to be loyal to Her. The joy of Ayodhya's women knew no bounds because their king Dasaratha had 353 wives, and every man in Ayodhya married multiple times following their role model Dasaratha. With this vow of Rama, the future king, the women were delighted polygamy was on its way out.

Vasistha asked the couple to exchange garlands. Rama decided to have a bit of fun. Rama was much taller than Sita and she could not really garland Him if he did not bend. But Rama decided to not budge from His position. Lakshmana immediately came to Sita's rescue; he touched Rama's feet knowing that He would bend to pick him up. Clever as She was, Sita seized this opportunity and put the garland around Rama's neck to waves of laughter rippling through the audience. Rama was impressed both with Sita's presence of mind and Lakshmana's cleverness.

One by one, all couples were tied in matrimony. All couples offered their respects to their parents, the great sages and to every elder who had come to bless them. Celebrations rang through every corner of Mithila; there was merriment in the air as if happiness was dancing on the streets. People could just not fathom the reason for feeling so irresistibly happy.

Of everyone's happiness, the most profound was sage Vishwamitra's.

But it was not the marriage of His disciples that had gladdened his heart. There was much more to his ecstasy.

vishwamitra heads north

Vishwamitra could now head onward and live a life dedicated to Rama. He had finally managed to unlock the door he had seen back when he was at war with Vasistha and he could now head home, his real home, the feet of the Lord Almighty. Vishwamitra handed over all his powers and knowledge to Lord Rama, his world. He lived up to his name – a friend of the entire world. Rama now had all the means and resources to protect the entire world and chase away the demoniac forces. An even greater task Vishwamitra accomplished for the benefit of the entire world was uniting Sita with Rama.[31]

Vishwamitra had carried out all his responsibilities and perfected his life by his service to Lord Rama. He now wanted to head North to spend the rest of his life by meditating on Lord Rama. He sought Lord Rama's permission to move on and embark upon his spiritual journey.

The next morning when Mithila was yet to wake up from the hangover of the intoxicating joy that had befallen the city, Vishwamitra walked into the horizon toward the Himalayas.[32]

---

[31] Sita represents a living entity, Rama represents God and Vishwamitra represents a spiritual master whose role is to connect the living entity with God, thus assuring eternal happiness.

[32] There is no further mention of Vishwamitra in the *Ramayana*. Vishwamitra's life embodying determination, focus and service, remains a perennial source of inspiration to spiritual aspirants. The hero of Book One of the *Ramayana*, Vishwamitra, had attained maturity in his devotion and had transformed from a *bala* (child) to an adult in his devotion.

CHAPTER 9

MIGHT IS NOT ALWAYS RIGHT

sweet sorrow of parting

Vishwamitra had headed toward the mountains now that his pupils were married. Dasaratha's job in Mithila was done and he decided to return home. He could not wait to celebrate his sons' successes and marriages in his own city with his own people. He could feel the throbbing expectation of all those who had not gone on this historic Mithila trip, instead staying back in Ayodhya to protect and maintain their city. When the entire royal entourage woke up early next morning in Mithila, it was as if a hive of bees had been stirred awake. They were buzzing with the excitement of returning home to more celebrations. What was even better was that they could take home with them Ayodhya's princes and their wives. Mithila had turned into one big bustling fair to watch the newlyweds. Soon, the brave and handsome Suryavanshi brothers stepped out with their beautiful and angelic wives for the customary newly married public appearance. Hoots and hollers and ooh and aahs rippled through the crowd. It was quite a commotion. Everyone wanted to get the best view. The crowd could not have enough of the royal couples.

Dasaratha and his queens could well imagine the hullabaloo that awaited them back home. Meanwhile, although heavy-hearted, Janaka and his brother Kusadhwaja were all set to send off their beloved daughters. They ordered expensive gifts and valuable things to be packed into palanquins and loaded on to elephants. These would accompany their daughters to Ayodhya. Countless things were being packed and stacked so that it seemed almost as if all of Mithila's precious belongings were being sent to Ayodhya. Soon the Maithils would have to bid their favourite daughters goodbye. Janaka and the Maithils had eyes brimming with tears. These weren't the sad tears a girl's family sheds on her leaving home for her in-laws' house. Instead, these were tears of joy and relief. Mithila's daughters were now in safe hands: The illustrious Rama and His brothers had received its most valuable treasures.

Sweet sorrow flowed through Mithila's veins as Ayodhya streamed out of the city. Janaka and Kusadhwaja, their ministers and all the sages walked the procession to Mithila's boundaries, bade everyone farewell and returned home. It seemed as if the waves had washed up precious shells on the beach and returned to the loving embrace of the ocean.[1]

Dasaratha's entourage was celebrating so much that it was like a sugar rush. People danced and sang throughout the journey home. In a carriage drawn by powerful horses, flanked by the chariots of his four sons, Dasaratha soaked in every ray of sunshine surrounding him. The smiling coy brides swayed along with the bedecked swinging palanquins perched on the strong shoulders of nimble-footed carriers. Trailing them was the mirthful sea of Ayodhya's citizens bracketed by the marching rows of Ayodhya's formidable army. Dasaratha cast his triumphant gaze all around. He was the master and protector of all he surveyed. The king of Ayodhya was floating in this seemingly everlasting uplifting moment.

---

[1] Often a guest is treated as a hen that only consumes and does not contribute. But in fact, a guest is like a hen that lays a golden egg; the golden egg of the opportunity to serve.

shattered sunshine

Dasaratha's reverie was shattered by a ear-splitting wail. The sinister cry seemed to come from above. The celebrations screeched to a halt under the trembling feet of the dancing revellers. Dasaratha looked up to witness the most ominous sight he had ever seen: hordes of birds hovering in the dark sky, screeching as if in excruciating pain. Dasaratha was certain this was a very bad omen. His heart pounding, he turned toward his spiritual guru Vasistha hoping for an answer and a solution, if this horrific phenomenon warranted one. Vasistha knew everything. Dasaratha hoped he knew what all this meant, too.[2]

Vasistha monitored the flight pattern of the distressed birds. It was a sure sign of an apocalyptic catastrophe. Vasistha then looked around and saw something very reassuring: the animals were going around in circles. The anxious Vasistha suddenly broke into an all-knowing smile. This swift emotion shift befuddled Dasaratha. Before he could ask his guru anything, Vasistha decoded the phenomena for his disciple: "The screeching birds definitely point toward an approaching calamity, but then the animals moving in circles bodes good news. The calamity will cause no harm." Dasaratha's frayed nerves were instantly calmed.[3]

Dasaratha soon realized that relief was only a split-second luxury. Soon the earth shuddered and shook as if a million elephants had

---

[2] Excess happiness is like a postdated cheque, which when cashed by Time, leads to suffering. Nature is an expert banker maintaining the perfect balance sheet of the currency of joys and sorrows.

[3] Some opportunities come disguised as disasters. Too much time is spent whining about the furore these opportunities create, rather than focusing on capitalizing on them.

stomped in unison. A violent dust storm whirled up in the distance and came swirling at great speed toward the entourage. The storm was on a rampage, demolishing everything along its way. Trees lay uprooted, lakes evaporated, bees swarmed out of their hives, wild beasts fled out of their shelters, snakes and rats rushed out of their holes and hapless birds spun uncontrollably in the storm. The ravaging dust blanket soared up to blur the sun and roll down a curtain of darkness. The shrieks and howls, the swirling dust and reigning gloom was more than any heart could withstand. Everyone in the faint-hearted procession fell unconscious, barring Dasaratha, Vasistha, the brave brothers, the shy princesses and some sages.

With each swirl toward Dasaratha's chariot, the storm seemed to wane in fervor. The moment it reached the chariot, it came to an abrupt halt. The thick dust plume settled to reveal the formidable force behind the destruction.

the axe-wielding rama

The past seemed to have returned to haunt Dasaratha, for towering over him was an intimidating broad-shouldered, barrel-chested hermit with a conical dreadlock knot on his head, wearing a two-piece deerskin – one covering his loins and another thrown across his torso. The passive, sagelike attire belied his warrior-like demeanor – glowering bloody eyes; rage-radiating flush face; hot heavy breath. Worse still were his menacing weapons – a huge bow in his left hand and a battle axe on his right shoulder. An axe-wielding hermit? Horror gripped Dasaratha as soon as he recognized the raging storm. He stifled a scream under his breath, "Parashurama! He's back!" Those 350 marriages of hairbreadth escape just whizzed past Dasaratha's mind. Alas! Now he was trembling before the very revenge-seeking sage he had been escaping from for so long. Even recollecting the horrific past sent tremors down Dasaratha's spine. How could this be happening? Hadn't Parashurama retired peacefully to the Mahendra mountains, forsaken His avenging rage against the Kshatriya (the warrior class) for mercilessly slaughtering his father? Why had He stormed back? Dasaratha had no answers; he did not know what to say and how or whether to plead for anything at all. Parashurama alone knew why He had returned!

The sages accompanying Vasistha bowed to this warrior incarnate of Lord Vishnu and paid their respects and eulogized Him with words befitting exalted sages.

Parashurama boomed: "A few days ago, a deafening roar shook the Mahendra mountains and spoiled My meditation. That instant I took a vow to meet the one responsible for the tumult. I am looking for Rama, the breaker of Lord Shiva's mighty bow."

Parashurama looked at Rama and appreciated the valor He displayed through the slaying of powerful demons and the breaking of Lord Shiva's bow. It really did not matter how unimaginable and astounding His earlier feat was, Parashurama had come all the way from the mountains just to test His skills on an equally powerful bow. Would Rama care to display His strength on Parashurama's bow? A slight, mysterious smile slipped through the corner of Rama's mouth. He knew that the ignorant Parashurama, too, was an incarnation of Lord Vishnu just like Him and was throwing a futile challenge at Him. Parashurama raised His massive arm, flashing His golden bow for all to see. He walked up to Rama and incited Him to string this new bow – the bow of Lord Vishnu. Could Rama string Lord Vishnu's bow with as much ease as He had Lord Shiva's? If Rama could actually achieve this feat, Parashurama promised a duel with Him. After having cast the challenge, the menacing Parashurama glared at the calm Rama.

Parashurama's provocation drove Dasaratha insane. His fears revisited him and he wondered how Rama would accomplish such a task? The protective father seemed to have conveniently forgotten that this son had not-so-long ago broken Lord Shiva's bow and even killed some formidable demons. Dasaratha stepped off his chariot and fell on his knees, imploring Parashurama to let go of this challenge. In all these years, Dasaratha had never had the courage to appear before Parashurama and had always chosen to hide behind weddings when the *Kshatriya* slayer came knocking. Now immense love for his son had given him the gumption to face Parashurama. He loved Rama more than his own life.[4]

Dasaratha pleaded with Parashurama and calling Him by another name, asked Him, "Bhargava Rama,[5] why do you want to take up weapons after having renounced them and ventured to the Mahendra? What would you achieve by threatening and challenging a child?"[6]

---

[4] Selfless love is the elevator that leads you up the great heights of sacrifice to prove your depth of sincerity. When you love someone, too much trouble is no trouble at all. When you hate someone, too little trouble is too much trouble. Love is the pill that peps you to do the impossible.

[5] The sweet-talking Dasaratha deliberately called Parashurama by His lesser-known name to identify Him as a descendent of the Bhargava dynasty renowned for exalted and peaceful sages. The name Parashurama meant the holder of *parashu*, or battle-axe, a name that reflected His violent nature. Dasaratha, by addressing Him as Bhargava Rama, tried to remind Him of His peaceful background and hence appealed to His calm side, if there was any, hoping his pleas would work on Parashurama.

[6] A human adapts to situations just as a chameleon changes colors to match its surroundings. The real color is often forgotten over constant color change to suit the environment. A subtle reminder of our real nature and color jolts us back from false pursuits.

Dasaratha's pleas went unheard because Parashurama's gaze was fixed on Rama. He raised His eyebrows as if asking Rama if He had the mettle to take up this challenge. But Rama's mind was elsewhere. He had never before seen His father on his knees begging for His life. Rama lauded Parashurama's commitment toward His own father, Jamadagni, and the fact that Parashurama's intense love and respect for His father had led Him to take up arms to avenge His father's death. Rama's appreciation impressed both Parashurama and Dasaratha. Rama was deft at pleasing many individuals simultaneously. Parashurama interpreted Rama's praise as not being judged for His killings, whereas Dasaratha interpreted it as Rama's high regard for the axe-wielding warrior. Rama's words meant different things to Parashurama and Dasaratha but He was also making a point of His own: If Parashurama had so much respect for His own father, how could He let another's father beg in front of Him? This, Rama pointed out to Parashurama, amounted to a double standard not worthy of a father-loving son.[7]

Rama then reprimanded Parashurama for doubting His abilities and yanked the bow off His hand. Even Parashurama, the warrior known to travel as fast as the mind with arms that moved as fast as the wind, was taken aback. Standing in front of the mighty Parashurama was just a boy who had snatched away His bow at lightning speed.[8]

---

[7] In overappreciating one's high personal standards of behavior, it is possible to underestimate another's.

[8] Finding fault with a person is like touching a raw nerve. When you touch a person directly on his weakness, he shrivels like a touch-me-not, shut to further interaction. But before touching another's faults, if you first touch upon the person's strengths, the person relaxes like the plant that allows an able and caring gardener to weed it. The person thus becomes ready to shed every fault you find, now feeling assured that you care.

Even before a perplexed Parashurama could react, Rama bent the bow, strung it and pointed an arrow toward the axe-wielding hermit. The confidence and the ease with which Rama maneuvered the bow told Parashurama that it had reached its true owner. This must be Lord Vishnu, He concluded. The two incarnations of Lord Vishnu – Parashurama and Rama – were standing next to each other.

Rama, bow in hand with an air of authority, asked Parashurama where He should shoot the arrow now that He had already drawn one. Rama did not want to kill Parashurama because He was a *brahmana* and was also related to His master Vishwamitra as the descendent of his sister Kaushiki. He gave Parashurama two options: He could either shoot the arrow at Parashurama's leg to disable Him or aim at all the powers and piety that Parashurama had acquired through years of meditation. Parashurama chose to sacrifice His piety and justified His choice: He had donated Earth, which He had won by killing the rulers, to Kasyapa *muni* because of which He no longer had the right to stay overnight on the planet. Parashurama decided He needed His limbs to keep His promise and head for His abode in the Mahendra mountains before nightfall.[9]

---

[9] The way Lord Rama dealt with the two bows is very interesting. He approached both the bows with extreme confidence. In the case of Lord Shiva's bow, He had no intention of taking up the challenge. Vishwamitra had urged him to take it up. Rama sought the blessings of Vishwamitra, respected the bow, lifted it and broke it. As far as Lord Vishnu's bow was concerned, Rama had not offended Parashurama, but Parashurama still insulted both Him and His father. Not stopping at that, Parashurama had acted arrogantly extolling his own powers. Rama magnanimously ignored his behavior and appreciated him for his commitment to his father before demonstrating His own powers, thus humbling Parashurama. As soon as Parashurama realized his mistake and begged forgiveness for his haughty behavior, Rama gracefully gave him the choice of punishment. Punishment should not be meted out merely to penalize, it should also serve the purpose of purification and rectification. This principle is emphasized in all mature forms of governance.

Rama's arrow swished through the air and sucked in all of Parashurama's piety and disappeared. Parashurama lay prostrate in front of Rama and acknowledged Him as the Supreme Lord, the master of all creation. Glad about being defeated by Him, Parashurama circumambulated Lord Rama thrice before leaving for the mountains to resume His penance.

Rama then invoked the ocean god, Varuna, and handed over Lord Vishnu's bow to him for safe custody. With Parashurama's departure, the gloom that He had brought along disappeared. The radiant sun smiled again and the celestial flower showers rained upon Lord Rama.

Time, which had frozen[10] when the colossal incarnations clashed, ticked back to normalcy and stirred awake the comatose entourage. Everyone woke up to the celestial flower showers. They knew deep down that their Rama had averted the ominous catastrophe. All was well again.

Rama assured Dasaratha that He was safe. With his son safe and Parashurama gone, Dasaratha embraced Rama as he shed tears of relief and joy. He wondered how often he would have to face situations that would threaten to tear Rama away from him. For now, Rama was with him, and that was all that mattered. Dasaratha ordered his entourage to hasten pace toward Ayodhya lest another calamity stall them.

---

[10] Even Dasaratha and the others who were conscious could not witness what transpired between Rama and Parashurama because the two were surrounded by the dust storm Parashurama had created. It was thus a private moment between the two incarnations. The past – Lord Parashurama – had made way for the present – Lord Rama.

life returns to ayodhya

Ayodhya's soil was parched for the shower of its sons' footsteps. As soon as the procession reached the border, the city sprung into celebrations. The streets were decorated and people began rejoicing. The city wore a festive look and was ready to welcome Lord Rama.

The three mothers, Kaushalya, Sumitra and Keikeyi ushered their daughters-in-law into their home with great pomp and glory. Many rituals were performed to invoke auspiciousness in their married lives. The generous King Dasaratha distributed limitless gifts to everyone in the kingdom. Ayodhya's soul had returned. Rama's return breathed life into a dead city.

Even as the celebrations continued, Dasaratha conveyed to Bharata his uncle Yuthajit's message about his grandfather's desire to meet him. Bharata immediately rushed to Keykeya with his loving brother and eternal companion Shatrughna.

Ayodhya, already a complete city, seemed even more complete with the arrival of the four new princesses. Rama and Lakshmana helped their father, Dasaratha, rule Ayodhya with great expertise; their training at the hands of Vasistha and Vishwamitra helped. Rama performed endless welfare activities for His citizens. Everyone in Ayodhya was enamored by Rama's kind and magnanimous attitude.

Rama was not just a good dutiful prince, he also made sure he was a dutiful husband. He spent a lot of quality time with Sita. Even sugar that most naturally dissolves in milk could not compare with the unfathomably natural love between Rama and Sita. He loved Her not only for Her exemplary radiance but for Her virtues as well. Not only Rama, Sita had also won over the entire family with Her goodness and humility.

Limitless joy surrounded Dasaratha. He was a proud king, a proud husband, a proud father, a proud father-in-law and a proud disciple. His life was picture perfect.

The perfect picture was not to be perfect forever, though. Dasaratha was yet to face the worst. All seemed to be well until a nightmare shook him out of his happy slumber – a nightmare that portended deep darkness and a never-to-be-filled void.

Was it some kind of prophesy? Was it a dream? Would it actually come true? Who would make it come true? An unknown fear gripped Dasaratha and left him motionless.

APPENDIX

24 QUALITIES THAT MAKE A TRUE HERO

Narada *muni* explained every quality in relation to Lord Rama. He highlighted how Lord Rama personified every quality mentioned by Valmiki. Anyone who aspires to be a perfect human would need to imbibe these qualities - and Lord Rama had them all!

The following are those qualities:

1. *Gunavan* - Great birth, wealth and education is all that one needs to be the best of all. Possession of even one of these infuses pride in the beholder. Further, the one who has them all indeed becomes arrogant! A person of virtue is the one who in spite of his great birth, wealth and education, is *sausilya* or amicable with everyone. Lord Rama had all three in completeness, yet He remained amicable with everyone. Lord Rama exhibited this quality by befriending Guha (a tribe leader), Sugriva (a monkey) and Vibhishana (a demon).

2. *Viryavan* - A person of power. Lord Rama exhibited this power during His battle with Khara, Dhushan, Ravana and Kumbakarna.

3. *Dharmajna* - The *dharma* (or duty) that Lord Rama followed is the *dharma* of protection, which assures salvation to those who completely surrender to Him. If anyone seeks His shelter, He gives up His life for them, provides for them and protects them.

4. *Kritajna* - A person of gratitude. Lord Rama graciously remembered every little act of service done to Him by others. A higher greatness on His part is that He ignored numerous disservices committed against Him by others. Most importantly, He was highly obliged to those who receive His services.

5. *Satyavakyah* - A person who strictly abides by his words is a *Satyavakah*. Lord Rama stuck to His promise given to His father. Despite His mother's and Lakshmana's appeal to disobey His father, He stuck to His words and principles. Furthermore, while on exile, Bharata pleaded with Him to return to the palace but bound by His commitment to His father's promise, He did not return and stayed back in the forest.

6. *Dridavratah* - A person who is committed to protect is a *Dridavratah*. Such a person gives protection to those who seek it, irrespective of other commitments (*Vrata*). Lord Rama gave protection to the Rishis of Dandakaranya as well as Vibhishan (ignoring the monkeys' reservations). His protection also came in other ways, viz. offering scriptures, sages and regular appearances as incarnations.

7. *Charitrenecha koyuktah* - A person of exemplary conduct, impeccable behavior and perfect to a fault; one who does the right thing at the right time. The test of nobility is not valor but conduct. Rama welcomed Vibhishan and accepted him as His brother and gave him shelter when Vibhishan wanted to take refuge under Him, despite fierce opposition from every member of the monkey army.

8. *Sarvabhutesu kohitah* - A person who ardently wishes and works for the good of all without any distinction. He serves others with an equable temper that remains unaffected by his personal likes or dislikes. Lord Rama did not look at Jatayu, the

vulture, as the lowest among birds. He served him as a son would his father.

9. *Vidvan* - A person who is the master of all wisdom. Lord Rama was well-versed in all the 64 arts and skills. He had mastered all the Vedas, was excellent at archery, knew all martial arts, rode all types of vehicles, could sing well, play all musical instruments, paint, dance, etc. Lord Rama not only mastered these skills but also mastered the art of using each skill at the appropriate time.

10. *Samardah* - A person who is competent beyond doubt or question. Sheer knowledge and strong determination are not enough; along with it one should have the capacity to put them to efficient and effective use. To accomplish any task, three things are essential - strong unwavering will and tenacity of purpose (*icchasakti*); complete and clear knowledge of the end goal (*jnanasakti*); and a high degree of skill and competence. All the three were exhibited by Rama during the killing of Ravana and Tataka. Without employing these three qualities, it would be impossible to kill such powerful demons.

11. *Jitakrodah* - A person who controls anger and summons it to his service when needed. Lord Rama demonstrated this quality twice - once when Sugriva neglected his duty and again while protecting Hanuman from the attack of Ravana.

12. *Dyutiman* - A person whose beauty casts a spell over men and women alike. Vishwamitra, Janaka, Sita and sages in Dandakaranya, all found Lord Rama attractive.

13. *Anasuyakah* - A person who is free from envy. Lord Rama saw no fault in Keikeyi or in Dasaratha even though they deprived Him of His rightful kingdom.

14. *Kasyabibhyati devascha jataroshasya samyuge* - A person whose courage never fails in the face of inseparable forces of hostility and opposition. Amid attacks from 14,000 soldiers of Khar and Dhushan, Lord Rama merely smiled. This fight seemed impossible to win, but in a matter of 48 minutes, He emerged victorious.

15. *Aryah* - A person who bonds closely with dharma and moves away from adharma. Lord Rama embraced the forest to follow the dharma of a son, which is to abide by the father. He stayed away from Surpanaka to abide by the dharma of a dutiful husband. Jabali *rishi* tried to use atheism as a tool to convince Lord Rama to come back to Ayodhya and become the king, Lord Rama reprimanded him very severely for abandoning dharma to achieve a personal goal.

16. *Sarvasamaschaiva* - A person who practices equality. Lord Rama's attitude was not warped by preferences nor distorted by prejudices caused by birth, wealth, status or power.

17. *Satpurusha* - A person who is eternal. Lord Rama is *sat* or eternal, He is *sat purusha*. *Jivas* who stick to Him attain their *sat* nature from Him.

18. *Pratibha* - A genius. Lord Rama's dealings with His brothers at so many instances and keeping them united despite several opportunities to break them shows His genius. His genius is also displayed by His ability to take the right decisions in the most trying of situations.

19. *Sarvalokapriyah* - A person who is loved by all. Lord Rama's demeanor brought all the extensive worlds into the ambit of His embrace.

20. *Sadhuh* - A person who is saintly. Lord Rama's saintliness is

the purity of His mind. Never in His entire life did He even think of harming another for His personal welfare. Even toward Keikeyi who actually cheated Him, He harbored no ill-will.

21. *Priyapraya vritti* – A person who is pleasant in behavior. Lord Rama's pleasant behavior and agreeable ways fascinated all who looked at Him.

22. *Prakritya kalyanimatih* – A person who is good and generous. Lord Rama thought of the good of all and worked toward its fulfillment.

23. *Anavagita parichayah* – A person who maintains a reserved disposition that distances from him the mean, the wicked and unworthy elements. Lord Rama only spoke words that were essential and when necessary. He stayed away from gossip and poking fun. Through this conduct, He naturally repelled the wicked and unworthy elements from His inner circle. When Surpanaka came and began babbling, He directed her to Lakshmana.

24. *Vinaya madhuro vachiniyamah* – A person who is humble, sweet natured, disciplined and whose words of wise counsel make him beloved to all. When the sages of Dandaka saw the sweetness of Lord Rama's personality, they forgot all their miseries and became absorbed in His beauty.

BOOK 2

SHATTERED DREAMS

SHUBHA VILAS

PREVIEW

SHATTERED DREAMS

CHAPTER 1

a restless night

Dasaratha was breathless from all the running. He had been running with all his might; he was panting and his tired aging legs were aching for this chase to end. His ashen face and horror-seared eyes longed for a familiar face. Frantic and terrified, he was fleeing from this dark, menacing monster. The monster had been chasing him around *his* Ayodhya, the city he had ruled for so long and knew every lane and bylane and every nook and cranny of. Yet he seemed to find no place to hide or no one to turn to. He was hoping to trick the monster off his back and escape into this familiar city, but with every step, the chase got worse. He seemed to be running past every memory, every incident and every event of his life as he tried to stay off the evil creature's reach. As every little detail of his life flashed by with each step that he took, he heard a blood-curdling, chilling shriek. Could it be the monster? Alas no! It was his past! How could his life let out such a spine-wrecking scream?

Between his delusions and his consciousness, Dasaratha realized that he was in fact fighting two monsters – the monster within and the monster outside. Everything had become a big blur. Which of the two monsters was he fleeing from?[1]

Dasaratha ran on until he reached the door of one of his ministers. His desperate knocks seemed to die silent deaths. None opened the door. The dark creature's thumping footsteps became louder and clearer. It felt as though it was marching to the sound of Dasaratha's loud heartbeat. Petrified at the thought of being captured, Dasaratha began running again. He looked around. Dead calm. The streets that he loved so much for their hustle and bustle now lay empty. Not a soul seemed to have ever walked or lived in Ayodhya. No citizens, no guards, no animal even. Where did they all go? This isn't the time to rationalize. Just run, Dasaratha told himself.

time seizes dasaratha

Just when Dasaratha was about to make it round the bend and manage to fox the creature, a huge furry hand gripped him. Time had "ceased" him. It was all over now. There was nowhere to run, no more to run. He had just run into Time. Dasaratha tried to wrestle out of Time's tight grasp. The harder he tried, the tighter it gripped him. No matter how much he fluttered and flapped like a bird in a snare, flipped and flopped like a fish in a net or scratched and scrambled like a rat in a trap, he just could not escape this unyielding grasp.

---

[1] The present on the canvas of life is the result of a multitude of past strokes. Rather than brooding over those erroneous past strokes that can no longer be undone, learn from them and apply those strokes of wisdom today to paint a beautiful future. As in a relay race, your past chases you to the present and the present runs toward the future. The baton to success always lies in the hands of the present.

By now, the sweat beads on his forehead burst and began pouring along his temples. Dasaratha twisted and turned in his sleep and his legs flapped helplessly, as if they were not his own. He wanted to shout for help, but fear had robbed him of his voice. Or, perhaps he had come to terms with his destiny. Dasaratha tried to make that one last attempt to escape the monster's grasp. He threw his mighty arms up to grab the monster's neck...Kaboom!

The deafening explosion jolted Dasaratha back to consciousness. He looked around. He was on his soft white bed, although still trembling and sweating profusely. A knocked-over heavy urn lay vacillating on the floor. Dasaratha was half relieved. I am still in my room! It was just the urn! I must have knocked it down in my sleep. There's no monster here. But what was that? It was a nightmare he wished would never come true. His heart hadn't stopped pounding, and seemed like it never would. It was a recurring nightmare that had left Dasaratha sleepless till the end.

The crashing urn brought ten guards rushing to the king's bedside. Dasaratha had half an urge to send them off to arrest the monster that had so traumatized him. Alas, a nightmare monster cannot be captured. He waved his bewildered guards away. The worried look on their king's face was indication enough to leave him alone. The guards returned to their stations.

The pensive king stepped off his luxurious bed and began pacing the room. Every bit of opulent furnishing in his room seemed lackluster. Everything around him had lost its sheen. Even the mirror in the corner of his room wore a sad look. Dasaratha walked up to the mirror and saw the angst that had traveled from his heart to his face. He had flashed endless happy smiles and worn the mask of calmness for the entire world, but the mirror reflected the truth: He was standing there forlorn, miserable, helpless. All the happy vibes he sent out at daytime were but lies that buried the truth of his nighttime horrors. These were dark dreams and dark fears he could not risk sharing with anyone. This was a battle he had to wage alone. How many more such dreams to endure? What do they all portend? Dasaratha was no fool. He had a premonition that something terrible was coming his way. How terrible? Dasaratha had no clue.[2]

How does one prepare for a danger one knows nothing about? Dasaratha looked hard at the mirror. Did it have any answers? Wait...did he just see...? The king abandoned his nightmare analysis to face a far more worrying reality: A strand of gray on his head! He looked again. Goodness! His head was teeming with gray! His duties as king had kept him too busy to even realize that he was graying, and growing older. Perhaps the monarch's white umbrella camouflaged the grays. There was no escaping the truth now: He was aging, and aging fast. He had been king for far longer than any other from the Ikshvaku line.[3]

moonbeam of hope

Just then a happy thought crossed Dasaratha's sad mind. As he broke into a smile, his worry wrinkles disappeared. He had spotted the moonbeam that would chase away his darkness. For two decades and

---

[2] How long can one go on with smiling faces and crying hearts? Either till the smile of the face goes to the heart or the cry of the heart reaches the face.

[3] The easiest way to forget your limitations is to shift the focus from self-absorption to active-facilitation. Dasaratha had not realized his shortcomings because of his absorption in his responsibilities.

a half, Dasaratha must have smiled countless times at the thought of this moonbeam – the bright spot in his life, the solution to all his ills. His moonbeam was Rama Himself – Dasaratha's life, his breath, his real wealth and luckily, also his eldest son.

Dasaratha had always thought of himself as a man with four arms – his sons were his arms. He loved all his arms equally, but always gravitated toward the strongest. He loved all his sons dearly, but he had an instinctive attraction for Rama and an innate connection with Him.

Dasaratha began pacing the room again. Only this time, it was not out of worry but out of hope. Dasaratha was restless. He wanted the sun to rise because sleep had become a nemesis. He could not return to that monster. He knew that it would sneak up on him the moment he shut his eyes, almost as if it lay hidden under his lids. Dasaratha kept staring toward the east through what was left of the horrible night. Half the night had been damned by despair and the other half buoyed by hope. Wasn't this what life was all about?[4]

At long last, the sun rose to rid Dasaratha of the anxiety of how long it would take for sunrise. His other worries were his own, and he had to deal with them all by himself. He dressed to go to his courtroom. As he slipped into his robes and tightened his waist belt, he gritted his teeth in firm resolve: His twin problems would have to be solved today.

Dasaratha rode on his royal elephant across the citizen-lined streets of Ayodhya. Hundreds stood waiting to greet and admire their powerful king and bask under his protective glances. But an array of weak

---

[4] Life is a combination of hope and despair, the one that dominates you carves your personality.

thoughts furrowed the mind of their powerful king. Who would protect him from these thoughts?[5]

Dasaratha's mind kept raking up his nightmares again and again, almost as if some evil force was trying hard to stop him from making the optimistic decision he was about to make. Suddenly, he winced. He wanted to shake his thought off the black serpent that had been the villain of the worst nightmare he had in days. The serpent had nearly strangled him to death. Just thinking about the horrid reptile left Dasaratha cold and perspiring. His thoughts somehow raced back to that time in his youth when he had made a weird promise. That promise was like a sword dangling over his head, waiting to pierce through it. That memory rattled him as did the thought of all the meteors that had hurtled toward Earth over the past few weeks. As the thoughts in his head grew louder with the sound of the gurgling pot in the river and the haunting shriek of a dying human, the applause and cat whistles of his subjects grew fainter. In his head, he could clearly visualize his glistening sonic arrow whiz past, hit its target and let out a shriek. These haunting visions kept draining him. The majestic king who surveyed his subjects was secretly hoping some higher power would show some mercy and save him.

No! For the moment, Dasaratha tried to talk himself out of his fear. "No! I will put an end to all this inauspiciousness in my life by doing the most auspicious thing. O mind! Disturb me not from fulfilling my desires." He decided to go ahead with what he had in mind.

Dasaratha decided to take a detour. Instead of going to the courtroom, he made his way to the "hope center" of Ayodhya. This

---

[5] Every protector needs protection. Being constantly reminded of such a need keeps the protector humble. Everyone in this world has a role to play and a role to depend on. Absence of the role they play causes despair and the absence of role they depend on (higher powers) causes hauteur.

was the center that had always stood like a beacon of hope for him as it had for all his ancestors, especially in trying times. All his dark thoughts and negativity seemed to plunge as the elephant took the turn toward the center. It was as if the dark powers had backed off, realizing that they could haunt him no more. Dasaratha jumped off his faithful elephant of many years to enter the safe haven. With his folded palms in a *namaste mudra*,[6] the king stepped into the temple of Lord Ranganatha, the nine-foot form of Lord Vishnu lying on his celebrated snake bed. Dasaratha lay prostrate in front of that deity and prayed for protection from all evil and for empowerment to make the right decisions. Dasaratha now felt truly blessed.[7]

---

the king's assembly

Dasaratha always entered the courtroom to blaring trumpets, booming drums, reverberating conches and hundreds of bowing heads. A regular day would have Dasaratha saunter in, with a nod here and a nod there, savoring the adulation of his citizens as he trundled to his throne. Something was different today. Dasaratha was in earlier than usual, his detour notwithstanding. Who would keep time on a day such as this? Certainly not Dasaratha! He walked briskly toward his throne with complete focus. He had determination and a sense of urgency. As he looked straight ahead to the throne he had

---

[6] An age-old yogic posture that indicates shelter-seeking.

[7] Prayer peppered with a feeling of helplessness is a tool to attract grace. But grace really descends when this prayer is unobstructed by the transparent wall of pride in one's abilities.

occupied for years and years, he seemed to be conversing with it. He had to do it here and now. The throne needed more security than he could offer.

The court was soon brimming with hundreds of citizens, sages and ministers. Today was not an ordinary court day, for the king had called in a special convention. Dasaratha had earlier invited all subordinate princes, chieftains and officers of the various cities and villages of his kingdom, army chiefs, public leaders, important state functionaries, his Big M (Dristi, Jayantha, Vijaya, Suraashtra, Raashtravardhana, Akopa, Dharmapaala and Sumantra) and his two spiritual gurus (Vasistha and Vamadeva) to this epic meeting. He had held his decision close to his chest till every important person of his kingdom had gathered to hear him. He had called the most important people of his kingdom, but not the most important people of his life. He had deliberately not invited Mithila ruler King Janaka, Sita's father, and Yuthajit, his wife Keikeyi's brother and Bharata's maternal uncle, keeping in mind the time it would take for them to reach Ayodhya. Dasaratha could not afford that time. Not for this decision he was about to make. Was the omission merely because of the distance his relatives had to cover? That the invitations had gone out to those living farther away seemed to suggest there was more to the omission. For now though, all but two of the most important people in Dasaratha's rule were seated before him.[8]

As Dasaratha walked briskly toward the throne, his invitees followed him, and it seemed as though an elephant king was leading his herd to the lake of joy. Only, this king was wounded. Dasaratha reached the throne, turned around and surveyed the audience. Such

---

[8] A complex mindset is indicative of the complexities of the past. An exception made on the basis of some excuse provides a glimpse of those complexities.

intoxicating respect, he thought. Dasaratha seemed in control despite the tumult in his mind. As he sat on his throne, every king, minister, every courtier and every citizen settled on their seats.

Dasaratha regarded every member in the audience. These were the loyal people who had helped him achieve and maintain supremacy over the entire world for such a long time. He was grateful to them all. Everyone had so many divine qualities that each person seemed perfect: They were knowledgeable, ready to sacrifice their lives, selfless, free from wrath even in the most provoking of circumstances; in fact calamities brought the best in them.[9] They were spiritual, far-sighted, wise, tradition-loving heritage-bearers who passed down every ounce of their virtues to the next generation. Everywhere Dasaratha turned, he saw loyal and caring faces. He could feel their effusive love for him. Often he had seen them maintain such calm and balance handling situations, keeping in mind the time, the place, the circumstances, the injunctions of ancient texts, the opinions of wise saints, the advice of loyal people and the sentiments of the citizens. Dasaratha's faith was reaffirmed. He was certain that seated before him were the right people to endorse his decision today.[10]

Dasaratha thought of this assembly of loyals as physicians gathered to calm his restless mind. Although they were many in number, these

---

[9] Calamity in friendship is absence of a person during sad times; calamity in governance is absence of courage in emergencies; calamity in culture is absence of determination during temptations; calamity in agriculture is absence of rain during cultivation; calamity in parenting is absence of time during development.

[10] Decision-making is akin to breathing. Just as in breathing there is careful balance between inhalation and exhalation, decision-making must be a careful balance between personal benefits (taking in or inhalation) and communal harmony (giving out or exhalation).

people were so inspiringly cohesive that they became one body and one mind when it came to serving the interests of their king and their kingdom.[11]

Each member of that audience loved Dasaratha and respected Vasistha. Dasaratha had always been like a father figure to them, treating them as his children and caring for their needs. Today, when everyone had gathered before him, Dasaratha gestured to his helps to shower innumerable valuable gifts upon all gathered in his assembly. He felt the joy a father would as he saw them receive their gifts.

"Hail King Dasaratha! Long live King Dasaratha, our protector!" A chorus of appreciation reverberated through the court. As the din continued, the adulation echoed inside Dasaratha's ears. Dasaratha! Dasaratha! Dasaratha! He had heard this several times, but none sounded as special as the first. With the chorus of his name echoing through the courtroom, Dasaratha traveled far away from the now to the then: a distinct distant memory.

---

the ten-chariot hero

"Dasaratha! Dasaratha! Dasaratha!" the demigods were shouting out in joy now. But it wasn't long ago that an attractive messenger from the land of the demigods (universal administrators) had crashed into the courtroom of the young King Nemi. "Help! The heavens are in trouble and the gods need your help in saving them from a never-

---

[11] Unity without loyalty to a common goal is like cement without water to seal bricks.

before-experienced calamity named Sambarasura!"

The youthful and ever-ready-for-a-fight Nemi ventured into the heavenly realm, beaming with pride that even the demigods depended on his valor. He was itching for the fight to begin, but the demigods thought it prudent to inform him about the complexity of the job at hand. The commander in chief of the demigod's army painstakingly expounded the illusory power of Sambarasura and about his abilities to use all kinds of weapons to perfection. Nemi was nonchalant; he had squashed far too many powerful and multiple weapon-wielding opponents with his mighty arms. The chief of the demigods noticed Nemi's arrogance and smirked. As he walked away, he warned: "Be ready for the surprise of your life when you face ten Sambarasuras."[12]

What did he just say? 10 Sambarasuras?! What would that mean? Who cares? Nothing is really difficult, thought Nemi.

Nemi's war-anointed, scar-seared left arm gripped his mighty bow, which he had mounted on the chariot floor. He was all set to attack the jeering Sambarasura he had spotted a little distance away. Nemi then stole a quick glance at his petite charioteer for this battle outing – his own favorite queen, the beautiful Keikeyi! The king was searching for traces of fear, but instead, steering the chariot in the direction of the heckling monster was the gallant Keikeyi with a glint in her eyes – the glint of anticipation of an adrenaline-pumping battle.[13]

During the terrible fight that followed, Sambarasura realized that

---

[12] A foolhardy person seems enthusiastic to the ignorant, but he seems ignorant to the wise. The fine delineation between overconfidence and self-confidence is determined by the reaction to good advice. When the water of good advice is poured, an overconfident person's already-filled jug rejects it, whereas a self-confident person's sponge absorbs it.

[13] Confidence is contagious; so is fear. Both act inversely. Confidence increases our capacity and fear decreases it.

Nemi was not the usual puny human, the kind he had swallowed by the dozen so often in the past. Sensing a tough battle with the mighty-armed Nemi, the demon unleashed his powerful illusory tricks. Nemi dodged each of those tricks and began shooting his sharp arrows at Sambarasura. It took a while for Nemi to realize that arrows from behind him had begun penetrating his armor. He turned around and was startled to see a Sambarasura clone standing right there! How? Yet another arrow pierced him from another side. He turned to fight another Samabarasura. Three of them! Soon a bewildered Nemi was being pelted with arrows from seven directions. Nemi was right in the middle of a foray of darting arrows, and all his energy was expended in just trying saving himself, leave alone attacking Sambarasura. The brave queen Keikeyi realized that her husband was in deep trouble. She urged him to hold on to the mast of the chariot and suddenly veered the chariot toward the sky and whisked the wounded king to safety.

Keikeyi patiently attended to her semiconscious husband and nursed him back to health. The ever-grateful Nemi thanked her for saving his life and decided to end the battle that he had left halfway. Once again, bow in hand and arrows sharpened, Nemi charged at the demon with full vigor. Soon, the seven Sambarasuras lay grievously wounded. But then three more appeared and locked Nemi in yet another high-pitch battle. By this time, the seven Sambarasuras recovered and Nemi was left fending off 10 attacking Sambarasuras from 10 different directions. Nemi's chariot kept circling in all directions – at times flying, at times veering sideways, at times charging headlong, at times moving backward but rarely surging ahead. Nemi himself seemed to be dancing as he dodged the whizzing arrows, rattling spears, pacey clubs and scores of other weapons that were being hurled at him simultaneously. It seemed like the dance of death.

Just as Nemi seemed to have an edge, an arrow hit a slot on his chariot wheel, almost dislodging it. The chariot began to wobble and Keikeyi knew she had to think and act fast. She stooped and inserted her finger into the slot to keep the wheel from coming off. The entire weight of the chariot rested on the brave queen's fragile finger. Nemi's eyes welled up with tears at the sight of his wife enduring excruciating pain just to save him. The king trembled with a rage that seemed to have transferred on to his sharp arrows. As Keikeyi fixed the chariot, Nemi shot arrow after arrow at the ten-cloned Sambarasura. Every arrow hit its mark, and soon Sambarasura was slain and had become yet another of the many glorious conquests of Nemi.[14]

"Dasaratha! Dasaratha! Dasaratha!" the elated and relieved demigods had cried. They had been watching the battle from afar. Nemi was now Dasaratha, the man whose chariot could move in ten directions!

a king steps down

"Dasaratha! Dasaratha! Dasaratha! Hail, King Dasaratha!" The loud adorations dragged Dasaratha back to the present – a grim present. Past glories were now history, and reminiscence served no purpose. The king had to refocus on the present, so he straightened himself.[15]

---

[14] If service is like a flower and genuine service attitude is like fragrance, then gratitude is like a bee that hovers over it. Relationships thrive when genuine service is acknowledged by active gratitude. Keikeyi was happy to serve and Nemi was grateful to receive. She provided assistance and he gave appreciation.

[15] One should not ruminate about glories of the past to act as the salve to ease the pain of the gloom of the present.

All formalities had been completed, and the most important people had assembled and settled down. Dasaratha began to speak – his voice an elegant blend of power and sweetness, deep as the thundering cloud but sweet as the whistling flute. Dasaratha spoke with the charisma of the king of the world, with clarity and from his heart.[16]

"The magnanimous city of Ayodhya thrives on the principle of sacrifice – a student lives not for himself but to serve his teacher; a husband lives to serve his wife; a king to serve his kingdom; the kingdom to serve the country and the country to serve dharma. The 'I' generation is a dangerous one, where everyone is only worried about 'I, me and mine.' When the mentality is who is going to serve me, it will keep a person dissatisfied. Even to breathe, one has to let out and let in air. This is nothing but giving and taking. One cannot be naïve and say, 'I will only let in and not let out, because I don't like giving.'

"The satisfaction of Ayodhya's citizens has been my life's sole purpose. Administrative schemes were laid out with sharp acumen, protective measures taken with great vigor and limitless charity granted with humble benevolence, all keeping this goal in mind. And all of this has not been my doing alone. To the degree a blind man depends on his stick, I have depended on the collective wisdom of all of you gathered here to make this kingdom what it is – a heaven on earth."[17]

---

[16] Superficial speech is shallow and sensible speech deep. Depth in speech is indicative of a person of substance. Harsh speech is bitter, sweet speech is pleasant. Pleasantness in speech is indicative of a person of kindness. A charismatic leader is a blend of substance and kindness.

[17] Being a genius is not so much about knowing everything as much as it is about knowing when to admit to the self that 'I don't know' and seek guidance.

Dasaratha drew a deep breath and continued in a tone that reflected his present predicament, "I am now weary, old age has decayed my strength and rendered me unfit to fulfill the demands of the royal crown. If the royal white umbrella above my head could speak, it would tell you a hundred tales of my valor and my ceaseless efforts to keep my people safe. But now, under the same umbrella, time has taken its toll on me and I am shriveling up as does a flower under the summer sun. The burden of righteousness is indeed heavy. I have been carrying it around on my never-resting shoulders across so many seasons. An aging man cannot do justice to the weight of a zillion expectations. I long for rest and wish to hand over this burden now. Like the bull that after years of slogging for its master needs care and rest, I, too, crave for some repose.[18]

"Hear my friends and well-wishers, Dasaratha, your king wants to pour out his heart. When time comes for a season to change, none can stop it. Only a fool would even think of attempting to stop the change. Coping with change and seeing nature's wisdom in the change is a sign of mature intelligence. Just as my ancestors of the Ikshvaku line had ruled this kingdom with paternal care, I, too, have trod the path of the glorious dead and served my kingdom with endless zeal. And just as the glorious kings of this dynasty, in time, had handed over the reins to able hands and focused on the next

---

[18] The burden of responsibility brings to the ground the one floating in the clouds of self-interest. Expecting responsibility to be fun is no different from a weightlifter expecting his weights to be as light as a mushroom. Treating people like chewing gum is akin to hedonism in a relationship. Use-and-throw works fine for chewing gum but not for people. Dasaratha, like many leaders, led a life of service to others, and the last thing such leaders expect is to be overthrown by being branded useless.

aspect of their lives, I, too, wish to do the same. I have been witness to some disturbing ill omens, which calls for a change of guard.[19]

"I was named Dasaratha because my chariot was trained to move in ten directions and conquer ten nemeses. A king is called *maharaj* and so is a renunciant. Why? Because a renunciant is a king in six inner directions. I am a king only externally but a prisoner internally. I now want to focus on conquering my six inner demons. Six aspects of nature teach us how to conquer these six inner enemies."

SIX *ANARTHAS* TO CONQUER

Lust: As long as fire is confined to a fireplace, it provides warmth. As soon as it surges and spreads, it unleashes disaster. Lust, like fire, should stay confined by self-control.

Rage: Water sprayed on the face from a sprinkler feels cool, but water gushing uncontrollably from a dam destroys villages sometimes. Rage, like gushing water, should be curbed to avoid devastation.

Ego: A frog, overestimating the harmony of its voice, croaks on and on only to attract a hungry snake. Ego and self-praise attract the snakes of time. The mouth needs to be sealed with the nectar of humility.

Greed: Accumulating water in a pot holds for as long as the pot

---

[19] Resistance to inevitable change is a result of nature's painful unpredictability of the consequences of change. The tendency of controlling minutely leads to the fear of losing control as a result of change. Change management is about gracefully changing the way we perceive change.

has no holes. Greed, which is the hole from which leaks the fluid of intense attachment to accumulation and leaves one thirsty for peace, needs to be plugged with satisfaction.

Illusion: A camel feeding on thorny cactus mistakes blood oozing from its tongue for nectar; a victim of illusion considers miseries to be cradles of happiness. Illusion needs to be curbed by acquiring real vision, which ensures clear action.

Envy: A man unconvinced about the poisonous effect of the *datura* plant may test it on himself before using it on his enemy. Would he live to see its effect on his target? Envy when harbored destroys the bearer even before impairing the target. It has to be nipped in the bud because when it grows, like a *datura*, it could fill the world with the fruits of evil and seeds of destruction.

Fire when not confined, water when not controlled, frog when not silent, the pot when holed, camel when not prudent and the *datura* when not nipped in the bud can all have disastrous consequences. So the flaws in fire, water, frog, pot, camel and *datura* plant are teachers in that they teach us how to subjugate the six inner enemies of lust, anger, ego, greed, illusion and envy.

Dasaratha's eyes darted from person to person in the courtroom to see the effect of his speech. He scanned everyone's expressions. He had just laid bare his life before everyone. What were they thinking? He could not read anything from their baffled, blank expressions. Perhaps he needed to communicate his thoughts more clearly.

"I want my eldest son Rama to take over from me, and I want to retire to focus on the deeper aspects of my own life. I have served you all for so long and now I request that you all grant me some time to serve myself, while there is still some vivacity left in me. Rama is already married to Sita, now I want to marry Rama to this planet Earth. I trust your decision more than I trust mine. So dear friends, please be forthright with your opinions about my decision so that a consensus can be reached at the earliest."[20]

Dasaratha stopped talking. There was silence; perhaps a pin would drop and be heard loud as thunder. The king was palpitating; mixed emotions ran through him. This deafening silence was killing him. The dark thoughts in his mind began to grow louder than ever now. He had pushed all of those aside to bravely declare what he wanted to. But why were they all so silent? Was everyone wondering why would Dasaratha, who had ruled so well for so many years, now hand over his kingdom to a novice, a young inexperienced boy, when everything was perfect in Ayodhya? What if all of them decided to reject this proposal? What if they felt Rama was not qualified enough to be king? God, please let them not think this way! Dasaratha decided to accept and abide by whatever conclusion everyone arrived at together. After all, wasn't this the kind of cooperation and mutual trust that had made Ayodhya invincible? But why was everyone silent? Speak something, this silence is stifling![21]

Suddenly Dasaratha's court erupted and everyone spoke in unison, and they said exactly the same thing: 'Icchaamah, mahaabahum, Raghuveeram.' A tumultuous uproar went up in the air, the vibrations

---

[20] Just as pressure between two powerful stones grinds grains to fine powder, consensus between neutral people results in well-rounded and impartial decisions.

[21] Decision-making in the kingdom of Ayodhya followed a circular system. Which point in a circle could be considered the most important? The center, naturally. In a circular system, the king was also one of the points on the circle but not the center. At the center was the welfare of the kingdom. The king was not a lawmaker, instead he was a lawkeeper. The king expressed ideas, all citizens laid down their opinions, and the churning of ideas and opinions resulted in a collective decision.

of which reached every corner of Ayodhya. It seemed as if the palace walls would crack. Though deafening, the sound was like music, like the cry of a muster of peacocks on seeing the first rainclouds. It was indeed a cry of joy!

"We desire (*icchaamah*) the mighty armed one (*mahaabahum*) Rama (*raghuveeram*)." A member of the assembly rose and spoke on behalf of everyone: "You have indeed ruled for a long time, you should now step down and allow the royal white umbrella to shield Rama."

Everyone in the audience smiled, but Dasaratha became sullen. Ironic! He should have been happy. It was his proposal after all. A downcast Dasaratha told them that it was wonderful that they had accepted Rama as their next king, but their enthusiasm left him wondering if they had always wanted him to relinquish the throne to Rama. Dasaratha began to have this unnerving feeling that he had been an unjust and unqualified king and that his subjects were patiently waiting for this day. He clarified his doubt with them so that he did not have to step down feeling rejected. A chieftain stood and said: "Your only disqualification is that you have someone as worthy as Rama for a son."

Another got up and said: "Rama has so many good qualities that the moment we think of Him, we cannot imagine anyone else leading us." Yet another rose to say: "Our situation is similar to that of a cow that delivers twin calves, confused about which of the two calves to give more love and attention to because she loves them both equally. Similarly, we love you and Rama equally so we are not sure whom to choose to be our king."

Now that his doubts were set aside, Dasaratha was beaming with each comment. The pride of a father had replaced the insecurity of a retiring king. Words of glory for his son were sweeter than honey. He knew these weren't just platitudes but showers of genuine appreciation toward Rama.[22]

triple virtues

Ayodhya's citizens considered Rama as the greatest of all Ikshvaku kings. A great person is labeled prodigious only if he is a combination of three virtues – magnificent talent, right attitude and spotless character. Rama embodied all these virtues.

Talent

Talent is like a sword, not to be merely admired but to be actually used. Just as Rama's quiver is equipped with multiple arrows, His personality is equipped with multifarious talents.

Rama not only knew all the Vedas by rote, he also knew how to apply them. His skillful use of all celestial weapons was not an arrogant display of power but a premeditated show of care.

His excellence in singing was not superficial melody but a love-awakening and hope-giving euphony. His oratory wasn't a long-winding river of discourse but eloquent drops of nectar. His grasp of public administration was abetted by a wary balance of reward to the

---

[22] Empty flattery soothes the mind, whereas copious appreciation touches the heart. Flattery engages only the tongue, while appreciation employs the eyes to observe, the ears to listen, the intelligence to analyze, the tongue to speak and the heart to feel. When eaten, the flattery fruit intoxicates and weakens, whereas the appreciation fruit gives strength and encouragement.

virtuous and reprimand to the wicked, avoiding excesses on either side.

Attitude

Talent without the right attitude is like sweet rice without sugar. Talent brings one to the brink of the bridge to success and right attitude helps one cross it.

The symptom of the disease of vanity is the desire to be approached by others rather than to approach others; the sweet-smiling Rama vaccinated Himself against this disease and initiated discussions using the elixir of humility. The symptom of the disease of intellectual snobbery is extreme self-reliance; Rama was immune to this disease because he gulped down the amalgam of submissive inquiry from three sources, the experienced (*vayo vriddha* – those possessing the wealth of age), the wise (*jnana vriddha* – those possessing the wealth of knowledge) and the cultured (*shila vriddha* – those possessing the wealth of character). The symptom of the disease of insensitivity is extreme self-concern and sheer indifference toward others; Rama was untouched by this disease because of the tonic of empathy he had obtained by partaking in the joys and sufferings of his people. Rama kept His mind healthy with the vitamin of gratitude for all those who did Him good, even if only once, and eliminated the toxins of lapses toward Him.

Character

Talent and attitude take one to success, but character helps one maintain it. Spotless character is a tripod of self-control, honesty and integrity.

Nature puts an ordinary piece of coal through extreme pressure to transform it into the most precious jewel. When an ordinary human happily subjects himself to the pressure of self-control, he transforms himself to a man of spotless character.

An elephant has two sets of teeth – a useless set (tusks) just for show because these cannot be used for eating and a useful set, to actually chew food. Just like the elephant, a man who lacks integrity has two sets of value systems – one for preaching (high standards) and another for practice (compromised standards). Rama's life was an open book. He chose to embrace invaluable principles and demonstrate integrity rather than make a compromise for self-interest and personal convenience. Rama's connection with the truth was the same as a cuckoo's connection to its sweet song – pleasant and constant.

One of the kings present in the assembly compared Rama to the moon when it came to making people happy, to the earth when it came to forgiveness, to the sun when it came to His radiance, to Brihaspati (the guru of the gods in heaven) when it came to wisdom and to Indra (the king of gods) when it came to courage.

Everyone took this opportunity to shower praises on Rama. An elderly minister rose, tears of affection in his eyes, and said that the entire kingdom was praying for Rama – across every stately mansion, every little hamlet, the young and the old were praying for Rama through the day. This observation touched Dasaratha. So many blessings for his son?[23]

All those praises from all those eminent people and the buoyant mood of everyone in the assembly was incentive enough for a

---

[23] The blessing of the strong is to facilitate the weak. The blessing of the weak is to strengthen the strong. Blessing is an intangible currency that helps one buy the ingredients for success.

beaming Vasistha, the spiritual guru of Dasaratha and the entire Ikshvaku dynasty, to get up and speak: "Dasaratha, rest assured that your decision to step down and hand over the reins to Rama is not only acceptable to everyone but also highly desired by all. We are waiting to see Rama seated under the white umbrella ride on the royal elephant across the streets of Ayodhya. In fact, we wish to see this lion of Ayodhya astride an elephant! Historic!"

Vasistha's assurance filled Dasaratha with immense hope and happiness. He quickly tried to make a rough calculation to compare the amount of joy he experienced now with that of the happiest moments of his life – this was twice the joy of hearing about Rama's birth, thrice the joy of Rama's marriage, four times the joy of Rama breaking Lord Shiva's bow and five times the joy of Parashurama's defeat.

Phew! Such relief! A huge burden was taken off Dasaratha's head. He suddenly felt giddy with happiness because his mind stopped tormenting him as soon as the court seconded his decision. He thanked everyone profusely for obliging and concurring with his decision. Let the celebrations begin! No more delays. Let the coronation take place the very next day, Dasaratha declared and walked off with Sumantra, his confidant, charioteer and minister, following closely behind.

Vasistha plunged into action. Right away, an executive organizing committee was formed; the finest quality of rice, milk and yogurt were packed for distribution to a hundred thousand *brahmanas*.[24] A host of

---

[24] The joy of giving is higher than the joy of the occasion of giving. But this joy of benevolence can be only perceived when the giver gives with gratitude. If the giver gives with arrogance, his act of giving will be perceived by a receiver as being punched by a boxer.

things, including gold, diamonds, worship paraphernalia, hundreds of natural herbs, floral garlands, corn, honey, clarified butter, new clothes, chariots, all kinds of weapons, four divisions of army, an elephant with special auspicious signs, a white fan, a flag staff, a white umbrella, a hundred shiny golden pots, a bull with gilded horns, a complete tiger skin, were listed for procurement before dawn. All doorways in the kingdom including that of the royal palace were to be swathed in sandalwood paste, decorated with floral garlands and smoked with fragrant incense. Prayers and oblations were to be carried out in every temple in Ayodhya with great pomp and reverence. Musicians and dancers were to perform in all corners of Ayodhya starting right away and make it to the royal palace by dawn... the list was endless! Despite his age, the enthusiastic Vasistha went on and on, poring over every tiny detail with great gusto. This was no ordinary occasion. For many, it was a once-in-a-lifetime event.

While Vasistha was busy making arrangements for the following day's ceremony, Dasaratha entered his private quarters with Sumantra. At last, he was free to speak his mind and express his emotions without the pressure of being watched by all. With tears of joy in his eyes, Dasaratha ordered Sumantra to beckon his life, Rama, to his presence.

---

a king steps in

About two hundred yards from him, Dasaratha could see a greenish beacon, effulgent like the sun flickering atop a golden frame. It took a while for the frail and world-weary eyes of king to realize that the gold-green light was actually the radiant body of his oldest son,

Rama, dismounting gracefully from his golden chariot with the help of Sumantra. Such beauty! How could anyone take his or her eyes off this boy? Two and a half decades had passed by just looking at Him, but now time stood still upon seeing Rama. Dasaratha had the most beautiful queens of this world for wives and the most beautiful objects to behold, yet all those beauties could not hold his attention.[25] But it was different with Rama, he never tired of looking at his beautiful son. As the world-famous hero Rama was getting off the chariot holding its mast, Dasaratha's eyes went up to the flag fluttering on top of the chariot. Soon that flag would bear the royal emblem.

The moment Rama stepped on to the ground, it seemed to light up. His walk resembled the vigorous gait of an elephant. His long arms draped in silk reached His knees. His enchanting face resembled the moon and was held high, as if challenging the moon that was now hiding. Carefully protected within the *bimba*-fruit red lips was a row of teeth, shiny as pearls.

Am I touching silk or is it butter? wondered Sumantra as Rama held him while dismounting from His chariot. How could these soft, delicate hands have broken Lord Shiva's mighty bow? As Rama alighted the steps toward Dasaratha's palace, Sumantra followed Him with folded hands, gazing meditatively at His delicate feet which seemed to dance as They climbed the royal steps.[26] Rama's lotus feet took Sumantra back in time by half an hour.

---

[25] Just as snow vanishes with warmth of the sun, the beauty of the objects of this world diminishes with passing time. Both the Sun and Time rise of their own accord.

[26] The stern posture of the eagle indicates confidence, the twitchy posture of the sparrow indicates fear and the callous posture of the vulture indicates meanness. Similarly, the folded hands of Sumantra suggested his loyalty and downward gaze revealed his modesty. The science of gestures indexes the traits of the mind and the moods of the individual.

Rama, Sita and Lakshmana were talking to each other, smiling. Sumantra had literally barged into Rama's palace and interrupted this happy discussion. But the three of them immediately rose from their seats and offered their respects to the elderly and wise minister. His presence heralded an instruction from the king. Soon, Sumantra was Rama's charioteer. Sumantra was more elated to hear that Rama would be king than he would have been had he himself been made king of the universe. Sumantra's joy increased manifold when he saw the effect Rama's chariot trip to Dasaratha's palace had on the citizens of Ayodhya.

Drum beats and loud music ushered the chariot along every street. People seemed to say that they were now in safe hands, protected from all misery. Sumantra noticed the scintillating effect Rama's charm had on Ayodhya's damsels, who shed their shyness and ran like deer to keep pace with Rama's chariot so that they could see His lotus face for a little while longer. Their eyes were like darts piercing Rama's shining body and lotus-like face. Rama's looks were driving everyone crazy. The minds of the girls were swept away by overflowing love that tore down discipline and etiquette just as a gushing river breaks the embankments. Their shamelessness surprised them. Even the men were reeling under the effect of Rama's personality. He was robbing the eyes and minds of all of Ayodhya with His beauty, His generosity and His virtues. Ayodhya's men behaved like cows separated from their calves and chased Rama's chariot just as they had chased butterflies in their childhood. Sumantra thought it was comical: so many royals running like crazy people. As Rama passed by, a wave of calm swept across the minds of people, in the way cool breeze would bring relief to people scorched by summer heat.[27]

---

[27] The simplest joys of nature cannot be replaced by the complex creations of man.

From atop tall buildings and palaces, flowers rained down from the hair of girls leaning over their windows trying to catch a glimpse of Rama. Some even swooned seeing Rama's broad chest adorned with a beautiful garland of fresh lotus flowers. Sumantra noticed the streets of Ayodhya were strewn with flowers. It seemed as though even the gods had showered some praise on Rama.

---

dasaratha's lament

"Accept my respects, O Lord of Ayodhya!" The sweet-voiced Rama's voice boomed across the room as He bowed down in veneration in front of His father with folded hands. The melodious voice brought Sumantra back to the present.[28]

Dasaratha lifted Rama up and pulled him close to his bosom. The loving embrace suddenly turned into a test – the mighty-armed Dasaratha tightened his grip to assess Rama's physical prowess. Now that Rama was expected to carry the burden of the world, would his chest and shoulders have enough power in them? As Dasaratha crushed the delicate body of Rama, he could sense the resilience and power beneath the soft exterior. Even a quarter of the power he had used in that embrace would have crushed an ordinary human, but Rama was oblivious of everything. All He felt was His father's loving embrace. Bravo, my son! Dasaratha thought.

---

[28] In a fountain, water that bursts upward with zeal comes down with grace. Similarly, respect when sent forth with genuineness, returns with elegance. Rama was respected because he was respectful.

Dasaratha released his bear hug and gently ushered Rama to the gilded throne in his palace and sat beside Him, pouring out his heart. The delight on Dasaratha's face upon seeing Rama was the same as seeing one's happy reflection in the mirror.

Dasaratha lifted his index finger and said: "Deep gratitude. That's what I feel toward the gods for having allowed me to live and rule this long. In all these years, I have carefully struck off all the five debts a human being incurs. By performing sacrifices, I am no more indebted to the celestials. By studying the scriptures, I have fulfilled my debt to those sages who wrote them and taught them. By donating wealth and food, I repaid my debt to the *brahmanas*. By relishing in the comforts of desire, I have fulfilled my debt to myself. And of course, by begetting a wonderful son like you, the debt to my ancestors, too, has been realized. I seem to have only one duty left to complete – place the imperial crown on your head. Everyone in Ayodhya wants to witness it, and this will be the fulfillment of my life's greatest dream, too.[29]

"I consider you a good friend, so I wish to say a few things although I am aware you already know of it. Yet, as your friend[30], it is my job to help you understand your responsibilities. A just ruler happily

---

[29] Clouds receive salty water from the ocean and return sweet water as rain. A cow eats grass and returns sweet milk. A coconut tree drinks water and returns nectar. What one receives is a debt that can be absolved by paying through selfless service. But being grateful vindicates one of the additional interest accrued.

[30] Only the inexperienced say that a father is only a father. He is in fact a protective father only initially, then a disciplining commander, then an encouraging teacher, then a transparent friend, then a respectable mentor and then a dependent elder. Holding on to a past role is like holding on to a moving car.

sacrifices the self at the pyre of world peace. The two swords that dangle above a leader's head are desire and anger.[31] A good leader keeps these swords from felling him with the help of the shields of satisfaction and patience. The secret of a leader's success lies in his able ministry and not his personal talent. Keep the ministers satisfied in every possible way – directly or indirectly. A leader without followers is no leader at all. A leader's ability is always weighed against the satisfaction of his followers – keep the people happy through well-thought administrative schemes, ever-brimming coffers and easy accessibility."

Saying so, Dasaratha rose and began walking restlessly across the room. He was not sure about how to convey the message he actually wanted to. Rama understood that there was more to this conversation. If it was such a happy occasion afterall, why was His father upset and worried? A happy man does not behave this way. What was behind this mask of happiness?

Dasaratha opened up. He told Rama that at this point in time, his life was like a mother's, who though happy at the thought of giving birth, still writhing in labor pain, is unsure whether to smile or cry. As he paced the room, Dasaratha clenched his fists, as if to stop the flow of time, and mentioned that bad signs were haunting him. He described all his horrifying nightmares, the ill omens he had spotted over the last few days, the falling meteors and even the royal astrologer's predictions that the planets Rahu and Mangal were stealthily approaching his birth star. These omens implied that the king would either die or meet with a fatal accident.

---

[31] For a good leader, anger and desire are his loyal servants, he displays them when required. The day these servants peep out without instruction from the master, that day marks beginning of the end of leadership.

Dasaratha told Rama that he could no longer trust his own mind these days as it seemed to have a life of its own. He wanted to crown Rama king before his mind forced him to change his decision. His mind right now was as restless as a monkey, as strong as an elephant, as turbulent as an ocean and as stubborn as the bull. How could any sane human rely on something so unpredictable? He wanted to expedite things while he still had some control over his unstable mind.[32] "It has to happen tomorrow," Dasaratha concluded.

Shifting his tone from that of concern to jubilation, Dasaratha requested Rama to remain celibate for the rest of the night and observe a fast with His wife, Sita and sleep on a couch made of *kusa* grass. As an afterthought, he also told Rama to ask His best friends to guard His palace all night. Sabotage was a weapon such ill omens often brought in their wake. What was Dasaratha expecting? He was not so sure if he was anticipating an attack from his disturbed mind or from somewhere outside!

Rama stood up to leave, sensing that His father had conveyed everything and given him enough instructions. As he was about to leave, Dasaratha muttered under his breath that the coronation should take place while Bharata was still away. Rama perked a brow, expecting a justification for that statement, but there was none. Instead, Dasaratha made two diametrically opposite statements: "Bharata is a righteous and compassionate brother and he will follow you. But men are inconsistent because of which sometimes impulse may throw up unexpected results." He then abruptly walked away.

---

[32] An unprotected and unpredictable mind is like an open pot of nectar. One blob of poison dropped into it will ruin all the nectar in it.

one king two bodies

Erect back, lotus posture, folded hands, a serene face, closed eyes, prayerful murmur – this was Rama's vision of His mother, Kaushalya. She was always the same every single time he visited her. Yet again, she stood there greeting Him as she always did. Rama admired her. She was the epitome of devotion and dedication.

What was surprising, however, was the presence of Sita, Lakshmana and Lakshmana's mother Sumitra in his mother's room. Their smiling faces at once implied that they already knew. Some guard or attendant desirous of earning either the favor of the Queen Mother or some extra wealth had perhaps informed her of her son's coronation the next day. His mother's prayer now was surely her way of offering gratitude to the Lord for showering such kindness upon her. Rama waited patiently, using this time to meditate on and appreciate his mother's divine qualities.[33]

Kaushalya gracefully got up to see her son. She walked up to Him with a knowing smile. Yet Rama formally informed her of His coronation the next morning. The happy mother poured out a river of blessings from her heart with joy and gratitude.

Rama then turned toward Lakshmana and Sita and told His brother: "Ayodhya will be ruled by one king in two bodies. Together We will rule the kingdom bestowed upon Us by Our father. I desire to rule the kingdom only for your sake." Conveying this, Rama departed to

---

[33] Muscles develop and strengthen when one pushes a heavy object away from oneself. Similarly, our capacity to show appreciation grows by pushing away the craving for self-appreciation.

His palace along with Sita to prepare for the fast and the other pre-coronation rituals.

---

darkness returns

Night fell on Ayodhya and a blanket of darkness enveloped the city. It slowly crept into Dasaratha, too. Dasaratha dreaded sunsets for it heralded the dark nights he did not want to face. He sat in front of his mirror, and once again, a strand of gray caught his attention. The gray glistened against the dark backdrop of the night, almost as if trying to say something to him. What is it? Why was he focusing on that one gray strand? Did the gray of the hair and the black of the night allude to something? What horrors lay ahead?

AUTHOR PROFILE

Shubha Vilas, a spiritual seeker and a motivational speaker, holds a degree in engineering and law with a specialization in patent law.

His leadership seminars are popular with top-level management in corporate houses. He addresses their crucial needs through thought-provoking seminars on themes such as 'Secrets of Lasting Relationships', 'Soul Curry to Stop Worry' and 'Work–Life Balance' to name a few.

He believes that a good teacher, no matter how knowledgeable, always sees the process of learning and teaching simultaneously as an inherent aspect of personal and spiritual growth.

Shubha Vilas periodically interacts with the youth in premier institutes across the country, inspiring them to live a life based on deeper human values. Close to his heart is his role as a guide and teacher to school children, teaching foundational values through masterful storytelling.

He also helps individuals apply the teachings of the *Bhagavad Gita*, the *Ramayana* and other dharmic traditions in dealing with modern-day life situations.

Connect with Shubha Vilas on
Facebook: https://www.facebook.com/ShubhaVilas
Twitter: @shubhavilas
Email: ramayana.shubhavilas@gmail.com

JAICO PUBLISHING HOUSE
Elevate Your Life. Transform Your World.

ESTABLISHED IN 1946, Jaico Publishing House is home to world-transforming authors such as Sri Sri Paramahansa Yogananda, Osho, The Dalai Lama, Sri Sri Ravi Shankar, Robin Sharma, Deepak Chopra, Jack Canfield, Eknath Easwaran, Devdutt Pattanaik, Khushwant Singh, John Maxwell, Brian Tracy and Stephen Hawking.

Our late founder Mr. Jaman Shah first established Jaico as a book distribution company. Sensing that independence was around the corner, he aptly named his company Jaico ('Jai' means victory in Hindi). In order to service the significant demand for affordable books in a developing nation, Mr. Shah initiated Jaico's own publications. Jaico was India's first publisher of paperback books in the English language.

While self-help, religion and philosophy, mind/body/spirit, and business titles form the cornerstone of our non-fiction list, we publish an exciting range of travel, current affairs, biography, and popular science books as well. Our renewed focus on popular fiction is evident in our new titles by a host of fresh young talent from India and abroad. Jaico's recently established Translations Division translates selected English content into nine regional languages.

Jaico's Higher Education Division (HED) is recognized for its student-friendly textbooks in Business Management and Engineering which are in use countrywide.

In addition to being a publisher and distributor of its own titles, Jaico is a major national distributor of books of leading international and Indian publishers. With its headquarters in Mumbai, Jaico has branches and sales offices in Ahmedabad, Bangalore, Bhopal, Bhubaneswar, Chennai, Delhi, Hyderabad, Kolkata and Lucknow.

SINCE 1946